MIND & SOCIETY FADS

Frank W. Hoffmann, PhD
William G. Bailey, MA

SOME ADVANCE REVIEWS

"This will be a book of wide appeal and general use. For the student of popular culture, it is a survey of social bulimia and ballyhoo; for psychologists and therapists, a reminder of quackeries and quick fixes; for English composition teachers, a smorgasbord of research topics from the pages of National Enquirer or Skeptical Enquirer or both; and for the general reader, a delightful but often disturbing display of the fallacies and foolery that all are heir to. Reference librarians should plan on keeping it handy."

Robert J. Higgs, PhD, Professor of English,
East Tennessee State University

"This fascinating encyclopedia of obsessions and diversions reveals that America, at times, has been the dupe of profiteers who, through skill and luck, instigated what became a fad. The majority of the entries, however, record a welcomed respite for segments of the public from a seemingly mundane mainstream. Some of these fads have been long forgotten, but even those of recent vintage are placed in a context that will be revealing to all but the most widely read social historian."

Gene DeGruson, MA, Curator of Special Collections,
Pittsburgh State University, Kansas;
Editor, *The Lost First Edition of Upton Sinclair's* The Jungle

Mind & Society Fads

HAWORTH Popular Culture
Frank W. Hoffmann, PhD and William G. Bailey, MA
Senior Editors

Mind & Society Fads

Frank W. Hoffmann, PhD
William G. Bailey, MA

Harrington Park Press
An Imprint of The Haworth Press, Inc.
New York • London • Norwood (Australia)

ISBN 1-56023-010-X

Published by

Harrington Park Press, an imprint of The Haworth Press, Inc., 10 Alice Street, Binghamton, NY 13904-1580

All illustrations courtesy of the Library of Congress.

Cover design by Steven Jenkins.

Library of Congress Cataloging-in-Publication Data

Hoffmann, Frank W., 1949-
    Mind & society fads / Frank W. Hoffmann, William G. Bailey.
       p.   cm.
    Includes bibliographical references and index.
    ISBN 1-56023-010-X (pbk. : acid free paper)
    1. United States—Intellectual life—20th century—Miscellanea. 2. United States—Social life and customs—1971- —Miscellanea. 3. United States—Social life and customs—1945-1970—Miscellanea. 4. Fads—United States—Miscellanea. I. Bailey, William G., 1947- . II. Title. III. Title: Mind and society fads.
E169.12.H635   1992
306.4'0973—dc20
                                         91-4132
                                          CIP

CONTENTS

ABOUT THE AUTHORS

Frank W. Hoffmann, PhD, MLS, is an associate professor in the School of Library Science, Sam Houston State University. His teaching responsibilities include library collection development, reference/information services, and a seminar of popular culture. His publications include *The Development of Collections of Sound Recordings in Libraries* (Marcel Dekker), *Popular Culture and Libraries* (Library Professional Publications), *The Literature of Rock* series (Scarecrow), and *The Cash Box* chart compilation series (Scarecrow). He received his doctorate from the University of Pittsburgh and his BA in History and MLS from Indiana University.

William G. Bailey, MA, MLS, has worked in the Information Services division of the Newton Gresham Library, Sam Houston State University, for the past 12 years. He is currently the head of the Reference Department. Due to his daily routine, he is constantly looking for new writing projects to fill information gaps. A fad encyclopedia appeals to his eclectic mind; he is already the editor/compiler of books on such diverse topics as police, longevity, and Americans in Paris. He holds an MA degree in English and American Literature from the University of Houston, and an MLS from the University of Texas at Austin.

Introduction

The entries in this volume will undoubtedly step on some toes. For *Mind & Society* we describe those fads that affect us more than any other. Ones that lodge in our belief system and obscure our logic, ones that hoodwink and taunt us with their folly. So that later we either smile at ourselves or wince. Hula hoops go out with the trash, these fads not so easily. Now, having worried you about what follows, let us set your mind at rest. In discussing fads, much of the problem stems from the word "pejorative." Doesn't fad denote frivolous, trifling, superficial? By calling something a fad, don't we reduce it to a mote of dust? Don't we disparage, belittle, and discredit anything we label a fad? Yes and no.

Fads sharpen our thinking. In *The Psychotherapy Handbook* (1980), editor Richie Herink and his contributors describe over 350 psychotherapeutic systems and techniques. Herink is quick to add, "This list is not definitive, however, since depending on how wide the net is cast, there may be said to be as many psychotherapies as there are therapists (or perhaps even as many as there are patients!)." A decade before, such a handbook would have been half the size. During the 1970s, psychotherapies proliferated like wildflowers. The market for people who wanted to curb their neuroses had expanded due to the restless 1960s and a new era of introspection. So from Freudian-Jungian-Adlerian soil, a field of psychotherapies popped up to meet the demand, along with a possessive guru for each.

Let's look at three of the more faddish mind cures. Christian psychotherapy used the Bible to teach conflict resolution and behavior control, ignoring that in the Old Testament an avenging, not a benevolent, God, settled most matters. Up until then the Church had had a corner on confessions and dispensed its medicine for free. Past Lives Therapy employed reincarnation to exorcize former evil selves and to put to rest earlier traumatic events. The prerequisite for entering this therapy was a firm belief in reembodiment and metempsychosis, without which you couldn't go home again and again and again. Exaggeration therapy worked wonders through "the humoristic aggravation of neurotic feelings of self-pity, and of neurotic complaining behavior, by the invention of increasingly dramatic stories until the client starts smiling or laughing." In layperson terms, the psychotherapist made fun of the client until he or she shook like jelly. If the client said, "Nobody loves me," the psychotherapist responded with, "Poor little me, half crippled, blind, clothed in rags, everybody spits at me when I walk down the street."

The list of faddish mind cures goes on. Oriental-influenced therapies included Aikido, Acupuncture, Buddhist Insight Meditation, and Tibetan Psychic Healing. Computer Therapy (watching fuzzy CRT characters pulsate on a screen as a calming influence) and Megavitamin Therapy (overdosing on an alphabet of dietary supplements) were also actually taken seriously by clients. But fad and foolishness formed the ultimate partnership with the Fischer-Hoffman Process: Fischer, a dead psychoanalyst, treated clients through Hoffman, a psychic.

These examples taken from Herink's handbook underscore the pejorative effect fad treatments exert on clinical psychology and, with trepidation, continue to exert. Even though today they appear less often, fad treatments still devalue the profession. For good reason, legitimate psychotherapists attempt to cleanse their ranks of pseudotherapists. Professor Henry E. Adams asks:

> How does psychology, and particularly clinical psychology, avoid being enticed into participating in current theoretical or therapeutic treatment "fads" which are epidemic, transient phenomena reflecting the public's and the profession's current political and sociological enthusiasm? Is it possible to prevent the training of "true believers" in clinical psychology? ["The Pernicious Effects of Theoretical Orientations in Clinical Psychology." *The Clinical Psychologist* 37 (Summer 1984): 92]

In answer, Adams suggests a six-point plan. Clinical psychologists should:

1. Adhere to a scientific approach at all times, not make a cult of one theory or treatment, and be more critical toward all theories and treatments.
2. Develop classification systems and measurements that are independent of theories.
3. Substitute empiricism for eclecticism, i.e., objective evaluation of individual theories instead of subjective mixing of convenient theories.
4. Realize that psychology may never settle on a comprehensive theory of human behavior; so it's best to devise theories that explain specific phenomena in light of the evidence.
5. Realize the majority of findings in the scientific literature that are statistically significant are of little practical scientific or clinical value.
6. Switch their interest from the potpourri of therapeutic techniques to formulating theories on the development and cause of aberrant behavior.

If Adams' plan were instituted, fad psychotherapies would have less chance to wreak their pernicious effect. However, our interest here is not in reforming clinical psychology, but in discussing the pejorative nature of fads. Negative labeling can also be positive. Adams demonstrated this when he admonished his peers to forego treating clients with "psycho-religions." True, a charismatic healer can help a client (even with Past Lives Therapy) if the client is susceptible to the brand of treatment offered. But more often than not, the faddish therapy produces a sham cure and the client looks elsewhere for a remedy.

Professor Arnold A. Lazarus gives a striking example of how a one-theory psychotherapist might get lucky. Suppose:

A woman with a sore throat consults a physician whose name she picks out of the telephone book. The M.D. into whose consulting room she is ushered turns out to be a gynecologist. Consequently, the patient undergoes a routine pelvic examination during which a mild infection is discovered. An antibiotic is prescribed resulting in the serendipitous remission of her throat ailment. This felicitous result might lead the patient to seek gynecological assistance for all future throat ailments. To analogize further from the field of psychotherapy, we would then have a doctor who would insist that the pelvis was the royal road to the pharynx. ["The Specificity Factor in Psychotherapy." *Psychotherapy in Private Practice* 2 (1984):43-44.]

Malpractice, if you will, forces the censure of suspect treatments. Therefore, in this respect, faddishness is beneficial.

So far, we have mashed psychology's toes to the point of excruciating pain (see also Primal Therapy, Feeling Therapy, est, Psychoanalysis, Sex Surrogates, Orgonomy, and Esalen). It's not that psychology offers a convenient whipping boy. We could have chosen any field to illustrate the pejorative nature of fads, since none is free of passing fancy. By all means turn to the entries for Creation Science, Language, Education, Business Management, and Biorhythm. But pop-psychology is the more familiar and seductive. As dedicated professionals work to deliver psychology from the throes of birth, faddishness will reoccur. The hope is that one day the science of psychology will override the uncertainty and speculation that now mark its existence.

The remainder of this volume, not concerned with intellectual fads, deals with society and its lively interest in itself. Societal fads differ by appealing more to the spirit, the heart, and the funny bone; no sophistry or browbeating here. Nor are societal fads likely to be pernicious, which makes them all the more entertaining. The qualifier "likely" must be added though, because ofttimes things go awry in the affairs of humankind.

For instance, the first entry, "Aerocar," tells how a starry-eyed inventor wanted to revolutionize personal transportation in America. His invention allowed the driver to change from land to air travel in minutes by turning a few controls. If a lake, a forest, or even a city got in the way the Aerocar simply took to the sky to bypass the obstacle. Prototypes of the Aerocar exhibited to the public brought shouts of glee from most everyone but stern government regulators. The Federal Aviation Administration and other agencies foresaw greater traffic fatalities with the Aerocar than ever before. It was too mind-boggling to think of millions of Americans taking off into the wild blue yonder, unpoliced with no center stripe parting the heavens. The Acrocar certainly appealed to society's spirit of freedom in the 1950s and 1960s and still does, but perhaps it is better left a fad.

Some other societal fads that will touch your heart or tickle your funny bone are British Coronations, Bundling, College Students, the Dionne Quintuplets, Genius Sperm Bank, Harmonic Convergence, Personal Names, and Talking to Plants. As diverse as they seem, these mind and society fads have one thing in common: the ability to redirect human behavior through specious reasoning or magnetic charm.

Aerocar

For futurists, the most wonderful invention of the twentieth century got final approval from the Civil Aeronautics Administration (CAA) in 1957. After seven years of strenuous testing, the Aerocar was ready for public consumption. Both airplane and car, it could take off from a 650-ft. strip of land, carrying two persons and enough fuel for a 300-mile flight, cruising at a speed of 100 mph. On the road, the Aerocar seated four persons and purred along at between 50 and 60 mph. Its engine was a marvel of dual purpose. In the air, a four-cylinder motor drove a pusher-type propeller "through a fluid drive of steel shot." Propeller, drive shaft, and folding wings were removable and collapsed into a neat package for towing trailer-like behind the car. The same motor provided three forward speeds and reverse, just like other standard cars not able to go airborne. Moulton B. Taylor of Longview, Washington, designed the Aerocar. He was dead certain that once approval came he could find a manufacturer to mass-produce his darling, and soon thousands of Aerocars would zoom into the air and reland at will.

Taylor's prototype cost $25,000 to build. He reckoned that off an assembly line the price tag would lower to $8,000, still a luxury item but affordable by many American families. He predicted great days ahead for the Aerocar and started looking for money to finance his dream. But almost before he could clear the 650-ft. strip to launch Aerocar skyward, he encountered bad weather. Federal regulations had all but put the Aerocar in a hangar-garage permanently. Taylor explains in a letter published in *Aviation Week,* April 16, 1962:

> This difficulty [in raising capital] has been greatly influenced by a completely unsuspected difficulty which the developer of the Aerocar did not envision, and that is the matter of excise tax. While the FAA has classified the Aerocar as an aircraft

which must be certified, the IRS has classified it as an automobile and it is, therefore, subject to the 10% manufacturers excise tax. When you add this obviously discriminatory tax to the other unknowns that you face when you try to interest the money people in getting into the project, you can see that we are really up against about three strikes before we start.

Taylor asked that all readers interested in helping a just cause write their congressmen and complain. Because, as he ended his letter, "Certainly flying chariots are going to be the mode of transportation in the future and, while Aerocar is one of the first, we certainly do not believe that the possibilities of development in this field should be stifled by such a tax rule."

Twelve years later, Taylor still did not have start-up money, but his tenacity was intact. He had taken the Aerocar through three models, improving it each time. His latest flying chariot could now soar through the air at 135 mph and scoot across land at 80 mph. Its streamlined good looks, not boxy like the prototype, imitated the best European styling. Converting car to plane took only five minutes, and for safety, if some part wasn't secure, the engine wouldn't start. Taylor had made many other technical enhancements to improve performance both in the air and on the ground. As before, Aerocar Model III satisfied all federal safety standards. Glib as ever, Taylor, in answer to the most often asked question, "What do you have to change when you want to fly?" replied only, "Your mind." Yet he couldn't change the minds of the money men. The mass production cost had risen to $15,000 per unit, and he figured it would take a minimum of $5,000,000 just to start production. Again, there were no takers. Optimistically, Taylor cursed the gods of venture capital and returned to his drawing board. There was so much left to be done. Why not have the wings and tail of the Aerocar telescope out from the body at the push of a button? No problem, he surmised, with the right design.

Taylor wasn't alone in his quest to sell Americans on the idea of flying chariots. Igor Bensen, the head of Bensen Aircraft Corporation in Raleigh, North Carolina, preferred a Gyrocopter to an Aerocar any day. His invention, also known as a Convertabird, seated one person in an open-sided, scaled-down helicopter for quick commutes. Since the propeller was on top of the vehicle and not behind it, the Gyrocopter didn't have to fold up like the Aerocar. The happy owner only had to make a few adjustments to switch from air to land travel. The Gyrocopter flew at 85 mph and drove at 50 mph. It could land on a piece of ground no larger than a tennis court, and the FAA gave it its blessing. In speaking to his own Popular Rotocraft Association, Bensen envisioned "A Chopper in Every Garage." He negotiated with Montgomery Ward to sell do-it-yourself copter kits for $470; the engine was an extra $450. As with Taylor's Aerocar, future skies and roadways appeared to be filled with Gyrocopters. But all the public demonstrations and hoopla that followed amounted to nothing more than faddish interest.

It was probably for the best that these two fanciful inventions didn't make it in the marketplace. American highway fatalities were high enough already without adding to their number. Cars converting into airplanes and vice versa would wreak havoc on safe travel especially in the air; if a traveler could reach a destination faster by air, then why drive? The result would be an overcrowding of the more dangerous airways, where there are no prescribed lines to stay within. There would have to be air traffic control towers every twenty miles to ensure that people wanting to fly or land could do so in a disciplined manner. The mere thought of Aerocars and Gyrocopters mass-produced and available to a neurotic public makes one praise the intelligence of the excise tax.

BIBLIOGRAPHY

Blodget, Robert. "The Aerocar." *Flying* 85 (December 1969): 53 + .
"It's a Plane, and a Car, Too." *Business Week* (February 16, 1957): 200-201.
MacDonald, Don. "Car that Makes Its Own Expressway: Molt Taylor's Aerocar." *Motor Trend* 19 (March 1967): 84-86.
"Taxing Problem." *Aviation Week* 76 (April 16, 1962): 134.
"Whirlaway Way." *Newsweek* 63 (March 30, 1964): 68-69.

Able to fly in air or drive on land, the Aerocar had all the markings of success until federal regulations prevented its mass production. The nightmare of providing air traffic safety also grounded the Aerocar. (1957)

Arica Institute

A Bolivian named Oscar Ichazo shepherded 54 Americans to the Chilean city of Arica in 1970. As spiritual leader, he took them there for intensive consciousness-raising so they could regain their "essential selves." The retreat was such a success that Ichazo immigrated to the United States and opened the Arica Institute in New York City. He became widely known to the public through an interview in *Psychology Today* (July 1973). When asked about how he got started, Ichazo replied:

> After a time of remaining home in Chile, I began to travel and study in the East, in Hong Kong, India, and Tibet. I did more work in the martial arts, learned all of the higher yogas, studied Buddhism and Confucianism, alchemy and the wisdom of the *I Ching*. Then I went back to La Paz to live with my father and digest my learnings. After working alone for a year, I went into a divine coma for seven days. When I came out of it I knew that I should teach; it was impossible that all my good luck should be only for myself.

In Arica, Ichazo told his followers there are three centers in the human animal: the intellectual (path), the emotional (oth), and the vital (kath). Of the three, the kath is the most important. It is located about four inches below the navel because "[w]e sense our basic unity with all life in our guts." If training goes well, the individual renounces ego (any mind games) and learns to rely on kath:

> Very early in our training we introduce a system of mentations that trains people to think with their entire bodies rather than only with their "minds." . . . We divide the body into 12 parts, each of which has a physiological and a parallel psychological function . . . eyes isolate forms . . . the colon, anus,

bladder and kidneys eliminate food, ideas and experiences that are unmetabolizable . . . the genitals reflect our orientation toward or away from life. . . . Once consciousness is homogenized into the entire organism, the head is emptied and it ceases to exert a tyrannical control over everything.

To join the Arica Institute cost $3,000 for 3 months, later reduced to $995 for 40 days (1980). For an extra charge, the institute's store sold such necessities as instruction manuals and meditation suits. Since Ichazo placed so much emphasis on the whole body being alive and "intelligent," his training required large amounts of time devoted to exercise. A free-lance writer, Winifred Rosen, took the training and recorded her experience in *Harper's* magazine (June 1973). Friends had told her that the Arica Institute fulfilled its promise to provide "a place of inner and outer peace, joy, and harmony." Each morning, a trainer stood before the group and announced how that particular day was special. It's "Monday. The planet is the moon. The color is silver. The spirit is assimilation." After several hours of meditation on the planet, the color, and the spirit of the day, the group changed over to gym work, such as yoga asanas, calisthenics, and ballet. Rosen elaborates:

There were many other exercises. The day was filled with them. From the moment of waking to late at night, we did nothing but "objective" exercises. All day, seven days a week, for three months. And we were frequently waiting for the breaks because the exercises were so boring to do.

All the physical activity brought results. Rosen and the others toned up and felt better about their bodies. But the rest of the instruction was ego-flattening and meant to be so. The initiates met in groups of nine to "process Karma." The trainer encouraged group members to reveal the "charged" incidents of their lives, especially sexual ones. Later, Ichazo lectured on the advisability of practicing sexual continence because sex wastes energy and causes suffering in the long run. It was readily apparent that the initiates lived on a very low level of consciousness and were full of harmful beliefs. Only complete obedience to Arica would save them from their living hell. At the end of three months, Ichazo summoned Rosen to his modern high-rise apartment. He told her she was very close to realizing spiritual truth, if only she would accept the fact that she was unimportant in the scheme of things—virtually nothing. To leap the last hurdle, she should show her good faith by working a full month in the Arica nursery. Rosen declined. She had her story.

Faddish interest in Oscar Ichazo roller-coastered after the *Psychology Today* interview. His own words exposed him for what he was. Ichazo's years of groping for an answer to life left him with little more than a jumble of incoherent ideas to pass on to the gullible. Here's a sample of his supposed profundity in response to a comment on modern society:

> But even the paralysis [from overstimulation by the media, computers, etc.] may be a sign of the end of the old order. In the ego-indolent fixation, for instance, right before the ego breaks there is tremendous exterior movement combined with interior paralysis. . . . The world is not limitlessness, so we must discover that humanity is one body. If the idea of reincarnation is real—and it is—then all the people who ever existed in the world are now alive. We all are now. Humanity is the Messiah and we are awakening to that fact. That is the meaning of the consciousness revolution.

BIBLIOGRAPHY

Keen, Sam. "We Have No Desire to Strengthen the Ego or Make It Happy: A Conversation about Ego Destruction with Oscar Ichazo." *Psychology Today* 7 (July 1973): 64-72.

Keerdoja, Eileen, et al. "Arica: The Same Old Yen for Zen." *Newsweek* 98 (November 9, 1981): 20.

Martin, Peter. "New Narcissism." *Harper's* 251 (October 1975): 45+.

Rosen, Winifred. "Down the Up Staircase." *Harper's* 246 (June 1973): 28-36.

B. F. Skinner

As different from Sigmund Freud as he could be, Burrhus Frederick Skinner shares one thing in common with the great Viennese psychoanalyst: both men unwantedly attracted faddish interest in their theories (see entry on "Psychoanalysis"). Over a long and productive career, Skinner, a behavioral psychologist, wrote a number of books, three of which sparked considerable controversy among his peers and a great deal of public consternation. The first of his books to set teeth on edge was *The Behavior of Organisms* (1938). In it he discusses his own invention, the operant conditioning chamber, or — as it came to be known — the Skinner box. Operant conditioning is only one of several types of conditioning; others include avoidance conditioning, differential conditioning, Pavlovian conditioning, and so on.

The Skinner box, constructed to demonstrate operant conditioning, worked like this. The box itself was a 12-inch cube. A small lever projected from one interior wall. When a rat inside the box depressed the lever, food dropped into the chamber for consumption. The rat continued to press the lever until satiated. Further conditioning occurred when the scientist changed the procedure for acquiring food. For example, if the rat received food only after ten lever presses, it frenetically slapped the lever to speed the process. Or, if food was forthcoming only after a wait of one minute no matter how often the lever was pressed, the rat learned (was conditioned) to wait until the minute was almost up, then hit the lever hard for the last few seconds.

Skinner devised many variations of operant conditioning experiments using rats, pigeons, monkeys, and humans. He concluded from his many years of experimentation that animal behavior can be predicted and, even more to the point, can be controlled.

The Behavior of Organisms, a scientific treatise, was virtually unknown to the public, so it couldn't have aroused faddish interest.

What did excite the public was misrepresentation of Skinner's laboratory work in relation to the rearing of his daughter, Deborah. Somehow the truth got twisted. The public thought that Skinner had placed his own child in one of his torture boxes and that he was a cold-hearted scientist who would stop at nothing to prove his theory. People envisioned poor little Deborah forced to press levers all day to satisfy her simple needs while the diabolical Skinner noted responses and continued to dream up new operant conditioning tasks for Deborah. He probably had her box tossed in among those containing rats and pigeons. And what if the rats and pigeons outperformed Deborah? Would her father punish her with electric shock? Public speculation only got worse.

The truth of the matter was that Skinner placed Deborah in an "air crib" — a glassed-in, insulated, climate-controlled environment — and not in a Skinner box. Deborah waddled naked in the air crib, free from ill-fitting clothes and diaper rash, so that she never experienced abrupt temperature changes. The air inside the crib passed through filters to keep it germ free and was so clean that Deborah only needed one bath a week. A 10-yard-long sheet of cotton on a spool installed at one end of the air crib and rolled through into a hamper at the other end provided Deborah with perfect diaper service. Since her environment was soundproof, she didn't hear harsh noises. Deborah could watch her parents through a large window, so she didn't feel alone. Often the Skinners took her out of the air crib for cuddling and play. By her own admission when she reached adulthood, Deborah said her 2 1/2 years in the air crib were tranquil ones. Her father proudly declared that Deborah was the happiest of babies. She rarely cried, and the air crib easily was as comforting as the womb had been. So much for Skinner's imprisoning his daughter to make her a slave to his experiments. Pleased with the results, Skinner marketed his air crib, but only a few sold (1,000+).

Published in 1948, *Walden Two* (see separate entry), unlike *The Behavior of Organisms,* became a bestseller, although not until the 1960s. A novel, the book pictures a utopian society reliant on Skinnerian principles of behavioral engineering. Walden Two's 1,000 commune members practice reinforcement for good behavior and nonreinforcement for bad behavior. Their goal is to eradicate all counterproductive actions, from malicious gossip to overt crime. They live in harmony with one another and stand as a model for the rest of the world to emulate. In *Walden Two,* Skinner transfers his lab observations to a human setting, albeit fictional. For years he had witnessed well-behaved creatures that responded to his dictates. Would human substitution be any different? He made rats and pigeons tow the line, why not people? During the experimental 1960s some of the younger generation embraced Skinner's utopia; others despised the mechanism of control. Those who liked *Walden Two* started communes in imitation of it; those who didn't flocked to more liberal communes that offered free love, drugs, and Bohemian living. Skinner's intention in writing *Walden Two* was to convince himself that behavioral engineering might work in the world at large. It was a mental exercise, a philosopher's conjuration. Skinner had no idea that his novel would provoke faddish interest and result in real-life replication.

Beyond Freedom and Dignity was published in 1971, the year Skinner turned 67. For a third time, the American public charged into conversation about the then-Harvard professor. Skinner implored humankind to save itself from the evils of undisciplined living:

> The intentional design of a culture and the control of human behavior it implies are essential if the human species is to continue to develop. Neither biological nor cultural evolution is any guarantee that we are inevitably moving toward a better world. . . . What is needed is more "intentional" control, not less, and this is an important engineering problem. The good of a culture cannot function as the source of genuine reinforcers for the individual, and the reinforcers contrived by cultures to induce their members to work for their survival are often in conflict with personal reinforcers. . . . These facts simply underline the importance of the threat posed by the literatures of freedom and dignity.

For Americans, denigrating freedom and dignity (the respect and honor of being a free human being) was too much. And there was that awful word again — "control." Who in his or her right mind would want to give up freedom and dignity for a society of lever pressers? It seemed Skinner would die an unhappy man unless everyone spent some time in a Skinner box. Most reviewers of *Beyond Freedom and Dignity* reacted strongly:

> From a scientific standpoint, he knows almost nothing about human beings. (*Book World*)

> He appears to understand so little, indeed to care so little, about society itself that the reader comes totally to distrust him. (*The New York Times Book Review*)

> He does not appear to notice that the behavior he wishes to insure by scientific control is identical to that extolled by Victorian schoolmasters. . . . (*New Yorker*)

> Only if the views of this book are for the most part rejected will it really have a good effect on the social environment. (*Saturday Review*)

Even in scholarly journals, a brain trust of intellectuals denounced Skinner's notions in *Beyond Freedom and Dignity*. However, for his life's work, his undeniable contribution to behaviorism, and his controversial stands, B. F. Skinner graced the cover of *Time* magazine, September 21, 1971. But faddish interest in him lapsed shortly thereafter. In 1987, Skinner wrote an article for *The American Psychologist* berating his peers for not attempting to establish psychology as a science. According to him, the only way to do that was to return to the roots of the discipline — behaviorism and laboratory experimentation. Forget psychotherapy and any other therapies not based on rigid cause-and-effect observation. Once again, the old behaviorist was trying to exert a little control on those around him.

BIBLIOGRAPHY

"Brave New Behaviorism." *Newsweek* 78 (September 20, 1971): 95 + .

Cole, C. E. "Vanderbilt Symposium on B. F. Skinner." *Christian Century* 89 (March 29, 1972): 376-377.

Day, J. F. "Behavioral Technology: A Negative Stand." *Intellect* 102 (February 1974): 304-306.

Klaw, S. "Harvard's Skinner, the Last of the Utopians." *Harper's Magazine* 226 (April 1963): 45-51.

Rice, B. "Skinner Agrees He Is the Most Important Influence in Psychology." *The New York Times Magazine* (March 17, 1968): 27 + .

"Skinner's Utopia: Panacea or Path to Hell?" *Time* 98 (September 21, 1971): 47 + .

The Bermuda Triangle

The three corners of the Bermuda, or Devil's, Triangle are Miami, Puerto Rico, and, of course, Bermuda. Within this large ocean area, ships and aircraft of every description have been lost — never to be found again. Because there are no remains for investigators to examine, each and every loss has been shrouded in mystery. The Triangle's sinister work began with the *Cyclops* incident in 1918 — that is, the first recorded incident. Surely the Triangle had been performing its disappearing act long before the twentieth century, going back hundreds of years. The *Cyclops* left Barbados early in March 1918 en route to Baltimore, Maryland. A grand ship, it stretched almost two football fields and sailed comfortably at 14 knots. Two weeks after the *Cyclops* had left Barbados, it had not yet arrived in Baltimore, and the U.S. Navy sent out a fleet of search ships to find the wayward vessel. But to no avail; the *Cyclops*, 236 officers and men, 67 extra Navy personnel, the U.S. Consul General to Brazil, two AWOL Marines, and three Navy seamen charged with murder had vanished somewhere in the Triangle.

The next major loss occurred in 1931, when the *Stavenger*, a Norwegian ship, dissolved into thin air. More losses followed: December 1945, Flight 19, a Navy training plane, and its supposed rescuer, a Martin Mariner; 1946, the *City Belle*, a Bahamas schooner; 1947, a U.S. Air Force *Superfortress*; 1948, a DC-3; 1949, the British ship *Star Ariel*; 1958, a private yacht, the *Revonoc*; and 1967, a 23-foot cabin cruiser, the *Witchcraft*. The last-named vessel spoke for the rest — some 40 ships and 20 planes in all — lost in the Triangle since 1918.

Charles Berlitz, author of *The Bermuda Triangle* (1974) and *Without a Trace* (1977), promoted the idea that supernatural forces might explain the losses. His two books captivated readers, particularly adolescents, and faddish interest in the Triangle rode the high waves. Several Triangle fads had already emerged in the early 1970s. First, the popular mystic Edgar Cayce told his followers that the lost island of Atlantis was behind it all. The ancient Atlanteans had possessed a rare stone that filtered the sun's rays to generate laser-like beams of energy. The magic stone, still on Atlantis at the bottom of the Triangle, had never stopped absorbing energy and occasionally misfocused the power on hapless crafts venturing overhead. Second, radio station WKAT in Miami broadcast a talk show to discuss the Triangle and share eyewitness accounts. The show received thousands of calls not only about the Triangle, but also about ESP, saucer sightings, mental telepathy, psychic phenomena, and the hoped-for reappearance of Atlantis. Third, to connect with saucer sightings, some people believed aliens from outer space used the Triangle as a base of operations. The aliens swooped down from the sky and whisked off earthlings for lab experiments. Fourth, and by no means least, Satan was to blame. God may have made the earth, but now part of it clearly belonged to his infernal highness. For people drawn to the occult, the Triangle was an eerie reminder.

Asked for an explanation, the U.S. Navy said the ocean south of Miami extending to Puerto Rico and up to Bermuda is naturally treacherous. Savage thunderstorms and other forms of atmospheric violence arise suddenly, violence no team of weather experts can predict. The real devil in the Triangle is the water spout, an ocean tornado that furiously sucks up water to produce great turbulence inside its cone. Such a hell-bent waterspout can rip a plane or boat to smithereens, making it "vanish." Another explanation is that some of the deepest ocean trenches in the world sink to oblivion in the Triangle. The mighty Gulf Stream pushes debris in its path at a rapid pace, so a sunken craft soon falls into an abysmal trench.

Joining in solving the mystery, Soviet scientists advanced several novel hypotheses. Alexander Yelkin surmised that lunar and solar tides cause ionized magma movement under the ocean floor, setting off magnetic disturbances. That action in turn disturbs the proper functioning of electronic instrumentation, causing misnavigation

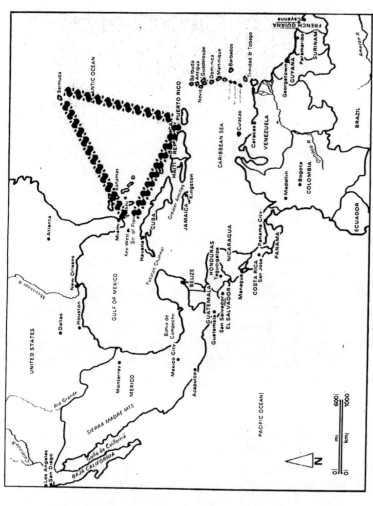

For centuries, ships have sunk, and more recently, aircraft have disappeared, into the watery grave known as the Bermuda Triangle. But it was not until Charles Berlitz wrote *The Bermuda Triangle* (1974) and *Without a Trace* (1977) that the phenomenon seized public imagination. Even though scientists explained the ocean area as one of great natural—not occult—turbulence, skepticism reigned.

and accidents. Nikolai Korovyakov also pointed to magma movement in the earth's core. Core expansion forces magma to rush upward to escape (e.g., volcanic eruptions). Likewise, an opposite action can occur when the core shrinks. Then suction in the core draws water into its fissures, which causes hurricanes and magnetic storms on the surface, possibly pulling in whatever else is up there. Other Soviet scientists looked at shifting earth plates and similar triangular ocean patterns to find a clue. But the safest guess came from Boris Filyushkin, a mere candidate of science in geography. Boris suggested that so many ships and planes have gone down in the Triangle because the area is extremely active. Not all of their captains knew what they were doing or how to avoid trouble.

Apart from all this learned supposition, librarian Lawrence Kusche at Arizona State University decided to check the facts surrounding each mysterious loss in the Triangle. For years, he had helped library patrons find Berlitz and wanted to know the truth for himself. He did, and wrote *The Bermuda Triangle Mystery – Solved* (1986). Kusche established that almost every spooky incident had a logical explanation. He discovered the following: there was no *Stavenger* under Norwegian flag in 1931; the *City Belle* did not vanish, instead it signaled for help and was rescued; a huge wave most likely hit the *Cyclops* broadside, opening a hole that filled so quickly with water there was no time to send out an SOS; and so on. Kusche concluded that Berlitz and others before him just kept repeating sea fables without ascertaining the truth.

Nautical statisticians report there are always a fair number of air and ocean vessels lost at sea each year. The Bermuda Triangle is but one area of the world where losses occur, and in reviewing losses worldwide, the Triangle doesn't appear any more hazardous. But there's no mystery in natural phenomenon, unless, perhaps, a space alien or the devil initiates the action.

BIBLIOGRAPHY

Berlitz, Charles. *The Bermuda Triangle.* Garden City, NY: Doubleday, 1974.
_____. *Without a Trace.* Garden City, NY: Doubleday, 1977.
"The Bermuda Triangle: Hypotheses of Soviet Scientists." *Oceans* 10 (September-October 1977): 58-59.

Kusche, Lawrence. *The Bermuda Triangle Mystery — Solved.* Buffalo, NY: Prometheus Books, 1986.

Smith, Marshall. "The Devil's Triangle." *Cosmopolitan* 175 (September 1973): 198-202.

Stewart-Gordon, James. "What's the Truth About the Bermuda Triangle?" *Reader's Digest* 107 (July 1975): 75-79.

Biorhythm

Dr. Hermann Swoboda, professor of psychology at the University of Vienna, and Dr. Wilhelm Fliess, a nose and throat specialist in Berlin, were the first to postulate a theory of biorhythm. Both men discovered biorhythm in the early 1900s and continued to write treatises about the phenomenon until their deaths. Actually, three rhythms comprise biorhythm: a 23-day physical cycle, a 28-day emotional cycle, and a 33-day intellectual cycle. Swoboda and Fliess collected evidence to substantiate the presence of the first two rhythms. The 23-day physical cycle predicts when a man's or woman's strength, endurance, and courage peak or ebb. The 28-day emotional cycle foretells highs and lows in sensitivity, love, and intuition. The third cycle, proposed by an Austrian engineering professor, Dr. Alfred Teltscher, determines when a person thinks the clearest and is most creative. All three theorists relied on observation and personal experience rather than on scientific proof for the basis of their claims regarding biorhythm. Swoboda noticed that, over time, illness in his patients followed a chartable course. Fliess also made charts, but his began with family trees and birth and death dates, which flowed in discernible cycles. Teltscher, on the other hand, not having patients to provide data, charted students' test-taking ability and found patterns developed that explained why even good students had bad thinking days. These and other empirical studies convinced Swoboda, Fliess, and Teltscher that biorhythms do indeed operate in human beings.

Belief in biorhythm makes perfect sense. Don't we all have good and bad days? Isn't all of nature governed by cycles? Don't the planets move around the sun, the moon around the earth, and the menses in a woman in cycles? Swoboda, Fliess, and Teltscher did their best to spread the word about biorhythm, yet few people listened in the early part of this century. Then, in the mid-1970s, Bernard Gittelson took center stage with his book, *Biorhythm: A*

Personal Science. A second printing followed one year after the first, with the result that thousands of Americans began to chart their own biorhythms. By this time, charting had grown more complex. Critical days are those when one of the three cycles hits dead bottom. Two cycles dipping together results in a double-critical day; three together, in a triple-critical day. A person whose chart shows a definite triple-critical day (i.e., cyclical lows for physical, emotional, and intellectual strength) had better stay in bed and not chance certain defeat.

For the uninitiated, Gittelson wrote a 68-page introduction to the personal science of biorhythm in which he recounted the findings of Swoboda, Fliess, and Teltscher, followed by "Biorhythm Charts of the Famous and Infamous," an appendix of birth charts, and another appendix of biorhythm charts—altogether 186 pages. Whereas the introductory part is engaging and credible, the biorhythm charts of the famous and infamous are pure Barnum. The reader sees indisputable proof that Marilyn Monroe took her own life August 5, 1962, because it was a double-critical day. Other charts pinpoint bad days that resulted in death for Clark Gable and Judy Garland. If they had only known, several airline pilots who crashed could have called in sick. Unknown to Senator Edward Kennedy, he experienced a double-critical day the night of Chappaquiddick. President Anwar Sadat made the decision to declare war on Israel on October 6, 1973, when his physical cycle (not his intellectual cycle) was at rock bottom. Lee Harvey Oswald, Jack Ruby, and Sirhan Sirhan committed their murderous deeds on critical days. It is glaringly obvious that Gittelson does not include charts for peak days predicting happy events, only doom and gloom. The message is: better watch your biorhythm or else!

Gittelson didn't go unchallenged. It was easy enough to chart biorhythm, given hindsight, but when he predicted that Reggie Jackson would have a bad World Series in 1977 his stock plummeted. During the 1977 series Jackson batted .450, hit five home runs—three in the final game—to beat the Los Angeles Dodgers, and became a legend overnight. Despite Gittelson's folly, he and George S. Thommen, who wrote *Is This Your Day?*, sold two million copies of their biorhythm books. In addition, while business was good, Gittelson's company, Biorhythm Computers, Inc., sold

1,000 personalized biorhythm charts a month for $9.95 each. Other entrepreneurs marketed biorhythm kits for predicting the outcome of sporting events (forget Reggie Jackson) and $50 biorhythm calculators for people on the go. To debunk Gittelson, statisticians played around with biorhythms. One in particular, Arthur M. Louis, looked at 100 pitchers on the days they threw no-hitters from 1934-1975 and at 100 heavyweight boxers engaged in title fights from 1899-1975. Louis found no significant correlation between biorhythm readings and individual performances.

Gittelson and Thommen aside, scientists continue to study biorhythm and have now ventured into mood research. On the practical side, British and Japanese industry, wanting to reduce accidents, chart worker biorhythms. Other useful applications of the theories advanced so far may be forthcoming. But thankfully, the personal science of biorhythm was a passing fad. What if the whole world had taken Gittelson seriously? Then millions of people would have sat granite-like with their eyes vacant.

BIBLIOGRAPHY

Gittelson, Bernard. *Biorhythm: A Personal Science*. New York: Arco Publishing Company, 1975.

Louis, Arthur M. "Should You Buy Biorhythms?" *Psychology Today* 1 (April 1978): 93-96.

Parlee, Mary Brown. "The Rhythms in Men's Lives." *Psychology Today* 11 (April 1978): 82-91.

Schadewald, Robert. "Biorhythms: A Critical Look at Critical Days." *Fate* 32 (February 1979): 7 + .

Simon, John. "Biorhythms: Pseudo-Science or Scientific Frontier?" *New Orleans* (August 1978): 12 + .

Thommen, George S. *Is This Your Day?* New York: Award Books, 1968.

Born-Again Christians

Typically, believers in Christianity reaffirm their faith each Sunday when they attend church. The more devout also pray regularly during the week. Both groups feel no need to make a public declaration that they are born again. They are Christians, and their quiet faith sustains them throughout a lifetime. But during the 1970s and into the 1980s, public declarations of having been born again reverberated across America. Stories of people suddenly finding Christ and just as suddenly rededicating their lives to Him saturated the media. Jesus Christ was alive and doing well in America, so well that politicians and criminals found it expedient to be born again, fortunes were made in His name, and religious bigotry seized society.

Exactly how does one become born again? Eric W. Gritsch answers the question in his book, *Born Againism: Perspectives on a Movement* (1982):

> You are born again when you (1) are baptized — as an infant, a second time as a believing adult, or without water and solely by the Holy Spirit; (2) have a traumatic conversion experience, speak in tongues, or change your life from one of egotism to one of sacrificial love for others; (3) believe that the Bible contains inspired and inerrant divine truth, reject "unbiblical" truths such as Charles Darwin's theory of evolution, or uphold monogamy and oppose polygamy; (4) expect the imminent end of the world, affirm the secret rapture of true believers before the Last Judgment, or discern your own time as the last thousand years of human history; (5) become a member of a moral majority defending the puritan ethic of marital sex, free enterprise in business, and public prayer in schools; or (6) hold that the United States has been called by God to be the defender of Christian ideals in an unchristian

world, or join an ideological crusade against godless Communism. This list of answers could easily be expanded.

The term "moral majority" Gritsch speaks of was adopted as a banner. Those born again repeatedly told the nation that they represented current thinking in America. Their opponents rebutted that these people were neither moral nor in the majority, but were splinter groups backed by enough money to get heard. The debate raged until it looked like the moral majority had more clout than expected.

A 1978 Gallup poll revealed that 84 million Americans 18 years or older had made a personal commitment of one kind or another to Jesus Christ. Many of them watched the "electric church" on television and felt divine fire in their bodies as they munched on pretzels. Such a sizeable number of Americans had to be molded into a constituency. In 1980, when Ronald Reagan became President after he defeated the ineffectual incumbent Jimmy Carter, the born-agains exulted. This transfer of affection was indeed curious. Only four years earlier, Jimmy Carter, who made many public declarations of having been born again, was the darling of the movement. But Carter didn't bring about "free enterprise in business," a move dear to the hearts of right-wing fundamentalists, rapidly enough. Hardly a Bible-thumper, Ronald Reagan believed in less government intervention in business and the infamous trickle-down theory, which kept the rich firmly in control of the nation's wealth. So Reagan was the man of the hour, born again or not. The moral majority politically blinded many Americans, who failed to see the upstart movement as one to gain power and wealth for some, not happiness and well-being for all.

One of the most publicized born-again conversions in the 1970s was that of Charles Colson, special counsel to President Nixon. Known as a henchman who could get any dirty deed accomplished, Colson faced a maximum sentence of five years and a $5,000 fine, or both, for attempting to defame Daniel Ellsberg in the Pentagon Papers trial. Caught red-handed, he accepted Christ as his savior and pleaded guilty. In his bestseller, *Born Again* (1976), Colson wrote:

And then I began to see it. The nation was in darkness; there was anger, bitterness, and disillusionment across the land. . . . God seemed to be saying that the renewal of our national spirit can begin with each person—with the renewal of individual spirit. "If you want to do something, submit yourself to Me and I will guide you" were the words implanted in my mind.

Given Colson's past, his detractors labeled him a hypocrite who discovered Christ just in time to save his hide (he served time anyway in a minimum security prison and was disbarred). Whether that was the case or not, Colson's conversion sparked a slew of other instant acceptances of Christ. People everywhere who had gotten in trouble took Christ into their hearts and were joyfully born again. What with conversions every day in the electric church and those seen on regular television, swift forgiveness for sins became big business. It seemed bearing witness before millions of people satisfied the soul like nothing else.

As the fad for self-declaration grew, Christ's name was heard in some unlikely places. Gorgeous New York models banded together and called themselves Models for Christ. Their prayer leader spoke these words: "I pray for all of Seventh Avenue. I pray that when Calvin Klein, Perry Ellis, Ralph Lauren and the other designers see these models, they'll see something different in our eyes." One born-again model asked to pose for a liquor ad answered "no," although her associate, also born again, agreed to pose "because the Bible says to honor your boss." Premarital sex wasn't so easy to reconcile. For the besieged models, choosing Christ over the mere mortals who wanted to sleep with them was trial by fire. But Christ won out for a time.

Christ also fared well in corporate boardrooms. Chick-fil-A's president and founder, Truett Cathy, a born-again Christian, decided not to open on Sunday, even in metropolitan shopping malls where people craved his chicken seven days a week. Cathy said, "Glorifying God is one of our corporate goals." Kenneth Wessner, head of ServiceMaster, an Illinois firm that manages hospitals, schools, and corporations, proudly admitted that his company's name means "service to the Master" and "master of service." The company's annual reports included biblical quotations and a religious essay. Randall's Food Market, Inc., a 35-store chain in Houston, refrained from selling alcoholic beverages because its chairman, Robert Onstead, was born again. By 1983, the Christian Chamber of Commerce *CCC Yellow Pages* listed some 1,000 born-again companies.

All wasn't that heavenly, though. The more zealous companies got into legal trouble by insisting on hiring only born-again managers and workers. In the marketplace, born-agains didn't like having to deal with nonbelievers and weren't afraid of saying so. Unless Jews accepted Christ, they were lost, as were other unenlightened people. The born-again companies prayed for big profits which Christ wanted them to have. It was the best management ploy going—to get workers to strive for Christ, the embodiment of love and perfection, rather than for a cigar-chomping Simon Legree who snarled at them. Born-againism showed up elsewhere as entrepreneurs discovered the name Christ ensured high earnings. Schools, day-care centers, recreation centers, clinics—just about every type of business enterprise—boasted of being exclusively for the born again. Thereby the faithful could count on the fact that only fundamentalist beliefs were expressed there, not godless humanistic viewpoints.

John Garvey observed in a *Commonweal* article: "For any Christian a belief in perfectibility is a dangerous thing . . . To say 'I am saved'—as if it were my decision that made the big difference—seems arrogant, presumptuous." The born-again movement lost some of its vigor when several of its top televangelists showed just how arrogant and presumptuous they could be. Jim Bakker, President of the PTL ("Praise-the-Lord") Club was accused of having illicit sex with female and male partners and of living grandly off the church's income. Eventually, Bakker was convicted of fraud in connection with the sale of partnerships in Heritage Village, a PTL resort development. When another prominent televangelist got into hot water, the end of the movement was near. Jimmy Swaggart, a minister of the Assemblies of God, admitted to paying a New Orleans prostitute to pose nude for him. Then, in defiance, Swaggart refused to undergo a two-year rehabilitation program imposed by his superiors because he didn't want to lose his $140 million-a-year television ministry or his Bible College. Bakker and Swaggart caught their fervent followers unaware, but not in a frame of mind to forgive and forget. The millions of dollars in contributions that had streamed into the coffers of the PTL began to slow, enough so that in 1988, the Reverend Jerry Falwell disbanded the Moral Majority, the conservative religious and political organization he had founded in 1979. After the scandals, few born-again Christians were proud to wear buttons on their lapels identifying them as such, and born-again bumper stickers, stationery, and calling cards disappeared quickly. All that was left to do then was for the disgraced televangelists to declare they were born again and start over. Besides, there was no rule limiting a person's declarations.

BIBLIOGRAPHY

Baig, Edward C. "Profiting with Help from Above." *Fortune* 115 (April 27, 1987): 36-41.

Colson, Charles. *Born Again*. Old Tappan, NJ: Chosen Books, 1976.

"Galluping Statistics." *America* 142 (June 14, 1980): 492.

Garvey, John. "The Prematurely Saved: Unecumenical Thoughts for Advent." *Commonweal* 105 (December 22, 1978): 805-806.

Savan, Leslie. "The God Squad." *Mademoiselle* 92 (January 1986): 116 +.

British Coronations

So far, there have been four coronations in this century: Edward VII on August 9, 1902; George V on June 22, 1911; George VI on May 12, 1937; and Elizabeth II on June 2, 1953. Edward VIII reigned as King from January 10, 1936, to December 10, 1936, but was not crowned in a coronation ceremony. He abdicated the throne to marry the American Wallis Simpson, who, twice-divorced, was not considered a suitable queen for the British Empire. All told, each coronation has inaugurated a whole kingdom of faddish interest for Americans. The unrivaled pomp and circumstance never failed to elicit the same questions. Why are there still kings and queens in the twentieth century? Ermine-wrapped royalty seems so archaic in the modern world. And what do British sovereigns do? They don't govern the lands they possess; Parliament handles that onerous task. It appears the only duties of a British sovereign are to look good for state occasions and to symbolize the glorious past.

But what of the inglorious present? The passing decades have witnessed the British Empire shrink in size and decline economically. Yet the British — even those on the dole — continue to approve of the Royal family living like, well, like kings and queens. In the terrible war year of 1917, George V and his queen received $2,350,000 in annuities paid by the British people, plus another $300,000 in revenues from the Duchy of Lancaster (*World Almanac*, 1918). In 1989, Elizabeth II and her husband had at their disposal approximately $6,599,745 in annuities paid by the British people (*Whitaker's Almanack*, 1990). Why do the beleaguered British permit such extravagance merely to prop up an antiquated symbol?

At each coronation these questions reemerged. The grandioseness of the medieval ceremony played out before a world of mainly have-nots has been for some Americans the height of arrogance.

But for unquestioning, enraptured observers, the coronation ceremony was a treat to behold. It involved so much pageantry that one
had to read a book to understand exactly what took place. British
publications on the subject state proudly, "The Coronation is in fact
a solemn contract of loyalty and devotion between Sovereign and
People." In brief, the stages of the coronation are:

1. The Entrance. The King or Queen enters Westminster Ab-
   bey, preceded by the highest dignitaries of the Church of
   England, and after private prayers sits in the Chair of State.
2. The Recognition. The church dignitaries present the Sovereign to the Church assembly. Silver trumpets sound.
3. The Oath. The Archbishop of Canterbury administers the
   spoken oath to the Sovereign. The Sovereign then, carrying
   the Sword of State, goes to the altar, kisses the Holy Bible,
   and signs the written oath.
4. The Anointing. The Sovereign moves to King Edward's
   Chair (dedicated for this purpose in 1297), over which four
   Knights of the Garter hold a canopy of gold cloth. The Archbishop of Canterbury anoints the Sovereign with holy oil in
   the form of a cross on the head, chest, and palms of both
   hands.
5. Presentation of the Spurs and Sword. The Lord Great Cham-
   berlain touches the Sovereign's heels with solid gold spurs,
   dating from the Coronation of Charles II, to signify the military character of the Sovereign. A lighter jeweled Sword of
   State is girt about the Sovereign with accompanying words,
   then the Sword is laid upon the altar. A peer draws it from the
   scabbard and carries it naked before the Sovereign.
6. The Investiture. The Sovereign receives the Armill and the
   Royal Robe, the Orb, the Ring, the Sceptre with the Cross,
   and the Sceptre with the Dove, each one highly significant of
   Sovereign duty.
7. The Crowning. The Archbishop of Canterbury lays the
   crown on the Sovereign's head. The peers put on their coro-
   nets. Silver trumpets sound. The Sovereign receives the Holy
   Bible, followed by the Benediction.

8. The Inthronization. The Sovereign leaves King Edward's Chair and goes to the Throne Chair.
9. The Homage. The clergy, princes, and peers pay homage to the Sovereign. Drums beat. Silver trumpets sound.
10. The Communion. The Sovereign descends from the Throne, goes to the Altar, removes the Crown, and kneels in communion. The communion completed, the Sovereign exchanges Robe and Crown before walking in procession. The final act of the Coronation is for the Sovereign to ride in the State Coach (first used in 1762) through the streets of London to the cheers of the crowd.

Americans could only read about the first two coronations, unless they were lucky enough to cross the Atlantic to be there in person. George VI's coronation was the first to be televised, and Elizabeth II's ceremony was an unparalleled media event. In connection with coronations, the Royal Jewels have been another source of faddish interest. To date, there are approximately 1,000 exquisite pieces in the collection, including the stones cut from the famous Cullinan diamond which, when mined in 1905, weighed over 3,000 carats. Because the Royal Jewels were rarely seen, they stimulated fervent delight at coronation time.

Perhaps not so ironically, King Edward VIII, who abdicated the throne for the woman he loved, melted more American hearts than if he had gone through with the coronation. To relinquish the crown of Great Britain to marry a commoner tainted by two previous husbands took courage. But by stepping down, Edward stepped into romantic legend alongside Romeo and Juliet, Tristan and Iseult, and Héloise and Abelard. Every detail of this incredible love story circled the globe faster than the marathon pilots of the day. In Sacramento, California, the proprietor of the Hotel Senator redecorated his bar with two 9-foot panels depicting the momentous event. On the first panel of the brightly painted mural, Queen Mary and the Archbishop of Canterbury look with horror at Edward sitting uneasily in full regalia on the throne. Edward avoids their grief-stricken faces to glance over his shoulder at Mrs. Simpson, who waits for him at the garden gate with her pet dog. The Prime Minister, Stan-

Elizabeth II became Queen of the United Kingdom of Great Britain and Northern Ireland and head of the Commonwealth in 1952. The coronation pageantry the
British revere, Americans puzzle over.

ley Baldwin, kneels at the King's feet, thrusting the crown forward for him to take. On the second panel, Edward, dressed in a suit and overcoat, with Mrs. Simpson, walks away from the court and its dejected members. What makes the panels even more delicious is that all the real-life characters except for Edward and Mrs. Simpson resemble huge playing cards, while an impish Cupid prances near Edward. One waggish commentator sort of championed the ex-king:

> [Edward] acted like something half-way human instead of a waxworks clothes-horse to hang an ermine kimono and metal hat on with as many rites and incantations as a voodoo funeral. . . . while neither the King nor his brother could probably make a living even in the Garden of Eden, George is a whole lot better puppet . . .

Surely this flippant remark came from the lips of an irreverent American. But no, it was the assertion of British General Hugh Johnson, whose syndicated column reached thousands of British, Continental European, and American readers. So much for undying respect for the Royal Family.

British coronations revive the beloved pageantry and earnest questions surrounding them. Faddishly, Americans delight in the ceremonies and buy paper crowns, plastic sceptres, and commemorative medallions by the carriage load. But we also wonder why the British allow such excess in a tough economic world, which makes us attend more carefully to our own President and the social expenses of running the White House.

BIBLIOGRAPHY

Blumenfeld, Ralph D. "The Story of the Coronation." [George V] *The Outlook* 98 (July 22, 1911): 616-624.

Bodley, J. E. C. "Coronation of Edward VII." *Fortnightly Review* 81 (April 1904): 650-661.

"Britain Prepares the Biggest Show on Earth." [Elizabeth II] *Look* 17 (May 5, 1953): 27-36.

Brogan, D. W. "Whys of that Paradox, the Coronation." *The New York Times Magazine* (May 10, 1953): 13 + .

Field, Leslie. *The Queen's Jewels*. New York: Harry N. Abrams, Inc., 1987.

Hayden, Ilse. *Symbol and Privilege: The Ritual Context of British Royalty*. Tucson, AZ: The University of Arizona Press, 1987.

Hunt, Francis. *The Book of the Coronation*. New York: Funk & Wagnalls, 1952.

Williams, Maynard Owen. "Along London's Coronation Route." [George VI] *The National Geographic Magazine* 71 (May 1937): 609-632.

Bulimia

The public first became aware of this eating disorder around 1980. At the same time, the American Psychiatric Association (APA), for its *Diagnostic and Statistical Manual of Mental Disorders*, third edition (*DSM-III*), devised diagnostic criteria for bulimia nervosa. Due to increased prevalence of the disorder, a later APA revision (*DSM-IIIR*, 1987) characterized bulimia as having these features:

A. Recurrent episodes of binge eating (rapid consumption of a large amount of food in a discrete period of time).
B. A feeling of lack of control over eating behavior during the eating binges.
C. The person regularly engages in either self-induced vomiting, use of laxatives or diuretics, strict dieting or fasting, or vigorous exercise in order to prevent weight gain.
D. A minimum average of two binge eating episodes a week for at least three months.
E. Persistent overconcern with body shape and weight.

These criteria, when put to the test, often reveal a lesser problem now recognized by psychiatrists as fad bulimia. As a result of careful interviewing, assessment measures, and the patient's response to counseling, the number of patients thought to be bulimic has dropped considerably. Primarily a disorder affecting girls in their late teens, bulimia can be a copycat behavior rather than a deep-seated mental affliction. Noting this, researchers have gone to college campuses to gather evidence to demonstrate the prevalence of bulimia. In a 1987 survey published in the *Journal of the American Medical Association*, researchers found that only 1.3% of college women and 0.1% of college men satisfied the *DSM-IIIR* criteria for bulimia. In a 1988 survey published in the *American Journal of Public Health*, different researchers found clinical bulimia in only

1% of college women and 0.2% of college men. In both studies, many more students "thought" they were bulimic and described bulimic-like behavior they had heard about as a personal affliction. But, again, they didn't meet the *DSM-IIIR* criteria. What happened between 1980 — the year news of bulimia broke out — and 1987 was the birth of a fad.

Not to be taken lightly, adolescents afflicted with clinical bulimia require psychiatric counseling. They are in no way part of the fad. Counselors now know how to tell the true bulimic from the faddist. Joan P. Cesari, member of the Counseling Psychology Department, University of Kansas, lists the differences:

1. The individual with fad bulimia experiences recurrent episodes of binge eating, but the amount of food ingested is considerably less than that consumed in cases of clinical bulimia.
2. The binge of persons with clinical bulimia consists of easily ingested, high-calorie food (i.e., junk food), whereas the person with fad bulimia will often report a binge consisting of a salad or a sandwich.
3. The secrecy and shame that surrounds the binge of a person with clinical bulimia is a major distinction between fad bulimia and clinical bulimia.
4. The termination of a binge by a person with fad bulimia usually occurs through self-induced vomiting [that is not habitual].
5. Persons with fad bulimia are also frequent dieters and have usually tried many approaches to weight loss.
6. Although some persons with fad bulimia show weight fluctuations their gains are usually no greater than 10 pounds because of the limited amounts and occasions of binges.
7. The person with fad bulimia rarely reports a depressed mood but almost always reports self-deprecating thoughts following a binge.
8. The person with fad bulimia has no history of anorexia nervosa or of clinical bulimia.

Teenage girls entering college want to be thin and thus attractive. The college years are when many girls look for a husband. Thin is in, so they grasp at any straws of hope. During the 1980s, talk about bulimia inundated most every college campus. If a girl wanted to look especially slender for a weekend date, she might have run several miles on a track, skipped a meal, and drunk prune juice. The next weekend, no date, so on Saturday night, in the company of other dateless girls or alone, she stuffed her face until her stomach hurt. Soon she and her girlfriends all knew the horrible truth — she had incurable bulimia! In the aforementioned research studies, some of the girls proudly told their friends they were bulimic. It was a status symbol. Besides, didn't famous Hollywood movie stars binge and purge all the time to keep looking good?

Fad bulimia isn't alarming if it doesn't worsen into clinical bulimia, or anorexia nervosa (self-starvation) which is life threatening. At present, the psychiatric community carefully monitors fad bulimia to see that it doesn't develop into clinical bulimia. For young girls, fad bulimia is most likely a rite of passage which they outgrow.

BIBLIOGRAPHY

Cesari, Joan P. "Fad Bulimia: A Serious and Separate Counseling Issue." *Journal of College Student Personnel* 27 (May 1986): 255-259.

Drewnowski, Adam, et al. "The Prevalence of Bulimia Nervosa in the U.S. College Student Population." *American Journal of Public Health* 78 (October 1988): 1322-1325.

Mitchell, James E., ed. *Anorexia Nervosa & Bulimia: Diagnosis and Treatment.* Minneapolis, MN: University of Minnesota Press, 1985.

Schotte, David E., and Albert J. Stunkard. "Bulimia vs. Bulimic Behaviors on a College Campus." *Journal of the American Medical Association* 258 (September 4, 1987): 1213-1215.

Bundling

During Colonial times, if, on a snowy evening, a suitor walked miles to visit his sweetheart, usually after the family meal he was asked to spend the night. His sweetheart coyly nodded approval, indicating that he was more special than her other suitors. After light conversation and perhaps a game of cards, the girl's parents bid the young couple goodnight. The blushing maiden went to her room alone, not to undress completely but to change her attire. She put on what was called a common dress, drawn at the neck and waist with strings knotted tightly, over cloth legs. Next, her suitor entered her bedchamber and removed any heavy outer garments he hadn't already taken off. Still wearing several layers of clothing, he got into bed beside her. They exchanged a few sweet words and fell asleep, bundled together.

That was the chaste scenario, although not the only one, as can be imagined. From contemporary accounts, most bundling was innocent — the young man tired from his walk and appreciative of a warm bed, the girl cautious and respectful of her father's rules. However, unwritten law did recognize the immediacy of natural impulses and decreed that any child born of bundling had to be sanctified by marriage. The less chaste scenario was purely for gain and fostered promiscuity. A husband might offer his wife or daughter to a known wayfarer or even to a perfect stranger for various reasons: money, favors, a quick marriage, appeasement of a lickerish wife, and so on. Henry Reed Stiles, the historian of bundling, has discovered several facts about the practice. The custom originated due more to convenience and necessity than to ulterior motives. Only the lower classes condoned it, not the upper. And bundling peaked in the years from 1750 to 1780.

As a custom, bundling had antecedents tracing back to the ancient Britons at the time of the Roman conquest. Eighteenth-century British, though, condemned bundling as that "peculiar American institution" to point out how immoral the colonists were. Actually, the dour-faced Puritans first made the practice acceptable, and they were hardly licentious people. For the Puritans bundling was a test of self-mastery, self-denial, and discipline.

Since bundling is considered a custom, can it rightfully be called a fad? From 1750 to 1780, bundling's peak years, there was a relaxation of moral restraint. Increased dissatisfaction with British rule sparked rebelliousness and made for unrest. Young men and women felt political friction in the air to match the fire in their loins. The tempo of life quickened, and so, too, did the need to experience physical love. Continued ravages of disease encouraged bundling. Smallpox, in particular, struck the lower classes, compelling procreation to fill out families.

Then why in 1780 did bundling lose its momentum? Stiles suggests that the upper classes, who had always frowned on the practice, were finally successful in putting an end to it. In 1780, the Revolutionary War was in full swing, with another three years of fighting ahead, so conscripting troops from the lower classes left few dewy-eyed males to go bundling. The upper class needed young men to bayonet British, and war was no time for playing bedsheet games. As a custom, bundling extended over many decades and provided respite for weary suitors or lascivious fun for expectant travelers. But as a fad, bundling marked a 30-year period in our history which preceded independence and, just as sure as Old Glory, stirred the souls of young men and women.

BIBLIOGRAPHY

David, Clement. "From Practices to Assumptions." *Catholic Education Review* 61 (1963): 328-334.

Ktorides, Irene. "Marriage Customs in Colonial New England." *Historical Journal of Western Massachusetts* 2 (1973): 5-21.

Stiles, Henry Reed. *Bundling: Its Origin, Progress, and Decline in America*. New York: Book Collectors Association, Inc., 1934.

Business Management

Historians have already labeled the 1980s the decade of greed. Reaganomics and the trickle-down theory produced a sunny climate of opportunism for aggrandizement. With the White House nodding approval of freer enterprise, it seemed almost un-American not to take advantage of the situation. The 1980s emphasis on get-it-now-while-the-gettin's-good affected management style, as did the economic ascendancy of other nations—Japan, in particular. Every few months, a new book told business how to drive workers harder to achieve maximum efficiency and make them like it to boot. America had lost its number one standing in finance and commerce. Thus, any book that could cure the ills of American business was worth its weight in equity funds (gold didn't perform well during the 1980s). So, in quick order, practically everyone who worked for a living got inoculated with the latest management fad. Most of the cures, though, turned out to be common sense, commonplace, and common knowledge. But that didn't stop frenzied managers from reciting the virtues of Theory Z, Intrapreneuring, and Skunk Camps.

Peter F. Drucker had been the top management guru for the last 40 years, having written 22 books on the subject (six of which were published in the 1980s). His advice was pretty much gospel until a whole boardroom of alarmists and envious scribes invaded his domain. Here's a sampling of how-to-manage books, some of which hit the big time, earning nifty dividends for their authors. Thomas J. Peters deserves to go first; his *In Search of Excellence* (1982) produced a $1.8 million royalty check which sent him in search of paper to write three sequels.

Peters, Thomas J., and Robert H. Waterman, Jr. *In Search of Excellence: Lessons From America's Best Run Companies*. New York: Harper & Row, 1982.

_____, and Nancy K. Austin. *A Passion for Excellence: The Leadership Difference*. New York: Random House, 1985.

_____. *Thriving on Chaos: Handbook for a Management Revolution*. New York: Alfred A. Knopf, 1987.

_____. *The Skunk Camp Promises*. New York: Alfred A. Knopf, 1987.

Kenneth Blanchard did well himself. As managers fired with a passion for excellence rallied workers, they learned from Blanchard how to conserve time.

Blanchard, Kenneth, and Spencer Johnson. *The One Minute Manager*. New York: William Morrow & Co., 1982.

_____, and Robert Lorber. *Putting the One Minute Manager to Work: How to Turn the Three Secrets into Skills*. New York: William Morrow & Co., 1984.

_____, and Drea Zigarmi. *Leadership & the One Minute Manager*. New York: William Morrow, 1985.

_____, et al. *The One Minute Manager Gets Fit*. New York: William Morrow, 1986.

_____, and Norman V. Peale. *The Power of Ethical Management: Why the Ethical Way Is the Profitable Way in Your Life & in Your Business*. New York: William Morrow & Co., 1987.

_____, and William Oncken, Jr. *The One Minute Manager Meets the Monkey*. New York: Simon & Schuster, 1988.

Evidently, Blanchard rushed around asking his associates — taking no more than one minute — for writing help. But back to our 1980s abbreviated bibliography on management cures.

Deal, Terrence E., and Allan A. Kennedy. *Corporate Cultures: The Rites & Rituals of Corporate Life*. Reading, MA: Addison-Wesley, 1984.

Naisbitt, John. *Megatrends: Ten New Directions Transforming Our Lives*. New York: Warner Books, 1982.

_____, and Patricia Aburdene. *Re-Inventing the Corporation: Transforming Your Job & Your Company for the New Information Society*. New York: Warner Books, 1985.

————. *Megatrends 2000: The New Directions for the 1990s*. New York: William Morrow and Co., 1990.

Ouchi, William G. *Theory Z: How Business Can Meet the Japanese Challenge*. Reading, MA: Addison-Wesley, 1981.

————. *The M-Form Society: How American Teamwork Can Recapture the Competitive Edge*. Reading, MA: Addison-Wesley, 1984.

Pinchot, Gifford, III. *Intrapreneuring: Why You Don't Have to Leave the Corporation to Become an Entrepreneur*. New York: Harper & Row, 1986.

Porter, Michael E. *Competitive Advantage: Creating & Sustaining Superior Performance*. New York: Free Press, 1985.

Now, did any of these books say something new about how to manage? Not really. They reminded American business of what needed to be done to increase productivity, and they supplied dronish managers with quick fixes and business schools with lecture material.

A library within the library — that on Japanese management technique — assumed even greater fad status. It was Pearl Harbor all over again as the Rising Sun handily defeated us. American business had no choice but to heed the Orient and eat a new kind of crow — sushi. After native and foreign writers clarified Japanese management technique, several points were obvious. First, American workers weren't Japanese. An ocean of cultural differences separated the two, as did resentment left over from World War II, the hated imbalance of trade in favor of Japan, dislike for Japanese regimentation, and plain old American hubris never to admit being second-class. William G. Ouchi in *Theory Z* — a primer of Japanese management technique — writes:

> The Japanese organization takes in only young people who are still in the formative stages of life, subjects them to multiple group memberships, and so inculcates in them the kind of devotion to co-workers that one sees in the United States Marines. It is not external evaluations or rewards that matter in

such a setting, it is the intimate, subtle, and complex evaluation by one's peers — people who cannot be fooled — which is paramount.

Soldier-like devotion and peer evaluation are two tenets of Ouchi's Theory Z; the promise of lifetime employment and nonspecialized career paths (i.e., employees learn new jobs to avoid burnout) are the remaining tenets. Some American businesses had been doing similar things all along and didn't see much that was revolutionary in Theory Z, while others jetted across the Pacific on JAL to explore the technique. Yet, at the start of the 1990s, in the management lexicon Theory Z was back at the end of the alphabet, especially after women executives read this bit of male chauvinism: "Every major firm in Japan has a large category of temporary employees who are mostly women. Even today, it is rare that a major Japanese firm will hire women into professional or managerial jobs."

Ouchi recognized the impermanence of new management techniques. He cautioned readers that quality circles (i.e., employee groups that periodically brainstorm on how to improve output) "are in danger of becoming the management fad of the eighties, replacing such previous fads as Zero-Based Budgeting and Management by Objectives." The University of Southern California's Center for Effective Organizations tracks management fads. The Center has discovered that company CEOs try out a fad after having briefly read or overheard something about it. In fact, that's how the fad spreads. One corporate head praises a management technique to high heaven, and then the others don't want to be left behind. The attitude is: Who knows? Quality circles might just energize the workers. Later, when the workers learn that their input has been tossed in the round file, it's time for the CEO to try another cure-all. During job interviews, nervous managerial applicants must extol quality circles or whatever the latest technique is to show that they are "on the cutting edge" of management thought. "I rely on good judgment" just doesn't get it.

Skunk Camp is a four-day retreat that immerses managers in Tom

Peters' theories on excellence. For $4,000 apiece, the participants meet at the Pajaro Dunes vacation development on Monterey Bay near San Francisco. There they get literature, T-shirts, tote bags, coffee mugs, and other memorabilia decorated with the skunk symbol. Peters borrowed the improbable name from Lockheed Corp's legendary cloistered R&D operation, the "Skunk Works." Skunk Campers attend well-organized lectures, group discussions, and brainstorming sessions that introduce them to practical ideas they can take back to their companies. They've heard some of the ideas before, but also some that are novel, which makes the experience worthwhile. They stay up late together, exercise together, and exchange war stories about Pearl Harbor II. Peters' main message throughout is that there are two ways for a company to prosper: by superior customer satisfaction and constant innovation. Both precepts embolden management to sprint off in every direction. Even if Skunk Camp eventually offends some noses and is discontinued, it wore a broad stripe in the 1980s.

As a defense mechanism, workers joke about management fads they must endure. Who hasn't gone to work on a Monday morning only to find out the whole organization will do things "differently" thereafter. If medical dictionaries were truthful, the definition for "ulcer" would be, "an inflammatory, often suppurating, lesion in the duodenum caused by management fads." Ernest D. Lieberman, in *Unfit to Manage!* (1988), charges that:

> Management has lost touch at root because in any big business or government operation, no one knows or can know everything important that goes on. . . . This fundamental ignorance is compounded by political, faddish, or greedy demands that run directly counter to productive realities, such as insisting that the Challenger launch on a frigid day, or ordering up a new "corporate culture" (attitudes and ways of doing things, not artwork) to be installed over the weekend, or demanding unreasonably high profits and uninterrupted quarterly profit increases even though they rob the future to do it. Despite their own ignorance, managements distrust what employees tell

them and don't want to hear what employees have to say, even though ground-level employees often know better than anyone what's really going on in the production process.

But ground-level employees don't get to go to Skunk Camp.

BIBLIOGRAPHY

Byrne, John A. "Business Fads: What's In—and What's Out." *Business Week* (January 20, 1986): 52-61.

Dunsing, Richard J., and J. Kenneth Matejka. "Fad Labelling: The Curse that Can Kill Organizational Change." *Management Decisions* 27 (January 1989): 37-39.

Lasden, Martin. "Fad In, Fad Out." *Computer Decisions* 17 (May 21, 1985): 74+.

Lieberman, Ernest D. *Unfit to Manage!: How Mis-Management Endangers America and What Working People Can Do About It.* New York: McGraw-Hill, 1988.

Migliore, R. Henry. "Business Fads: What's In, What's Out; What's Helpful, What Isn't." *Industrial Engineering* 19 (June 1987): 16-21.

College Students

Some of the most outrageous fads originate on college campuses. Tradition and the excess of youth dictate that it be so. A shelf of books could be written on the antics of college students by sifting through every school newspaper and interviewing alumni. That would be a formidable but fun task. Since a thorough examination can't be made, a "best of" college fads will have to suffice. Three exemplars covered at length in this volume are goldfish swallowing, Veterans of Future Wars, and Eastern mysticism, not to forget streaking included in Volume II, *Sports & Recreation Fads*. The most important point to note about college fads is how rapidly they spread. Regular fads lumber along like elephants compared to campus-born ones. Not that college students are apish imitators—it has more to do with competition and school spirit. There's also the added enticement of trying to get away with something administration frowns on. That's when the kicks really begin.

Before exposing the history of panty raids, mention should be made of Babylonian revels. In 1920, the 19th Amendment gave women the right to vote. Directly after, they poured onto college campuses to challenge society even more. To show their independence, the young women puffed cigarettes and drank gallons of illegal booze. All this indulgence culminated in world-record necking parties, pregnancy, and secret marriages. College administrators didn't know what to do about the Babylonian revels. Were they a fad or the future of coed life? Perhaps it had been a mistake to pass the 19th Amendment and admit more women to college if they were there simply to entice the men into debauchery. But just as student wickedness threatened to engulf the staid halls of academe, young women settled down and got serious. Instead of trying to outsmoke, outdrink, and outneck men, the spiritual daughters of the suffragettes applied themselves to something bigger—to outthink the cocksure Adams of the world.

Since the 1920s, Babylonian revels have shaken campuses time and again in faddish ways. Right after World War II, Apache parties were just the thing to spice up a dull weekend. Returning soldiers had seen the real Apaches in Montmartre night clubs. They were Parisian hoodlums who wore striped sailor shirts and tight-fitting pants. Their women, likewise, had on striped tops or blouses worn off the shoulder. An Apache male looked very masculine with a cigarette dangling from his lips and one eye covered by a beret. In sync, an Apache female showed a lot of leg in mesh hose visible through a slit skirt. For entertainment, the male tossed his woman around the smoke-filled dance floor like a sack of *pommes de terre*. If he didn't break her bones, they had a good time. A liberal G.I. Bill allowed veterans to attend college to instigate Apache parties. All it took was a little ingenuity and some paint to transform a plain room into a Montmartre dive. But for the tops in Babylonian revels, revisiting Imperial Rome via a toga party made the 1970s much more decadent than the tame postwar period. When college students shouted "To-ga! To-ga! To-ga!," it meant only a thin sheet separated modesty from Eros.

By best reckoning, the first panty raid occurred in 1899 at the University of Wisconsin, Madison. Four hundred pajama-clad males rushed Ladies Hall and came away with a reported "204 articles of clothing." But "lace riots" and "silk sorties" didn't really attain fad status until the 1950s. In the spring of 1952, a University of Michigan student uncased his trumpet and played "Serenade in Blue" out his dorm window. The clarion call spontaneously mustered about 600 males in the street, who began to chant, "To the women's dorms!" Feverishly, the males marched ahead. Once at their destination, they broke in side doors, pushed away coeds, and pillaged rooms for lingerie. Assaulted but not undone, some of the girls poured water on the raiders from their windows. Then, in a counteroffensive, 500 females sallied forth to the men's dorms to retrieve their intimate apparel, only to be stopped by the prune-faced Dean of Women. Quiet reigned again around 1 a.m. The next day, psychology students interviewed both warring camps in an effort to understand their curious expression of pent-up libido. That same spring, University of Missouri males broke windows and kicked in doors at two nearby girls' schools, their quest as well for the holy garment. At the University of Vermont, police used tear gas and fire hoses to repel panty raiders. At the University of Tennessee, the story was the same, except the lustful males pelted the police with eggs and shot out street lights. At Stanford University, 500 undaunted males burst through police and faculty guards to enter a women's dorm.

All told, there were 40 incidents in 1952. Unamused, college administrators across the country informed male students that panty raiders could lose their college deferment; perhaps the Korean War was a better place for such bold bandits. The threat succeeded until the war ended in 1953. One of the last big panty raids took place on May 21, 1956. Close to 100 University of Kansas males drove 12 miles to Baker University and parked outside Alpha Chi Omega sorority. Aware of what the outsiders wanted, the boys from Baker confronted them. The rival rooster groups strutted and pecked at one another to see who got the hen feathers. Ten days later, the University of Kansas dismissed 58 of its roosters.

One college administrator, when asked by journalist Andrew Hamilton to explain the panty raid phenomenon, replied, "Many deans are convinced that if coeds would refrain from squealing so delightedly or waving unmentionables out the windows, panty raids would be no more fun than collecting laundry." But the coeds did, and only a cold fish would think purloined panties unexciting. Professor Clarence A. Schoenfeld, in *The University and Its Publics* (1954), attributed the mania to spring fever:

> The most critical period of all is the April-May epoch, which produces campus outbursts as regular as the calendar itself. So predictable is this period of undergraduate flux that its causes may actually be profoundly biological, related somehow to the rutting of the buck deer and vernal craziness of the ruffed grouse.

Profoundly biological it was, as all nineteen-year-old males can attest.

The 1960s stimulated society in many ways. Those who were there can recall any number of zany happenings. Even today, the 1960s play well on television, surpassing the pale 1970s and the colorless 1980s in interest. During the fabled decade, college students bugged out on a regular basis. That didn't mean they went on entomological field trips; rather, they skipped class for a week or more to attract attention. There were specified bug-out times: at the beginning of a semester, just before midterm exams, close to finals, or whenever absence looked like academic suicide. All a student had to do to bug out legitimately was not to tell anyone. If friends knew where the absentee was, that nullified the bug out. However, most universities had favorite destinations, and the poor grinds back on campus knew where the absentees were. For instance, University of Texas students bugged out to Juarez, Mexico; University of North Carolina students to Nags Head Beach; Stanford University students to Squaw Valley; University of Michigan students to Newport, Kentucky; and blueblood Harvard students to Paris. Upon returning, the romantic and mysterious absentee told incredible tales of adventure: the days melted away like honey on bread; food and wine spilled out of a cornucopia; the opposite sex pleaded for ecstasy; and incidentally, the weather wasn't bad. Then the question: Why did you bug out in the first place? And the answer(s): too much pressure, I failed a test, my girlfriend left me, I wrecked my car, or the most nonchalant — no reason.

Caltech students are famous for dreaming up technical high jinks that make national news and inspire others to outdo them. *Life* magazine reported their 1963 project in full because it was so exceptional. The Caltech students organized a Piano Reduction Study Group "to reduce a piano in the shortest possible time to such a state that it may be passed through an aperture of 20 centimeters in diameter." The reducers had to use handtools of less than 15.4 pounds each, and only splinters weighing no more than 17.6 ounces were allowed to pass through. The Study Group bought four old spinets and set to work with a vengeance, racing against the clock to destroy each one. Picture this. Six husky males hammer a wooden piano as if they were Thor tossing lightning bolts. To their side stands a board with a small circular hole cut in it. As soon as the first fragments split off, the reducers feed them through the hole. On the other side of the board is a fast-growing pile of piano debris with keys strewn around like dominos. Caltech's best time was 10 minutes 44 seconds. However, Wayne State University shocked the

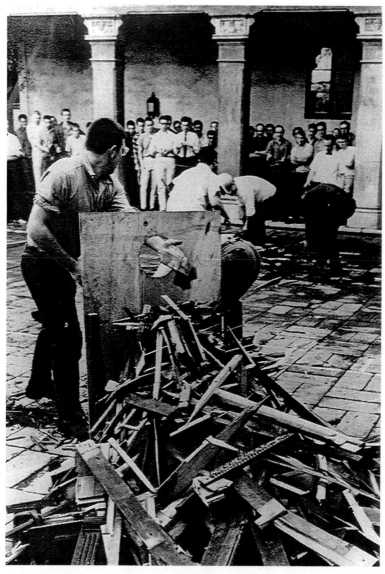

How do you pass a piano through a circle 20 centimeters in diameter? Easy: you demolish it first with regulation handtools of less than 15.4 pounds, as these Caltech students did in 10 minutes 44 seconds. Alas, though, a short time later Caltech lost its world record to Wayne State University. (1963)

group when it reduced a piano in 4 minutes 51 seconds and bragged that "Chopsticks" never sounded better.

Nonverbal communication — the art of saying everything without saying anything — arose as a general society fad in the 1960s. College students, being the innovators they are, toyed around with the pop-psychology notion. The Social Atmosphere Committee, a student group at Columbia University in the heart of New York City, recognized that no one stayed on campus. There were too many city distractions to compete with. But when students ventured into the Big Apple, they played roles and didn't meet anyone or feel at ease because of the fakery involved. To solve the problem, the Committee adopted nonverbal communication and selected as its motto "Warmth." The Committee secured an attic room 120' × 30', enough space for 50 people to mill around in. They painted the walls with free-form patterns in reds, blues, and greens. A Warmth member exuded:

> There's only one rule — no talking. And there's no plan; everything is improvised. At the start it's a little hard to get with it — nonverbal communication is very strange at first — but people are soon caught up in it, and you find yourself doing things you never thought you'd do. I mean, all the normal constraints are off, and everybody becomes a part of what's happening. It's one place where people can enter each other's fantasy lives.

One girl in the Warmth room wove cloth strips around some overhead pipes. A boy and a girl puffed into opposite ends of a cardboard cylinder. Some of the group just started bouncing up and down. A girl stuck her head and arms through a piece of plastic foam. A boy held a sign that read, "Touch the sacred blue egg. Free." The egg turned out to be a balloon. Warmth members painted one another wherever they desired. Musicians improvised a kind of Indian raga for anyone who wanted to dance. A couple held hands stiff-armed for a boy to limbo under. When the simulated pole got so low that the boy fell on his back, two bystanders stopped bouncing and carried him off in a mock funeral service. And this occupied only the first 30 minutes in the Warmth room! With so many great things to do non-verbally, the Columbia students were left speechless.

BIBLIOGRAPHY

"Babylonian Revels." *New Republic* 41 (February 11, 1925): 299-300.

"Bed Sheets Bonanza: Toga Party Craze." *Time* 112 (October 23, 1978): 88.

Brickman, William W. "Higher Jinks and Higher Education." *School and Society* 84 (July 7, 1956): 11-12.

"Bug Out!" *Esquire* 58 (September 1962): 94.

"Campus 'Panty Raiders'—How Many Await Draft?" *U.S. News & World Report* 32 (May 30, 1952): 26.

"Gronk!" *The New Yorker* 43 (April 1, 1967): 32-34.

Hamilton, Andrew. "Madness on Campus." *Saturday Evening Post* 228 (April 28, 1956): 26+.

"Life Goes to an Apache Party." *Life* 21 (November 18, 1946): 144-146.

"Mad Fad for Stir-Crazy Students." *Life* 54 (March 8, 1963): 43-45.

Shah, D. K., and R. LaBrecque. "To-ga! To-ga! To-ga!" *Newsweek* 92 (October 2, 1978): 92.

Couéism

Before arriving in the United States in 1922, Dr. Emile Coué (*kway*) visited England to lecture about self-healing through auto-suggestion. The British newspapers translated his most famous saying and the pithy basis of his treatment as, "Every day, in every respect, I grow better and better." Upon his landing here, American newspapers printed a different translation, "Every day, in every way, I am getting better and better." The slight change in translation, creating a little rhyme, became an advertising slogan of exceptionally persuasive power. Soon Americans from coast to coast knew of Coué through the rhyme which they repeated like parrots. "Every day, in every way, I am getting better and better," was not only fun to say but advanced Couéism rapidly. Autosuggestion was a type of self-hypnosis that had to sink into the subconscious to be effective. Dr. Coué called the subconscious "imagination" to distinguish it from other thought processes. An article in *Current Opinion* (April 1923) made this clear:

> The quintessence of the Coué idea may be summed up in his thought of the supremacy of the imagination. What he says, in effect, to people who suffer and who want to conquer their suffering, is: "Do not use your will! Do not use your conscious mind at all! Make no struggling efforts! All these things hinder and get in the way. It is the subconscious mind that cures, not the conscious, it is the imagination that does it, not the will."

Poor Sigmund Freud. For all his work and that of other psychoanalysts who butted their heads against a wall of disbelief, the public's immediate liking of Dr. Coué must have been unbearable. The darling Frenchman from Nancy won hearts wherever he went by telling audiences to concentrate on health, not sickness. Dr. Coué liked to use the metaphor of the orange peel in his lectures. He would say that pieces of orange peel cause broken legs, so the smart thing to do is to keep the peels swept up. The peels are all those unhealthy tendencies, bad habits, antipathies, passions, and hatreds that block happiness. Autosuggestion sweeps away the peels and replaces them with solid footing. In literal terms, Dr. Coué taught his patients to think "I can," not "I will." The difference is that "I can" addresses the imagination, where it takes root to ward off negative thoughts, whereas "I will" commands the conscious mind, which is obstinate and forgetful.

Dr. Coué, like other charismatic healers—whether legitimate or fraudulent—was himself the true source of healing power. Often by his reputation and presence alone he performed miracles. An American physician, Dr. George Draper, traveled to the Coué clinic in Nancy to observe daily operations. Dr. Draper witnessed a crippled woman supported by two other women enter a room of the clinic. The woman couldn't walk on her own due either to organic spinal cord disease or major hysteria. In a few minutes, Dr. Coué had her walking around the room without assistance, demonstrating that major hysteria was the problem and autosuggestion the cure. As practiced by the master, humor played an essential part in Couéism. Dr. Coué would "strip disease of its dignity" by ridiculing the affliction, though never the patient. Dr. Draper reported that the kind-hearted Frenchman made so many clever remarks aimed at reducing the fear of disease while making rounds in his clinic that patients laughed long and hard. Their laughter alleviated much distress and eventually allowed them to overcome their afflictions. Dr. Coué also implanted in his patients the suggestion that physically they were sound, and they had only to believe in their good health to regain it. The art of suggestion/autosuggestion and jokes, not drugs or medical experimentation, were the sole bases of Couéism. Because most of the patients who came to Dr. Coué suffered from psychosomatic illness, his success rate was high and his notoriety as a miracle worker ensured.

No question of fraud ever reared its ugly head. Dr. Coué was seen as an angel of mercy who derived complete satisfaction from helping others. His clinic in Nancy was free and open to all needy patients. What money he did make came from publication royalties and donations. Dr. Coué had gotten the idea of autosuggestion from reading an American pamphlet on how to be a winner in business. Well versed in traditional hypnosis, Dr. Coué knew too often the person under the spell awoke abruptly, which negated any good effects. Autosuggestion prevented this from happening and could be employed by the patient at any time without having to return to a hypnotist. The repeating of the slogan of Couéism, "Every day, in every way, I am getting better and better," by Americans in the 1920s was a good-natured fad that may have benefited them. But since it was a fad and not a lifelong habit as advised by Dr. Coué, those unsightly orange peels reappeared.

BIBLIOGRAPHY

Coué, Emile. *How to Practice Suggestion and Autosuggestion*. New York: American Library Service, 1923.
_____. *My Method: Including American Impressions*. Garden City, NY: Doubleday, 1923.
"Coué Reestimated in the Light of His Visit." *Current Opinion* 74 (April 1923): 469-471.
"Growing Better with Monsieur Coué." *Current Opinion* 73 (November 1922): 586-587.
"A Physician's Plea for Coué." *Literary Digest* 76 (January 6, 1923): 24-25.
Williams, Otto. "Healing by Autosuggestion." *Living Age* 313 (May 20, 1922): 467-472.

When boy meets girl, wooing fads go with each kiss. Animal attraction may never change but the mating dance does. One decade it's romantic love, the next booze and fast cars. Quite often instead of acting on natural impulse, Americans follow the crowd.

Courtship and Marriage

The *Royal American Magazine* published from 1774-1775 included a feature new to periodicals of the day. "The Directory of Love" offered advice to the lovelorn—those piteous souls entrapped in Cupid's snare. If the Revolutionary War hadn't intervened, the Directory, which ran for only a few issues, might have become a fixture. One letter from "a rich old man of sixty years" asked how he could regain the affection of his 18-year-old bride. She flirted with all the gay young sparks leaving him "almost crazy about it." In answer, the anonymous advisor, Philalethes, felt not one drop of sympathy, ". . . for youthful madam, instead of being fixed to the husband she wished for, and which her years demanded, finds herself joined to a parcel of dried bones, and a most unsubstantial withered body." Two hundred years later, the Directory of Love is a newspaper staple, and in syndication a modern Philalethes patters on every question of love from the sacred to the profane. Still, even as an institution, advice to the lovelorn follows faddish dictates. Eavesdropping on someone else's empty or broken heart has only a short-lived appeal for most readers.

The wearing of wigs in the seventeenth and eighteenth centuries became a personal statement of queerly perceived beauty and social class second to none. Back then, men and women courting one another donned outlandish hirsute creations in a parade of vanity unmatched to this day. To impress a lady, a man lacquered a "bigwig" to his head. The full-bottomed hairpiece curled and cascaded over his shoulders entrancingly, with either high peaks sticking straight up from the forehead (2″ or more) or with a simple part in the middle. However, as luxuriant as the full-bottomed was, it had to go. The unventilated curls caused sweaty pockets of itchy scalp to form underneath. The wearer, then, had to reach for a scalp scratcher of elegant design to bring temporary relief. But when cheek-to-cheek in the midst of finalizing a rendezvous, it was unseemly for a gentleman to claw at a bit of dermatitis. To alleviate some of the problem, wigmakers created the *toupet* style. Smaller and neater, the wig hair flowed back from the forehead over a custom-fitted pad. For additional adornment, the *toupet* wearer chose either pigeon's wings (softly curled side hair) or boucles (tightly bound horizontal curls starting at the temple). Also, for a more groomed look, a courtier could afix on his head the tie, Ramillie, or bag wig. Usually to accompany these styles black ribbon secured one or two long tails of hair in the back. The hair might hang loose like a pony's tail or dangle in a braid.

Well aware of male peacockery, women rose to the occasion and outpeahened them. The daring ladies mounted wigs such as these on their heads: the staircase, the hedgehog (hair cut ragged all over to resemble quills), and the "Cupid's Tower." As the names imply, the emphasis was on soaring height, requiring a wig dresser to stand on a stool to add such essentials as ostrich plumes, jewels, and spools of satin ribbon. Yet, curls, altitude, and gewgaws just weren't enough. The wig dresser had to spray grey or white powder over his creation to cover it completely. Then and only then was the wearer ready to face a judgmental world. What made wig-wearing faddish for colonials not in the upper crust was that it pandered to continental ways. Living in America, chauvinistic British and French set the style. The Old-World gentry wanted to disassociate themselves from the common people just as much as the common people wanted to forget them. Prior to the Revolutionary War, the temptation to look grand like European men and women of distinction affected some colonials. But after the war, Americans shunned hirsute flamboyance altogether.

With the redcoats licked and "Cupid's Tower" a thing of the past, postwar Americans avidly read and practiced elegant manners. Having just won freedom from Great Britain by virtue of rugged fighting and coarse tactics, their desire to return to civility was strong. Our barbaric image needed refining and our population replenishing, so a bouquet of etiquette books taught young people how to exchange pleasantries to hasten courtship. Some of the books were ridiculously faddish and included odd chapters of information. For example, *A New Academy of Compliments* (1795) contained an analysis of moles: "A mole on or near the private parts, promises ability in duty, vigor in love, and success in [having] many children.'' The language of the fan explained how a woman could communicate her interest in a man across a crowded room. In her porcelain hand, she fluttered the come-hither device to speak her deep longing.

It was also essential to learn one's etiquette before visiting a spa. Saratoga Springs in the 1830s was just the place to practice pleasantries. Due to improved transportation routes which brought people in from hundreds of miles away, Saratoga Springs flourished as the preeminent spa of the day. Now, the ostensible purpose of going to Saratoga or to any other spa was to drink the beneficial waters, but the true purpose was to find a "genteel" person to court. Spas were great meeting grounds for singles who, in their best clothes, put on airs. Entering a ready-made society of fine ladies and gentlemen was exhilarating. A hog butcher could act the part of a dandy and woo a seamstress who carried herself like a queen. This make-believe world of rare gentility wasn't without expense. Pretenders had to eat many bowls of potato soup before they could dine at Saratoga on venison in burgundy sauce. Somehow in the rage to have nonstop fun, imbibing the medicinal waters got lost. Saratoga renewed interest in itself throughout the nineteenth century by offering other pleasures to the public like horse racing, gambling, concerts, and lavish accommodations. But all these extras spoiled the earlier emphasis on providing a beautiful setting for courtship free from distractions.

Popular art visualized what the etiquette books tried to teach. In the 1850s, a young man snickered at a picture of a female heart divided into various "lands" like a map. Demarcated were love of admiration, coquetry, selfishness, sentiment, fickleness, love of dress, and love of display. Likewise a young woman amused herself by looking at a male heart with its lands: economy, love of money, love of ease and freedom, which she would change shortly. For wedded couples, depictions of marital strife reminded them that their blessed union could split in two. A lithograph such as "The Discord" sold well. Here's what it looked like: a husband and wife tug at a pair of trousers which symbolize family rule. The man is fully dressed except for his contested pants. He says, "I rather die than let my wife have my pants! A man ought always to be the ruler!'' His equally resolute wife thinks, ''So help me woman is born to rule and not to obey those contemptible creatures called men!'' At her side their daughter pleads, ''Oh Pa, let go, be gallant or you'll tear them.'' At his side their son pleads, ''Oh Mama, please leave my Papa his pants.'' Behind the husband a male friend urges, ''Fight courageous for sovereign authority neighbor; or your wife'll do to you as mine has done to me. She'll pull your hair off your head and compel you to wear a wig!'' And behind the wife a female confidant goads her on, ''Brave Sarah! Stick to them, it is only us which ought to rule and to whom the pants fit the best.'' Board games also attempted to shape courtship behavior. Invented by a clergyman's daughter, ''The Mansion of Happiness'' challenged players to move 67 spaces to reach ''happiness'' by landing on virtues, not vices. The object was to avoid getting mired in such ruts as ''audacity,'' ''cruelty,'' ''immodesty,'' or ''ingratitude.'' One unlucky spin of the teetotum could mean a major setback, landing a player in ''the pillory'' or ''the stocks''—for the truly immoral—''the summit of dissipation.'' Courting couples played the game lightheartedly but also to observe one another's attitude toward Christian ethics.

The English economist Thomas Robert Malthus (1766-1834) affected American courtship behavior in a salutary way. Malthus fretted about overpopulation and how teeming humans would eventually deplete the earth of its resources. Inspired by Malthus, Richard Carlile wrote *Every Woman's Book; or, What Is Love?* (1828) which implored British women to use birth control immediately. An American, Robert Dale Owen, taking his cue from *What Is Love?*, published *Moral Physiology* (1830). Owen recommended coitus interruptus as the most reliable form of birth control. The sponge method (absorbent material attached to a penny ribbon) wasn't as good, and a ''delicately prepared skin'' (priced at $1) for insertion in the woman cost too much for the average American. At the same time, a Massachusetts doctor, Charles Knowlton, published his contraceptive guide, *The Fruits of Philosophy*. Knowlton advocated spermicides for Americans who didn't want to live the Malthusian nightmare. Sulphate of zinc and sugar of lead were two of his harsh inhibitors, although plain vinegar was probably the best contraceptive, and during winter months ''spirits'' could be added to any of the spermicides to keep them "active." Knowlton suggested that bachelors fearful of sex urges restrict their diet to milk and vegetables; a man who consumes meat, turtles, oysters, and red wine encourages lust.

Both Owen and Knowlton suffered the consequences of being too frank. Moralists accused them of wanting to make all women prostitutes. It was much better for young girls to grow up believing babies came from cabbage patches than for them to know details about contraceptives. These early books sold well even though people who wanted to read them were afraid to admit they did. Moralists preached against Owen and Knowlton, using horrific words like "unnatural measures" to spit out their contempt. Contraceptives were a fad of the devil, and those who used them, philanderers and hussies. What all this posturing accomplished was to keep women pregnant year after year, creating families of ten or more children.

Another method of contraception that engendered faddish interest was John Humphrey Noyes' coitus reservatus. In his utopian community at Oneida, New York, Noyes made love with women for an hour or more without ejaculating, thereby pleasing them first and foremost. Sexual intercourse as a gymnastic art was certainly a novel idea for most Americans. Yet more audacious, Noyes wrote that sexual intercourse should be "a purely social affair, the same in kind with other modes of kindly interchange, differing only by its superior intensity and beauty." This assertion and the fact that such a sexual Valhalla existed in upstate New York fostered enormous faddish interest. Once again across America, as with Owen and Knowlton, moralists denounced Noyes and his so-called "Perfectionists." People questioned whether a righteous woman could actually enjoy sexual intercourse, and by the way, how did Noyes exhibit such exquisite self-restraint?

Before leaving the topic of contraception it should be noted that an interesting fad affected its opposite — conception. In the halcyon days of hoped-for fertility prior to gloomy Malthus, Thomas Ewell, U.S. Navy surgeon, advised couples to make love outdoors. Ewell had observed Negroes coupling in the hay, under trees, and alongside river banks (where else could they go?) with good results. There were always lots of black babies around. So Ewell inferred that something in the fresh air stimulated procreation. Naturally, to thwart conception a couple only had to stay indoors and breathe fetid air composed of "carbonic acid or azotic gas."

During the nineteenth century, the taboo subject of contraception grew like a weed in the garden of romance. But it didn't choke out faddish interest in courtly love altogether. Famous genre painters like William Sidney Mount (1807-1868) depicted scenes of endearing courtship that captured public fancy. Mount's painting entitled "The Sportsman's Last Visit" shows two young gentlemen wooing a comely maiden. The rugged sportsman in hunting costume is about to lose out to a less robust but well-dressed gentleman for the affections of the girl. The painting achieves two objectives: beauty and moral utility. Mount instructs viewers that marrying a footloose sportsman, no matter how handsome, isn't the prudent thing to do. Another Mount painting, "Winding Up," also speaks didactically. This time, inside a modest dwelling, a young man holds a skein of yarn which his beloved is winding into a ball, the lesson being that woman must tame the beast in man and harness him for domestication. Similar to Mount in skill and intention, Francis William Edmonds painted "Sparking," in which a young couple sit side by side in front of a warming fire. With her eyes downcast, the maiden in shawl peels apples while her wooer leans toward her in silent adoration. These courtship scenes and others like them weren't considered serious art that would win awards. Nor were they intended to be anything more than an attempt to interest the lovesick public in itself.

Love for love's sake withered toward the end of the nineteenth century and would never bloom fully again. Writers such as Edward Bellamy, Lester Frank Ward, Thorstein Veblen, and Theodore Dreiser looked askance at courtship and marriage. They saw the whole process as one driven by economic need and class preservation rather than one based on mutual attraction and free choice. Their notion of the "marriage market" dominated thinking for several decades, but so, too, have other notions of how Americans meet and mate. From 1900 on, each decade has focused on the meaning of love in a particularly faddish way. Perhaps the marriage market appeared more real to Bellamy et al., with the rise of urbanization. But as a new phenomenon, no, the marriage market had been around a long time. Reacting to this condemnation, magazine writers in the first decade of the twentieth century tried to reestablish pure love as the end-all and be-all of courtship and marriage. Typical of the journalistic sermons, Charlotte Perkins Gilman defined the "Five Kinds of Love" in a *Harper's Bazaar* article (1908). Her handful were desire, gratitude, sympathy, admiration, and devotion:

> It [true marriage] should have as an absolute requisite Desire — else the parties contracting had best remain mere friends. It should pile up from year to year rich stores of Gratitude for countless mutual favors and sweet usages. It should involve from the beginning the true Sympathy that would have drawn them together if of one sex; friendship can carry Cupid when he sleeps. It ought to have deep wells of admiration — each for each. And it will outlast all shock and change if it draw deepest of all on Devotion: the selfless service that asks nothing and gives all.

So, for the time being, love returned to nineteenth century Christian ideals. However, the 1920s tore the valentine in half by asking, "Can the modern girl love?" Gilbert Frankau gave his analysis in *The Forum* (1922):

> For there is nothing prudish about your modern girl. . . . She has, to sum up, no reticences either of thought, speech, or action. . . . She does not, as her predecessors, "dream." She has no time for dreaming. From the moment when she wakes in the morning until the moment when she goes to sleep at night, her every hour, her every minute is full. . . . To begin with, she is too selfish, too self-centered, too set on the pursuit of what she considers pleasure, to abandon herself to that self-sacrifice which is love at its best.

Already women's liberation had begun in earnest and with it the startling viewpoint that marriage was a blatant tyranny imposed by men on women.

Then came the 1930s and satin-pillowed film romance. Greta Garbo, Clark Gable, Jean Harlow, and Douglas Fairbanks, Jr. turned courtship into an art nearly impossible to imitate. Moralists charged courting couples with insincerity; having watched too many movies, couples only toyed with affection. Henry Morton Robinson, writing for *North American* said:

> It is much more fun to play a game than cope with reality, especially when that game provides in bounteous measure all the excitement and variety that actual life yields so charily. . . . The game of romantic love is peculiarly an infantile substitute for reality, a play-dream that has expanded far beyond its original limits, and now magnetizes with its powerful appeal all that is infantile in our lives.

Love? Infantile? How dare Robinson say such a thing! Didn't the silver screen portray love truthfully? Clemence Dane was no help either. She warned against the kind of love that is "chocolate-box idealism":

> It [love] fosters the belief that a woman's happiness depends on her beauty and that a man's main worth is his physique. Love as we meet it in the films, in the magazines, in the press, and to a certain extent in modern fiction is a synthetic emotion which is rapidly debauching popular taste.

During the 1940s and World War II, Americans didn't have time to play at love. The whole world was about to turn into one vast graveyard. Film still celebrated the perfect couple joined, but as the movie of the decade, *Casablanca* (1942), aptly made clear, higher ideals, patriotism, self-sacrifice, and — in the case of Rick — cynicism overshadowed romantic love. No matter, movie audiences knew that Rick — "I stick my neck out for no one" — was really a sentimentalist faking a sneer.

The 1950s were the Doris Day years and sportive courtship was in vogue. American women envied Doris: she looked so fresh and alive, her charm was limitless, and she always got her man. But that was in the movie theater. At home, a new word threatened the domestic bliss Doris Day embodied in her film confections. That word was sex. Marriage manuals flooded the market, manuals that concentrated more on sexual performance than on Charlotte Perkins Gilman's fifth kind of love, "the selfless service that asks nothing and gives all." According to the manuals, men and women were supposed to ask for everything and get it all. Paul H. Landis wrote this for *Reader's Digest:*

> Physical love is important to marriage. Granted. But we have gone to extremes in stressing its technical aspects. Many wives feel that there is something wrong with them — or their husbands — if they cannot achieve the kind of response they've read about.

That response was simultaneous orgasm, a sexual fad that forced husbands and wives to fake ecstasy so they could howl in unison with one another. As if ardent couples couldn't figure out sex for themselves, marriage manual dictums carried over into the next decade.

In the early 1960s, Harriet Van Horne voiced a lament before total sexual freedom broke loose:

> The marriage manual has replaced the slim volume of verse on the engaged girl's reading list. . . . Love, the post-Freudian generation may tell you, is what happens in Victorian novels and old movies on television. Love is for squares. . . . In a world that fails to honor the romantic tradition, that takes a let's-be-practical approach to courtship and marriage, it is woman who is most cruelly cut down. Without romance, a glory passes from her life.

Also prior to Janis Joplin's wailing, "Get it while you can," Ernest Van Den Haag declared in *Harper's Magazine:*

> When sexual objects are easily and guiltlessly accessible, in a society that does not object to promiscuity, romantic love seldom prospers. For example, in imperial Rome it was rare and in Tahiti unknown. . . . Love flowers best in a monogamous environment morally opposed to unrestrained sex.

Well, for the remainder of the 1960s, love flowered all right but not in a monogamous environment. Young and mature Americans experimented with varieties of love, causing enough commotion for the societal shift to be called a revolution. All of a sudden, taboo sexual relations were okay. Married couples faddishly toyed with adultery condoned by the concept of "open marriage" and took drugs not to see God, but to heighten their lovemaking. Single people were even freer to express their libido promiscuously, interracially, homosexually, communely, however. By the mid-1970s, Dr. James Ramey, Director of the Center for the Study of Innovative Life Styles, wrote in his book, *Intimate Friendships*, that any number of sexual relationships was fine. A person should seek broad connections with many partners to form a nexus of love.

Not convinced that intimate friendships would work, Shere Hite updated the Kinsey reports on male and female sexual behavior published in 1948 and 1953, respectively. Hite, a feminist, reversed the order of research; first she studied female sexuality (1976), then followed with a study of male sexuality (1981). And for good measure, she gave women the last word in *Women and Love: A Cultural Revolution in Progress* (1987). The most incandescent finding from Hite's initial survey was: 70 percent of women who don't achieve orgasm during intercourse have abundant orgasms from clitoral stimulation. Why was this revelation so earthshaking? Because the eminent sex therapists Masters and Johnson considered a woman's inability to have an orgasm from penile thrusts a sexual dysfunction. Thus, men made 70 percent of the women who responded to the survey feel sexually inadequate when they weren't. Hite's study of men indicated that males "define love as sex, and sex as penetration and ejaculation within a woman." This Cro-Magnon view of men also included charges of emotional sterility and pigheaded ego maintenance. According to Hite, the battle of the sexes had never been so bloody. The final book of the triad, *Women and Love*, severed what slender ties remained. Hite concluded that most women — married and single — don't feel emotionally satisfied in their relationships with men and consequently look to female friends for empathy. And what's more, female discontent with males sinks even deeper into resentment. To climb back out, women must reject the male world and male cultural values and live their lives free from domination.

Purported to reflect the thinking of all American women in the 1970s and 1980s, Hite's books caused a faddish ruckus. It was all too obvious that men in the studies got bashed, having been portrayed very unsympathetically. Most of the female respondents protested too much about males — to the point of bitterness or hysteria that defies common sense. Seemingly, Hite manipulated her data to support her own feminist ideas. Happy women, sexually fulfilled by men, do exist, but rarely in Hite. Critics asked, given her bias for feminism and exclusive survey methodology, what of Hite can be believed? And should a "social scientist" communicate to a gullible public such sweeping indictments from a prejudiced survey? For these reasons and others, Hite isn't held in the same esteem as the objective zoologist Alfred Kinsey.

BIBLIOGRAPHY

Bailey, Beth. *From Front Porch to Back Seat: Courtship in Twentieth-Century America*. Baltimore, MD: The Johns Hopkins University Press, 1988.

Burns, Sarah. "Yankee Romance: The Comic Courtship Scene in Nineteenth-Century American Art." *The American Art Journal* 18, 4 (1986): 51-75.

Cable, Mary, and the Editors of American Heritage. *American Manners & Morals: A Picture History of How We Behaved and Misbehaved*. New York: American Heritage Publishing Co., Inc., 1969.

Dane, Clemence. "What Is Love?" *The Forum* 94 (December 1935): 335-338.

Frankau, Gilbert. "Can the Modern Girl Love?" *The Forum* 68 (November 1922): 917-922.

Gilman, Charlotte Perkins. "Five Kinds of Love." *Harper's Bazaar* 42 (January 1908): 63-65.

Haag, Ernest Van Den. "Love or Marriage?" *Harper's Magazine* 224 (May 1962): 43-47.

Herman, Sondra K. "Loving Courtship or the Marriage Market? The Ideal and Its Critics, 1871-1911." *American Quarterly* 25 (May 1973): 235-252.

Hite, Shere. *The Hite Report: A Nationwide Study on Female Sexuality*. New York: Macmillan, 1976.

_____. *The Hite Report on Male Sexuality*. New York: Alfred A. Knopf, 1981.

_____. *Women and Love: A Cultural Revolution in Progress*. New York: Alfred A. Knopf, 1987.

Landis, Paul H. "Don't Expect Too Much of Sex in Marriage." *Reader's Digest* 65 (December 1954): 25-28.

Lystra, Karen. *Searching the Heart: Women, Men, and Romantic Love in Nineteenth-Century America*. New York: Oxford University Press, 1989.

Ramey, James. *Intimate Friendships*. Englewood Cliffs, NJ: Prentice-Hall, Inc., 1976.

Robinson, Henry Morton. "Sons as Lovers." *North American* 237 (March 1934): 232-238.

Rothman, Ellen K. *Hands and Hearts: A History of Courtship in America*. New York: Basic Books, Inc., 1984.

Van Horne, Harriet. "Romance vs. Sex Appeal: The Battle Women Lost." *Reader's Digest* 80 (February 1962): 60-62.

Craniometry and Polygeny

In the nineteenth century, these two perverse beliefs achieved great popularity because they supported biological racism. Craniometry deals with skull measurement to determine the dimensions and proportions characteristic of a particular race, sex, developmental stage, or somatype. Polygeny holds that humankind descended from two or more independent pairs of ancestors. Together, these theories gave Caucasians the "scientific" backing to rank themselves unflinchingly above all other races, with Negroes and Indians at the bottom of the heap.

Samuel George Morton (1799-1851), a prominent Philadelphia physician, contributed greatly to natural history by collecting over 1,000 specimens of skulls sent to him from all over the world. His collection easily surpassed any other at the time — a truly wonderful Golgotha, as it was called. Morton studied the skulls for the better part of two decades, publishing his findings in three superb works: *Crania Americana* (1839), *Crania Aegyptiaca* (1844), and a summary paper on the entire lot (1849). Many beautiful drawings and concise tables of data added immensely to the authority and, if you will, charm of the treatises. But not so charming, Morton's purpose in all this collecting and describing was to rank races according to cranial capacity (i.e., the bigger the skull, the bigger the brain, the greater the intelligence). Morton painstakingly measured each skull with special apparatus, including a tin cylinder, glass tubes, water, a float rod, a mahogany rod, and white pepper seed. Meticulous down to the last detail, he wanted to ensure the accuracy of his incontrovertible chain of being. Clearly, the white pepper seed et al. told the story. Modern Germans, English, and Anglo-Americans topped the hierarchy with a mean cranial capacity of 92 cubic inches. Other groups of modern and ancient Caucasians followed closely behind. Then came the Malayans and Polynesians — 85 cubic inches; the Mongolians — 82 cubic inches; the African, American, and Australian Negroes—83 cubic inches; and finally the North and South American Indians—79 cubic inches. The largest skull belonged to a German—114 cubic inches; the smallest to a Negroid Australian—63 cubic inches.

Being a pure scientist, Morton perhaps did not realize the danger inherent in his findings. The Declaration of Independence and the Jeffersonians had already proclaimed all men equal. But Morton's data denied this; genetically, Caucasians were the master race, Negroes and Indians, their servants. News of Morton's veracious skulls circulated quickly. No one knew or probably cared that Morton had solicited his skulls from wherever he could get them. Unlike a modern-day anthropologist, he did not retrieve them himself from the far corners of the globe; therefore, some fraud or mistaken identity occurred. Concerning Morton's accuracy, Harvard Professor of Geology, Stephen Jay Gould, has remeasured the cranial capacity of the skulls and discovered a sizeable discrepancy. Gould's corrected values place Native Americans on top with 86 cubic inches, then Mongolians—85 cubic inches; modern Caucasians and Malays—85 cubic inches; Ancient Caucasians—84 cubic inches, and Africans—83 cubic inches. Gould contends that Morton "unconsciously" manipulated his data. For example:

> Morton chose to include or delete large subsamples in order to match grand means with a priori expectations. He included Inca Peruvians [small skulls] to reduce the Indian mean and excluded Hindus [also small skulls] to raise the Caucasian mean.

Even though Morton's contemporaries were unaware of his suspect collection methods and rigged data, they should have doubted that cranial capacity has anything to do with intelligence. But then again, the august voice of science had spoken.

Now for polygeny. Born in Switzerland and already a famous naturalist, Louis Agassiz (1807-1873) immigrated to America in the 1840s. Shortly after arriving here, his observation of American Negroes—he had never seen a black in Europe—convinced him that they were an inferior race. Not only were blacks less than whites, Agassiz decided, they were also a separate species. Or, put more directly, in the beginning there had been a white Adam and a black Adam. No other explanation seemed possible. Whites and blacks could never have evolved from one common ancestor. Keep in mind that Agassiz based polygeny on observation alone. He watched field hands and house servants; he didn't make the acquaintance of educated Negroes. Because of Agassiz's charisma and scientific standing, people willingly believed what he said. This quotation from an article in the *Christian Examiner* (1850) is an Agassiz gem:

> There are upon earth different races of men, inhabiting different parts of its surface, which have different physical characteristics; and this fact . . . presses upon us the obligation to settle the relative rank among the races, the relative value of the characters peculiar to each, in a scientific view. . . . As philosophers it is our duty to look it in the face.

And if it were a black face, it was looked at from a commanding view. Agassiz continues:

> We entertain not the slightest doubt that human affairs with reference to the colored races would be far more judiciously conducted if, in our intercourse with them, we were guided by a full consciousness of the real difference existing between us and them, and a desire to foster those dispositions that are eminently marked in them, rather than by treating them on terms of equality.

Midway through the American Civil War, S. G. Howe, a member of President Lincoln's Inquiry Commission, asked Agassiz for his opinion on emancipating the slaves. In an impassioned letter, the polygenist remarked:

> Social equality I deem at all time impracticable. It is a natural impossibility flowing from the very character of the negro race [for blacks are] indolent, playful, sensuous, imitative, subservient, good natured, versatile, unsteady in their purpose, devoted, affectionate, in everything unlike other races, they may

but be compared to children, grown in the stature of adults while retaining a childlike mind. . . . Therefore I hold that they are incapable of living on a footing with the whites, in one and the same community, without being an element of social disorder. (August 10, 1863)

Of Agassiz's assigned character traits, it is difficult to see why good natured, versatile, devoted, and affectionate are inferior qualities. This list reveals quite a lot about the Aryan Agassiz, since presumably, he exemplified opposite traits. Like Morton, Agassiz had his ardent followers. Unlike Morton, Agassiz had to defend his views more often. Polygeny butted heads with creationism; the Bible said nothing about greater and lesser humans emerging from God's hand. Polygeny openly endorsed geographic segregation; Agassiz maintained that Negroes, having arisen from the cauldron of Africa, should stay there. By virtue of skin color alone, whites were happier in Vienna and blacks, the steamy Congo. Polygeny abhorred miscegenation — but let Agassiz speak for himself:

Conceive for a moment the difference it would make in future ages, for the prospect of republican institutions and our civilization generally, if instead of the manly population descended from cognate nations the United States should hereafter be inhabited by the effeminate progeny of mixed races, half indian, half negro, sprinkled with white blood. . . . I shudder from the consequences.

The polygeny debate raged on, making Agassiz look more foolish with each passing year except to those who agreed with him. His death stilled the controversy somewhat because with his demise, biological racism lost a persuasive spokesman. Thought to be one of the two greatest naturalists of the nineteenth century — Charles Darwin was the other — Louis Agassiz wrote in a letter to his mother that the sight of a Negro's palm placing food before him was so offensive it turned his stomach. And from this innocuous experience, he formed a faddish theory equal in perversity to craniometry.

BIBLIOGRAPHY

Agassiz, E. C. *Louis Agassiz; His Life and Correspondence.* Boston, MA: Houghton Mifflin, 1895.

Agassiz, Louis. "The Diversity of Origin of the Human Races." *Christian Examiner* 49 (1850): 110-145.

Gould, Stephen Jay. *The Mismeasure of Man.* New York: W. W. Norton, 1981.

_____. "Morton's Ranking of Races by Cranial Capacity." *Science* 200 (May 5, 1978): 503-509.

Stanton, William. *The Leopard's Spots: Scientific Attitudes Toward Race in America, 1815-59.* Chicago, IL: The University of Chicago Press, 1960.

Creation Science

God created the earth and all living things only 6,000 years ago. The "sudden appearance of highly developed forms of life" on earth was His work. Humans and apes in no way share a common ancestry—in fact, evolution is a sham; the fossil record that seems to support evolution does not—the fossils are the remains of pre-Noachian Deluge life, and the universe is no more than post-Noachian Deluge detritus left over after the "vapor canopy" (massive amounts of water suspended in the heavens) burst and poured down causing the Deluge. Creation science teaches these basic tenets and delves into other intriguing areas of Bible truth to explain how our world came to be. Most children learn about creation from studying Genesis and have done so for centuries, whether at home, in a religion class, or at Sunday school. Nothing new, but during the 1980s, when fundamentalist teachers asserted that there was such a thing as creation "science," they stirred up a hornet's nest. In the past, telling the "story" of Genesis to a child did no more harm than entertaining him or her with tales of the Easter Bunny or Santa Claus. But to formalize creation science and insist that it be taught in conjunction with the theory of evolution prodded self-absorbed scientists into jousting with the enemy.

The wily creation scientists took a different tact this time from their more inflexible stand at the Scopes Trial in 1925. Then it was winner take all: teaching Darwin's godless theory of evolution had to stop. In the 1980s, they simply asked for parity. Or did they? Anthropologist Alice B. Kehoe declared:

> Scientific creationists are part of a movement that seeks to establish through governmental policies a particular doctrine contrary to the principles of the United States Constitution [separation of church and state]. The movement is strongly authoritarian, patriarchal, militaristic, and opposed to public

support of social welfare programs. This New Religious-Political Right represents not just a disagreement about scientific interpretations but a serious effort to buttress the economic and political power of the traditional American bourgeoisie.

The days of making lighthearted monkey jokes were gone. To prove that creation science was truly a science, several "weighty" journals were initiated to inform the faithful and silence the doubters. The most prestigious one, *Creation Research Society Quarterly*, bore this proclamation on its title page: "Haes credimus" ("This we believe"). The articles inside deliberated a number of thorny questions such as, "Was the Pre-Flood Animal Kingdom Vegetarian?" The conclusion is—yes it was, which explains how Noah fed the carnivores aboard the Ark without them eating each other and how some Old Testament figures lived to be as old as 900 years. Doubtless, both groups munched on cabbage and carrots to achieve longevity. Researchers interested in "Survival of Freshwater and Saltwater Organisms in a Heterogeneous Flood Model Experiment" began by filling a 55-gallon aquarium with fresh water, to which was added "Instant Ocean" from the pet store and an assortment of saline-dependent sea creatures. When more fresh water and saline-hating creatures were poured on top, many of the living things suffered or died. The researchers surmised that during the Flood, pockets of unmixed water allowed some dispossessed creatures, not on the Ark, to survive, since Noah couldn't possibly have boarded two of every living thing on one small craft. Another puzzle solved in the pages of *Creation Research Society Quarterly* concerned what Noah did with all the animal excrement that piled up inside the Ark. Noah, a practical man directed by God, didn't just shovel it out into the floodwater; that would have been a 24-hour a day job for all the humans aboard. Instead, he turned the animal droppings into fertilizer to enrich the ecosystem he had improvised for growing fresh food (fits in neatly with the vegetarian "truth"). The author of this bit of biblical sleuthing went on to say that the Ark, usually pictured as having only one window, must have had more than that for needed sunlight and ventilation. "Is the Destruction of Plants Death in the Biblical Sense?" addressed the knotty problem of what Adam and Eve ate before expulsion from the Garden of Eden. Since there was no such thing as death prior to original sin, Adam could hardly have roasted a goat, chicken, or trout over an open flame. Holy Scripture reveals that God told man and the animals to "be fruitful and multiply"; however, He did not extend the same invitation to plants (then what does "fruitful" mean?). Therefore man and the animals could gorge themselves on plants and not fret about having to kill their fellow leafy creatures.

These "rigorous" articles enraged the scientific establishment, making amused tolerance of their fatuity no longer an option. The warring camps battled in print, in the media, and, finally, in the Supreme Court. Louisiana had passed a law to make certain that creation science and evolution would be taught in tandem to achieve "balanced treatment." None of this sat well with 72 Nobel laureates and 17 state academies of science, who made it known to the Court that creation science was the most transparent religious dogma and not science in any sense of the word. Seven Supreme Court justices declared the Louisiana law unconstitutional; Justice Antonin Scalia and Chief Justice William H. Rehnquist dissented. They argued the decision to strike down the "balanced treatment" law rested on "impugning the motives of the supporters" (i.e., that creation science was wholly motivated by religious aims to supplant belief in evolution). Other states on the verge of passing similar laws postponed or abandoned pending legislation in light of the Supreme Court's decision.

To be fair, though, while the scientific establishment has reams of proof to support evolution, its theory of how the world began is about as mystical as the biblical account:

> In the beginning, the "big bang" created the heavens and the earth. Now the earth was a formless void, there was darkness over the deep, and Nature's spirit hovered over the water. Nature decreed, "Let there be light, and there was light. . . ."

BIBLIOGRAPHY

Bennetta, William J. "Scientists Decry a Slick New Packaging of Creationism." *The Science Teacher* 54 (May 1987): 36-43.

Gould, Stephen Jay. "An Essay on a Pig Roast." *Natural History* (January 1989): 14-25.

Harrold, Francis B., and Raymond A. Eve, eds. *Cult Archaeology & Creationism: Understanding Pseudoscientific Beliefs About the Past.* Iowa City, IA: University of Iowa Press, 1987.

Hitt, Jack. "What Did Noah Do with the Manure?" *The Washington Monthly* 19 (February 1987): 25-28.

"Science and the Citizen: Science, 7; Creationism, 2." *Scientific American* 257 (August 1987): 14.

Death Education

In the last 20 years teaching young people about death has seemed necessary. Hasn't the horrific twentieth century warranted it? Kill-crazy photos from four major wars etch indelible images in our minds. Our popular culture — particularly film — wallows in blood, gore, and death. Once, censors had only gratuitous sex to complain about; now it is gratuitous slaughter of human beings that disturbs them. And well it should, when Rambo and Robocop grit their teeth just before annihilating everyone in their path. As the camera pans over the carnage, the viewer comes face to face with more than Hollywood magic. He or she sees the specter of what the twentieth century has been and most likely will continue to be into the next century. The race to build more destructive nuclear bombs, from the atomic to the neutron, has also burdened our daily thoughts. We expect imminent genocide if belligerent countries ever deploy their missiles. And worse yet, we envision that a giant mushroom cloud, then empty space, will be our last glimpse of earth. All these threats of the "knell that summons thee to heaven or to hell" mandate the teaching of death education. Or do they?

In medical and nursing school, death education is a necessary part of the curriculum. Doctors and nurses must know how to cope with the daily occurrence of death in the hospital. A major part of their job is to deal effectively with grieving loved ones and at the same time control their own emotions. Surprisingly, formalized death education for the medical profession also just emerged in the 1970s. Before that, it was left up to the individual to temper his or her nerve through experience. By his own admission, famed heart surgeon Michael De Bakey (1908-) felt personally responsible every time he lost a patient, even though the patient's chances to survive were next to none. It is important here to distinguish salutary death education from that which has shown itself to be faddish. Death education for professionals versus that for general students provides a good example of the difference between purposeful and wasted instruction.

Two professors at Penn State University, James M. Eddy and Wesley F. Alles, respond to, "Why should death education be taught?"

> By examining death, individuals often develop a greater understanding, appreciation, and reverence for life. When individuals are given the opportunity to examine factual information and to clarify personal values, it is probable that their anxiety will be reduced, which will enable them to pursue life with enthusiasm and confidence. Discussion of death can help to legitimize one's inner feelings toward death. It is hoped that through death education the denial of death can be replaced with a personal philosophy that accepts death as a fact of life.

Following are some educational activities in which young people learned how to accept death as a fact of life. High school students were asked to select one literary passage concerning death that most closely reflected their personal belief. The images ran the gamut from those of utter destruction to immense delight in death. Next, elementary school children compiled a scrapbook of newspaper clippings that classified the causes of death, especially the ones that most affected elementary school-aged populations. For high school and above, students completed a personal death inventory, answering such questions as, "Are you afraid of death?" "Have you made plans for your final days?" and "Do you believe that there are people to whom you wish to make peace with, express gratitude to, praise, thank, or express love to prior to your death?" Middle school students visited a cemetery to make gravestone rubbings, then responded to the questions, "Do you want a gravestone if you are buried?" and "If yes, what inscription would you want on it?" Also for middle school, students focused their attention on death notices in local and national newspapers. They examined each notice for purpose, similarity or uniqueness, and amount of information given. Another type of inventory, this time for junior high and high school students, ascertained their death-related fears. Non-death-related fears were included because they mask death-related fears. For example, walking in cemeteries or pregnancy do not in themselves cause death but might engender in some students death-related fears. For a last illustrative activity, elementary school students listened to their teacher read a book about a dying animal. The animal could be either wild or a pet. Afterwards, the class discussed its reaction to the book and the meaning of death; then the children listed emotions connected with death and drew pictures of themselves grieving for a dead animal.

Death education classes also required students to write position papers on a controversial death issue, study cryogenics, debate the religious aspects of death, play "Run For Your Life" — what would you do if you only had a limited time to live, and envision what might precipitate the deathblow(s) to earth. Death educators have been quick off the mark to establish their curriculum, but they haven't been so eager to assess the impact of death education on young sensibilities. In a telling report (1979), investigators Jon W. Hoelter and Rita J. Epley discovered this about college courses in thanatology:

> Because many death education students exhibit favorable attitudes toward suicide, report a high number of suicide attempts, and enroll in such courses to reduce fear of death, the therapeutic function of death education is a crucial issue. It may be that many students are not interested in acquiring a deeper understanding of the many facets of death but, rather, are attempting to substitute a course on death for needed professional counseling. . . . Students should be informed at the onset of a course dealing with death that research has not, as of yet, shown such courses to aid in resolving certain personal problems related to death.

Paradoxically, teaching children and adolescents about death has not raised parental hackles like sex education. During the same time that death education (i.e., the most morbid aspect of living) struggled for a foothold, classroom instruction about sexuality (i.e., the most vivid aspect of living) met with considerable resistance. At home, it was all right for little Jack or Jill to present his or her parents with crayon sketches of dead things. But let little Jack or Jill hand over a picture of sperm piercing a quivering egg, and the principal would hear about it next morning. Death education has been another one of those "new studies" that diverts students from learning fundamental skills. As a fad, it has galvanized educators more than students, who being young and vivacious are more interested in squeezing every drop out of life.

BIBLIOGRAPHY

Dickinson, George E., et al. "Death Education in U.S. Professional Colleges: Medical, Nursing, and Pharmacy." *Death Studies* 11 (1987): 57-61.

Eddy, James M., and Wesley F. Alles. *Death Education*. St. Louis, MO: C. V. Mosby Company, 1983.

Fulton, Robert, and Greg Owen. "Death and Society in Twentieth Century America." *Omega* 18 (1987-88): 379-395.

Hoelter, Jon W., and Rita J. Epley. "Death Education and Death-Related Attitudes." *Death Education* 3 (1979): 67-75.

Because they were the first quintuplets to survive birth, the Dionnes made over $1 million in endorsements, movie contracts, and visiting rights for their surprised parents. Callander, Ontario had never been much of a tourist spot until the stork flew in with the basket of five. (1934-1940)

Dionne Quintuplets

"I'm the kind of fellow they should put in jail," said Oliva Dionne, a French Canadian farmer living with his family in Callander, Ontario. On May 28, 1934, his 24-year-old wife, Elzire, gave birth to five infant girls whose total weight was less than 13 1/2 pounds. If that wasn't crime enough, the Dionnes already had five children, and Mrs. Dionne was far from menopause. Cecile, Marie, Yvonne, Emilie, and Annette—the Dionne quints—weren't supposed to survive. Dr. Morris Fishbein, editor of *The Journal of the American Medical Association*, told the press there had been only 30 cases of quintuplets recorded in the last 500 years, and of those, at least 1 or more of the infants had died within 50 minutes of birth. Those facts riveted world attention on the Dionne's four-room frame house, including the profit-minded notice of several freak show managers. Mr. Dionne, who stated he was not "built for hard work," immediately accepted a $250 per week guarantee and 30 percent of the gate receipts to show off his progeny. His parish priest had told him it was all right. But first the infants huddled together precariously in a basket had to live long enough to go on the road.

The "skinned squirrels," as one Canadian backwoodsman dubbed the quints, were fed milk, corn syrup, and water with an eyedropper at three-hour intervals to overcome their two-months premature birth. The local physician Dr. Allen Roy Dafoe found several young mothers to breast-feed the quints because the eyedropper method did not supply the natural nutrients the girls needed to grow. Sensing a big story, Hearst's *New York Evening Journal* and *Chicago American* got into the act and donated a hot water incubator (the Dionne's house was not wired for electricity). Other gifts flowed in from across the border. If five tiny human beings could prosper against the odds, then medical science could do anything. Dr. Dafoe employed two Red Cross nurses to watch the girls around the clock and kept a case history of the unfolding miracle himself. He also insisted that anyone entering the nursery area wear a sterile gown and gauze mask, though admittance was limited. Only one photographer who wanted pictures for science was allowed in, while others with less noble aims clamored outside for equal privileges. Later, a Canadian provincial judge declared the Dionne quints "international characters" and therefore accessible to all photographers and media people. One of the quints, 3-pound, 14-ounce Marie, had a tumor on her thigh. The world held its breath until Professor-Emeritus Howard A. Kelly of Johns Hopkins University applied radium to vanquish the malignancy. Dr. Kelly had a summer lodge near Callander and was more than happy to assist.

Meanwhile, the Dionne parents were pushed further into the background. To break the freak show contract Mr. Dionne had hastily signed, Attorney General Arthur W. Roebuck appointed Dr. Dafoe, Grandfather Dionne, and two other responsible parties as guardians of the quints. Meddling authority usurped not only Mr. Dionne's parental rights but also Mrs. Dionne's. She and Dr. Dafoe disagreed on what the quints should eat once they had passed safely through the nursing stage of development. Mrs. Dionne wanted to feed the girls what she had fed her first five children: thick soups, cooked vegetables, rice, and fresh cow's milk in hearty amounts. Dr. Dafoe blocked her wishes and instead made sure the girls got pasteurized milk, cod-liver oil, and Vitamin C. His prescribed diet of pea soup, fruit, fruit juices, strained vegetables, and cereal in small amounts seemed like wimpy fare for building tissue and bone. But Dr. Dafoe explained that his scientific diet prevented a host of childhood diseases and about the tiny helpings, fat babies were not necessarily healthy ones. Mrs. Dionne grumbled; she liked roly-poly cherubs, and Dr. Dafoe didn't know what he was talking about.

The freak show gambit nixed, Mr. Dionne nevertheless counted the zeros on a $250,000 check from 20th Century-Fox. His girls were to star in three movies. Another check for $50,000 was in the mail, plus a profit-sharing agreement. The windfall, along with promotion money already in the bank, totaled more than $500,000. A witty advertisement made the rounds telling people how they, like Papa Dionne, could earn big money from only a few minutes easy work in the privacy of their bedroom. Of the three Fox movies planned, the first, "The Country Doctor," charmed the public, who begged to see the astonishing quints in action. A sequel followed, "Reunion," in which the beloved country doctor from the previous smash hit is the guest of honor at a banquet attended by the 3,000 children he has delivered during his career. With the Dionne quints waddling around (age 2), the country doctor must straighten out a number of humorous entanglements. He calms a suicidal film star, tricks a U.S. governor into adopting a child, sparks a stalled love affair, and saves an old friend from losing his young wife. This time, however, moviegoers fidgeted in their seats; the quints were not in every scene! During filming, the real Dr. Dafoe made his presence known by demanding strict hygienic measures only slightly different from those enforced in the nursery. When not shooting the film, the actors had to wear gauze over their faces and continually spray their throats with antiseptic.

Another central figure in the Dionne quints craze was Fred Davis. Somehow he obtained sole permission to photograph the quints for the *Toronto Star*, whether they were "international characters" or not. Anyone wanting a picture of them had to go through Davis and his distributor, the Newspaper Enterprise Association. As one can imagine, requests rained in. The quints in every type of pose — dressed alike and laughing or pouting or looking open-eyed at the camera — any picture sold. Even Davis' stories about how he displayed the patience of Job to get the girls to act right for the camera sold to magazines. But seeing the quints in movies or on a postcard was not enough. Sightseers drove from everywhere to Callander. It's unclear who came up with the idea to build a fenced-in playground for the quints to frolic in for the public. Perhaps one of the freak show managers or some Canadian entrepreneur convinced Mr. Dionne of the potential goldmine. As soon as the observation gallery was completed, people lined up. The "Visitors Information and Instructions" sign read:

Any Person In Possession Of A Camera Will Be Refused
Admission To Playground Building
Please Maintain Silence And Keep Moving
Do Not Speak To Children

You May Enter As Often As You Wish During Visiting Period
But In Order To Be Fair To Visitors You Must Keep Moving
Toward Exits
9:30 AM To 10:00 AM
2:30 PM To 3:00 PM Weather Permitting

Visitors anxious to see related landmarks stopped at a cottage where midwives who had actually touched — and even kissed — the quints were on exhibit. Gas could be purchased at Callander's five-pump station, a memorable experience because each pump bore the name of one of the quints. Also for sale were authentic pebbles taken from the quints' nursery yard and a whole assortment of other memorabilia. Dr. Dafoe's house was a "must see" and, of course, the Dionne homesite.

On the quints' third birthday, no one doubted that medical science in the person of Dr. Dafoe had defeated the angel of death. Cecile, Marie, Yvonne, Emilie, and Annette were about as healthy as children could be. The Dionne parents may have given faint light to the girls, but Dr. Dafoe had made them burn brightly. At a time when civilization appeared on the brink of destruction, he was a genuine hero. About Dr. Dafoe, appreciations such as this in *The American Magazine* (March 1937) expressed the common feeling:

> But through civil suits, exploitation, rows in the nursery, and rows with the Dionne family, through political storms and three exciting years of fame, fortune, and world acclaim, the little girls have had through their lives the unbroken thread of the good doctor's love and solicitude. If they have been the elves who changed his life, he has been the kindly heart who has saved theirs — the Santa Claus of the brownies.

Because the Dionnes were the first quints to live beyond the birth trauma, signaling the dawn of a new pediatrics, they captivated the public completely. Since the Dionnes, three sets of sextuplets have been born and survived: to Susan Rosenkowitz in Mowbray, Cape Town, South Africa, 1974 (3 males, 3 females); to Rosanna Giannini in Florence, Italy, 1980 (4 males, 2 females); and to Janet Walton in Liverpool, England, 1983 (all female). But the Dionnes were the ones almost every American family wanted to play with for a day.

BIBLIOGRAPHY

Burton, Walter E. "Photographing the Dionne Quints." *Popular Science Monthly* 130 (February 1937): 32 + .

"Dionne Quintuplets." *The New York Times* May 29, 21:7; May 30, 19:5; and May 31, 40:2; 1934.

"Dionnes: Johns Hopkins Radium Relieves Quintuplet's Tumor." *Newsweek* 4 (August 18, 1934): 20.

"Hardy Quintuplets: They Symbolize Triumph of Science Over Older Forms of Care." *The Literary Digest* 121 (May 16, 1936): 19.

Kelley, Hubert. "What 5 Babies Did to a Town—and a Man." *The American Magazine* 123 (March 1937): 28 + .

"Quintuplets Make Headlines." *Newsweek* 3 (June 9, 1934): 20.

"Quintupling Assets: Another Quarter-Million Enriches the Glamourous Dionnes." *The Literary Digest* 122 (August 22, 1936): 26.

In the late 1960s, young Americans sought Indian gurus for spiritual guidance. The religion of their parents lacked mystery and was too judgmental. Eastern religions followed simple rituals and just plain felt good. The restless generation admired anyone who could sit still for an hour thinking peaceful thoughts.

Eastern Mysticism

When asked to explain what transcendental meditation (TM) was, the Maharishi Mahesh Yogi replied serenely, "It is the transference of attention from the gross state of thought to the subtle state of thought until the source of thought is reached and the mind transcends the source." Not sure he had clarified TM, the Maharishi added, "The nature of outer life is activity. Inner life is all silent and quiet. At this quiet end is absolute being, non-changing, transcendental bliss. Being is bliss-consciousness. Life without the conscious basis of being is like a ship without a rudder." To enter the subtle state of thought, the Maharishi advised his followers to select a sound or syllable and keep it secret. Then, twice daily for 30 minutes, each person was to repeat his or her "mantra" to still the savage beast within. That is all there was to the new religion of TM—no Bible, no Torah, no original sin, no confessional booth, no fear of hell, just the disciplined recitation of h-m-m-m-m or o-o-o-o-h. Actresses Shirley MacLaine and Mia Farrow adored TM, and the pied pipers of youth, the Beatles, journeyed to the Maharishi's bliss academy near New Delhi, India, to be closer to the fount of wisdom.

But most Americans in the late 1960s could not afford a ticket to India, so they had to settle for imported TM. Disciples materialized everywhere to satisfy Western curiosity: on university campuses, at city parks, in vegetarian restaurants, in retail stores, wherever people might gather to try TM. College students benefited the most as these testimonials show:

> In the week immediately following my initiation into meditation I cut my hair, returned to my family's house, got a job and registered in school for the fall. (New York student)

> My hair has gotten much thicker since I started meditating. One of the physical signs of anxiety is that the veins in the

scalp contract. Now, the blood can flow freely. Also, I think my intelligence has grown. (Girl in Cincinnati)

Hey, would you believe it? All the guys in my fraternity house have stopped taking drugs and started on meditation! (San Francisco student)

Hair fixation aside, these jubilant meditators knew the value of a good mantra. As the Maharishi told every new gathering, "This age demands streamlined methods without sacrificing quality." Mantra recitation was alacrity itself. And no fledgling hedonist could ignore the Maharishi's main message: "Life should not be a struggle; men are born to enjoy; every man has full freedom of action; do not suffer when you can enjoy; enjoy what you are and it will be good." Followers loved the Maharishi; he giggled like a child. He was plump, not emaciated like Mahatma Gandhi, and also unlike Gandhi, he wore hip shoulder-length hair and a full beard. The Maharishi dressed in a "dhoti" and sandals; around his neck hung a string of beads exactly 108 in number, representing the 108 verses of Hinduism's sacred gospel, the *Bhagavad Gita*. Back in India, some Hindus considered the Maharishi a saint and his movement to regenerate the world through meditation, a godly pursuit, while the orthodox criticized him for not adhering to self-abnegation as the path to enlightenment. In America, the Maharishi flew in his own twin-engine Beechcraft to spread the word; he also cut two meditation LP's—a far cry from sitting on a bed of nails next to the Ganges. Along with TM's good vibrations, other associated products sold quickly. The *Bhagavad Gita* in translation and mesmerizing sitar music had to be bought to create the proper pre- and post-TM atmosphere. Paisley cottons made great clothing and wall decorations. Brass incense temples mushroomed on every coffee table. "One of the charms of meditation," said a mantra reciter, "is that you don't have to believe in it for it to work." As silly as that sounds, the TM craze served a good purpose. Experimenting with LSD had grown rampant among youth. By substituting a proven stress reducer, TM lessened use of the hallucinogenic.

The Maharishi Mahesh Yogi wasn't the only guru pitching Eastern mysticism to American bliss seekers. In New York City alone a novice could choose from Yogi Dinkar at the spiritual Regeneration

Center on West 57th Street, Swami Bhaktivedanta at the Society for Krishna Consciousness temple on lower Second Avenue, or Swami Satchidananda of the Integral Yogi Institute on West End Avenue. All three adopted TM's use of mantra, but added something extra. For instance, Krishna Consciousness temple followers chanted these words for up to an hour at a time: "Hare Krishna, Krishna Krishna, Hare Hare; Hare Rama, Hare Rama, Rama, Rama, Hare Hare." The refrain translates into "Hail to God"; it accompanied a dance of joy set to tambourine music. To earmark the decade of the 1970s, *Life* magazine published an article on the quest for spiritual survival: "Never before in history has a single society taken up such a wide range of religious and near-religious systems at once." Besides TM, Americans embraced most all Eastern "isms": Buddhism, Hinduism, Sufism, Taoism, Vedantism, Yogism, and more. In a coattail (dhoti) effect, other Americans took to witchcraft, Tarot card reading, and frequenting occult bookstores. But what of the Western religions? One indication that they, too, were prospering showed up in divinity school reports. Applications to enter Yale Divinity rose 23% and Chicago Divinity, 20% to 25% (1970). The *Life* article told about Americans engaging in Nichiren Buddhism, Franciscan piety, the *I Ching*, or *Book of Changes*, white (good) witchcraft, and solitary yoga done in the desert or on a mountaintop. The article concluded with a story of some young seminarians, for whom Eastern mysticism was not the way, dedicating their lives to Christ. As one said, "Experiencing God is the highest high, the ultimate trip."

Fascination with Eastern mysticism, not Eastern religion because that would have required total commitment, prevailed for a few more years. All the time, most of those who worshiped TM could not have explained its origin, Hinduism:

One of the most distinctive features [of Hinduism] is the belief in "samsara," the round of birth, death, and re-birth, understood as a cycle of transmigration from one living form to another. . . . Another important and pervasive belief is the doctrine about the universal Self (Atman) and Ultimate Reality (Brahman) based on the teachings of the Upanishads. Brahman is the ground of all reality and existence. . . . The single-minded pursuit of the knowledge of Brahman, implying the attainment of moksha, has always been accorded an enormous prestige in the Indian tradition, yet it has remained the privilege of a small minority. The life of most Hindus is less directly concerned with seeking moksha than with conforming to the demands of dharma [which] prescribes what people ought to do, and governs every aspect of human conduct, including the duties that are an essential part of everyday life. (*The Encyclopedia of World Faiths*, 1987)

Among Hindus there are four social orders: the Brahmans or priests; the Kshatriyas or princes, rulers, and warriors; the Vaishyas or traders and merchants; and the Shudras or serfs. In short, Hinduism teaches that life is a jungle full of wild beasts ready to devour you. The only means of escape is to attain spiritual freedom. For a tiny minority this is possible, but for the rest, strict obedience to duty is all life holds in store.

The despair of Hinduism did not overshadow the pleasure young Americans found in chanting mantras in a paisley-draped room. Few TM inebriates knew about the tenets of a religion that relegated people to a bottom-heavy caste system. Nor could they equate themselves with a society of paupers who prayed to repeat their sad lives over again for eternity. The fad of Eastern mysticism closed its eyes to the poignant song of India but sat wide-eyed in lotus position at the feet of a guru surrounded by more flowers than Miss America.

BIBLIOGRAPHY

Hedgepeth, William. "The Non-Drug Turn-On Hits Campus." *Look* 32 (February 6, 1968): 68-78.

Horn, Paul. "A Visit with India's High-Powered New Prophet." *Look* 32 (February 6, 1968): 64-66.

"The Quest for Spiritual Survival." *Life* 68 (January 1970): 16+.

Wainwright, Loudon. "Invitation to Instant Bliss." *Life* 63 (November 10, 1967): 26.

"Year of the Guru." *Life* 64 (February 9, 1968): 52-59.

Education

In May 1949 the regents of the University of California system (eight campuses) began requiring all faculty to sign a loyalty oath. After swearing allegiance to the State of California, the professor then had to affirm, "I am not a member of the Communist Party." The regents meant business with their "sign-or-get-out" ultimatum that mocked academic freedom. Soon the McCarthy era would make an even greater mockery of personal freedom. For one interminable year, from 1949 to 1950, the loyalty oath handcuffed higher education in California. Most all faculty could have signed the oath with a clear conscience, but that wasn't the point. The oath infringed on their ability to teach basic concepts. If a history or economics professor just mentioned Marxism, he or she invited dismissal. On August 25, 1950, the UC Board of Regents fired 31 professors who refused to disavow communism. That was perhaps the blackest day for American higher education. Two years later, in the fall of 1952, the California Supreme Court handed down its decision in *Tolman v. Underhill* that effectively put a stop to loyalty oaths. The Court ruled not for academic freedom per se but against the UC system for mandating its state employees sign the oath or lose their jobs. No other state employees faced such a demand. Prior to the California hysteria, going back to the 1930s, other incidents like this had occurred. The difference then was the loyalty oath ploy was not used. Professors who discussed not only radical politics in class but also sex, race relations, evolution, and other unseemly topics found themselves out on the street. By 1949, summarily dismissing a professor was not as easy as it had once been. So the centuries-old loyalty oath briefly came back into vogue.

Forced to run the fidelity guantlet in the 1950s, professors fared no better in the next decade. This time they scurried through armed student lines. Whether a professor espoused Marxism, Zionism, or Voodoo didn't matter as long as he or she made the course work "relevant." Petulant students insisted that everything taught must apply to their lives and be utilitarian. "How relevant are Plato's dialogues to Kennedy's New Frontier?" "Would Hamlet fight in Vietnam or desert to Canada?" "Would Freud delight in free sex or cringe at it?" Two academics, Neil Postman and Charles Weingartner, agreed it was high time to pursue relevance. In their book, *Teaching As a Subversive Activity* (1969), they stated unequivocably, "The survival of the learner's skill and interest in learning is at stake." Dull lectures on metaphysical poetry and Palladian architecture were clearly irrelevant. Moreover, irrelevancy extended to the teaching of geometry, philosophy, history, linguistics, or any discipline that didn't lead to the acquisition of job skills. Relevant college courses were those students could cash in on.

The consensus was that professors wiled away time in class talking about what was dear to their hearts, not always imparting useful information. But what was useful? A liberal arts education gave the recipient improved reason and a sense of cultural heritage. But those two immense attainments were not enough. Students wanted more say in what and how they were taught. So the blue jean brigade shuffled around campus muttering, "Nothing's relevant," and challenged their professors to descend from the empyrean and give them earthly manna. Few professors acquiesced to the demand to transform universities into trade schools. What they did was redesign the curriculum while reminding students that getting a college degree was the most relevant thing in their young lives — even if the students had to take exams on metaphysical poetry and Palladian architecture.

Because public school education is more restrictive than higher education, fads commandeer the classroom almost effortlessly. In conjunction with the 1960s more-power-to-the-people movement, educational vouchers got a start. A parent obtained a voucher from a publicly accountable agency that entitled the bearer's children to free education at a public or private school of the parent's choice. In return, the selected school received cash for each student enrolled. The better or more popular schools prospered, while the poorer ones had to improve their standards or close. Supposedly, the voucher system benefited minority and indigent students the most. The disenfranchised would no longer have to languish in substandard neighborhood schools. The Harvard Center for the Study of Public Policy came up with the voucher idea and broadcast it widely, hoping for immediate adoption. But there were few takers. Vouchers infuriated educational organizations, religious groups, and private schools — all of whom foresaw a dismal future ahead. What nonsense, they said, to realign carefully planned school districts and disrupt students' lives with unnecessary bother. Educational vouchers got tossed on the fad pile, although a little later, a similar proposal shook the nation. The new remedy for equalizing educational opportunity, which also included unnecessary bother, was calling busing.

Once the buses began to roll, delivering minority students to predominately white public schools, educators had to resolve the language barrier problem. Hispanics in Texas and California spoke English haltingly which retarded their progress in class. In answer to the predicament, bilingual education activists got laws passed to provide classroom instruction in both Spanish and English. Their triumph prompted blacks to ask for the same consideration. Blacks wanted, at the very least, for their own schools to recognize black American English as a vital language. Thus, a black child could answer a roll call with, "I here," or at day's end say, "I be goin'," and not have a teacher fuss and fume. Known as bidialectalism, the movement was short-lived. Few educators — no matter how sympathetic they were to black pride — approved of hearing neighborhood argot in the classroom. A white kid couldn't say, "I ain't got no homework," so why let a black kid say, "It's a book that be on the desk." Besides, bidialectalism would seriously handicap a black student's chance to make it in the outside world. However, this realization didn't forestall accusations of racism or pandering to whites. Just as a fad bears scant resemblance to custom, bidialectalism differed enormously from bilingualism.

During the 1970s, deschooling fit in well with vouchers and bidialectalism as a prominent educational fad. The reason given for deschooling was that regular schooling endorsed a "hidden curriculum." Throughout the world, teachers taught students a specific ideology such as fascism, liberalism, Catholicism, socialism, and so on, embroidered with some nonpartisan knowledge. Deschoolers despised the blatant propaganda and advocated learning from the world through free choice and humanistic education, rather than learning about the world from doctrinaire teachers. Orwell's ominous year 1984 was rapidly approaching, and no one wanted to see Big Brother face to face. The deschoolers hoped computer technology and video transmission would link the world, thereby making it impossible for any single ideology to seize control of people's minds. But the main spokesperson for deschooling, Ivan Illich, saw error in this:

> Unfortunately, these things [technology] are used in modern media to increase the power of knowledge-bankers to funnel their program-packages through international chains to more people, instead of being used to increase true networks that provide equal opportunity for encounter among members of the majority. Deschooling the culture and social structure requires the use of technology to make participatory politics possible. Only on a basis of a majority coalition can limits to secrecy and growing power be determined without dictatorship.

The deschoolers blew a lovely bubble that burst on contact. Unfortunately, almost all measures that call for global change fall into the fad category (see Reconstructionism).

Here are some more educational fads briefly noted:

- "Adversary model of education": Two evaluators scrutinized a school program; one listed all the positive aspects, the other all the negative. They competed head to head to persuade the decision maker who was right. This method of evaluation depended more on the analytic ability of the evaluator than on a real assessment of the program. (1970s)

- "Dalton Plan": Each student signed a contract that projected for one month the amount of school work he or she would complete before negotiating the next contract. This trade-union effort proved to be too authoritarian in the classroom. (1920s)

- "Direct instruction": Promoted as highly task-oriented teaching that involved goal setting, active learning, regular instruction, and student accountability. These, of course, are the attributes of all good teaching. Who wanted to pay for indirect instruction? (1970s)

- "Existential counseling": The counselor viewed the world through the eyes of the student to help the student make free choices — because an individual must accept responsibility for his or her own actions. With apologies to Sartre, what other kind of counseling is there? (1970s)

- "Free school": Did away with internal and external authority, traditional rewards and punishment, and other hindrances found in most schools, and added unconventional subject matter to the curriculum to teach counterculture aims. Passed away with the hippie movement. (late 1960s into the 1970s)

- "Gary Plan": Platooned students either to study traditional subjects or to engage in special activities held outside the classroom. Begun in Gary, Indiana, the plan operated day and night, switching students back and forth to "maximize" learning. This exemplar of progressive education got too expensive and monopolized too much time. (1910-1920)

- "Man: A Course of Study": Funded by a $4,800,000 grant from the National Science Foundation, MACOS focused on man's ability to master his environment. Critics disliked the federal government dictating curriculum, especially the implied notion that science — not God — has all the answers. Before objections killed the program, some 500 school districts were using MACOS. (1970s)

- "Nongraded school": Abolished grade levels in elementary school. This spared slow learners the trauma of failure and allowed fast learners to advance quickly. Parents relied on the teacher to keep them informed of their child's progress. Follow-up research showed little evidence in favor of the nongraded approach. A bright child might pass on to middle school before being emotionally ready or an average child be held back too long by a minor deficiency and become more traumatized. (1960s)

As educators concoct new theories and methods, they also coin new language to explain themselves. Often the language is faddishly stilted and downright pedantic. The following pre-1965 terms, thankfully, have blown away like chalk dust:

- "Action research": to see how something works in practice versus armchair research
- "Articulation": to ease the transition of a student from one educational unit to another, i.e., from elementary school to junior high
- "Credentialing": the process of teacher certification
- "Deliberate-abstractor": a student who learns slowly
- "Delimitation": to fix the boundaries of
- "Effectuate": to bring about
- "Ideational": relates to thoughts or objects not immediately present to the senses
- "Interest inventory": what a student likes most
- "Reading consultant": remedial reading teacher
- "Realia": objects or activities used to relate classroom teaching to real life
- "Sociogram": students name three favorite and three disliked classmates for the teacher to analyze

Conceivably, with this glossary of choice pedaguese, one teacher might have said to another:

> I'm currently involved in action research on student articulation up to the college years. Now that I'm through with credentialing, I can devote more time to assessing delimitations and effectuating a solid hypothesis. I want to concentrate on deliberate-abstractors who have ideational problems and weak interest inventories. Heaven knows I've tried reading consultants and realia in the classroom, but I keep getting impossible sociograms to straighten out. What should I do?

BIBLIOGRAPHY

Dejnozka, Edward L., and David E. Kapel. *American Educators' Encyclopedia*. Westport, CT: Greenwood Press, 1982.

Esler, William K. "The American School Dilemma: On the Upside of the Third Wave." *Clearing House* 57 (October 1983): 53-55.

Gardner, David P. *The California Oath Controversy*. Berkeley, CA: University of California Press, 1967.

LeSure, James S. *Guide to Pedaguese*. New York: Harper & Row, 1965.

Postman, Neil, and Charles Weingartner. *Teaching As a Subversive Activity*. New York: Delacorte Press, 1969.

Rist, Ray C., ed. *Restructuring American Education*. New Brunswick, NJ: Transaction Books, 1972.

Einstein

The German physicist Albert Einstein (1879-1955) first advanced his "special theory" of relativity in 1905. Ten years later, he added his "general theory" of relativity and by 1920 was hailed as the hero of the new physics. Einstein's revolutionary thought challenged the best scientific minds of the day, leaving many of them unsure of what he meant. If Einstein were correct, then several Newtonian laws (e.g., the theory of universal gravitation and the corpuscular theory of light) were no longer valid. What heresy had this man wrought? Ripping out a handful of pages from Sir Isaac Newton's *Philosophiae Nauturalis Principia Mathematica* (1687) was unthinkable. But Einstein did and inadvertently created a fad.

For expert or layperson, the difficulty of understanding relativity made the theories paradoxically more attractive. The mere mention of Einstein set in motion a lot of head-scratching and feeble attempts to explain his highly abstract ideas. Enough was enough; a public cry went out: "Ask Einstein to make himself clear." The hero of the new physics tried in a newspaper article published by the London *Times* (1919):

> The special relativity theory is the application of the following proposition to any natural process: Every law of nature which holds good with respect to a coordinate system must also hold good for any other system, provided that the two are in uniform movement of translation. . . . In the generalized theory of relativity, the doctrine of space and time, kinematics, is no longer one of the absolute foundations of general physics. The geometrical states of bodies and the rate of clocks depend in the first place on their gravitational fields, which again are produced by the material systems concerned.

Einstein continued to "clarify" his theories in this manner, glazing even more eyes and twisting even more eyebrows than previously.

Once again, enough was enough, so *Scientific American* sponsored an Einstein Prize Essay Contest. To spice up the event, Eugene Higgins, a wealthy American bachelor living in Paris, offered $5,000 to the winner. No doubt, soon the world would have its simplification and know why Newton was moth-eaten. Physicists and astronomers from the most prestigious institutions sent in their essays, as did other independent thinkers. With all this brainpower at work to crystallize relativity, it was just a matter of time (no pun intended) before Einstein would be intelligible to a six-year-old. Surprisingly, L. Bolton, a staff member of the British Patent Office, won the contest, much to the chagrin of the professional ranks. "Zodiaque" (L. Bolton's nom de plume) had this to say about the general theory of relativity:

1. Associated with every gravitional field is a system of geometry, that is, a structure of measured space peculiar to that field.
2. Inertial mass and gravitational mass are one and the same.
3. Since in such regions ordinary methods of measurement fail, owing to the indefiniteness of the standards, the systems of geometry must be independent of any particular measurements.
4. The geometry of space in which no gravitational field exists is Euclidean.

And L. Bolton took first prize for clarity! In a state of frenzy, the public renewed its questioning: Was Einstein truly a genius? Was relativity the most important scientific discovery in the last 200 years? And, if it was, what in God's sweet name was relativity? As these uncertainties swirled around, the brighter journalists writing for every major and minor publication stepped forward to joust with relativity. A profusion of articles followed, and some clarification began to emerge. What the public finally gleaned from Einstein was that time could be made to stand still, and a human being living in a time warp could enjoy eternal youth. Now that was a revelation! Of course, Einstein's elixir was about as easy to obtain as a drink from Ponce de Leon's Fountain of Youth. The longevity seeker had to be launched into space and travel at a rate faster than the speed of light before conquering inexorable time and mortality. Like dizzy atoms,

so many relativity articles bombarded the public that a journalist for
The Nation wrote tongue in cheek:

> Read one exposition firmly and quietly, and if you do not at
> once see that nothing [in the universe] is fixed and absolute;
> that we are living in a glorious whirl in which time and space
> can gaily exchange places like partners in a Virginia reel, turn
> no more to Einstein but to your private cellar. You can be
> intoxicated only by a brew beneath the attention of physicists.

The Einstein craze raced on, not quite at the speed of light, but
close. The doubting Thomases who arose to challenge Einstein, the
public's awe of the man who had proposed something few understood—making him look even more like a bona fide genius—and
his little formula, $E = mc^2$, catapulted Einstein into every conversation. Never before had an ivory-tower thinker been so celebrated.
One of his detractors, Capt. T. J. J. See of the U.S. Navy, said,
"The Einstein doctrine that the ether does not exist, and that gravity
is not a force, but a property of space, can only be described as a
crazy vagary, a disgrace to our age!" The captain's last name was a
godsend for humorists who wrote that See saw more than Einstein
in their seesaw battle over Newton. But the preponderance of commentators took for granted that Einstein was a genius and relativity
a masterstroke of theorizing. A bit of early proof came when scientists photographed a total eclipse of the sun and discovered the light
rays around it did indeed bend rather than remain straight as previously thought—just as Einstein had predicted. Almost 15 years after the Einstein craze began, a writer for *Scientific American* (February 1934) summed up the phenomenon:

> Everybody agrees that Albert Einstein is one of the great ge-
> niuses of all time. His researches in mathematical physics
> have revolutionized science. . . . However, when we try to
> find out what it is all about—just what changes are taking
> place in the theories of science and philosophy—most of us,
> after more or less reading, give it up and content ourselves
> with wondering about the simpler, but more insoluble problem
> . . . how Professor Einstein managed to get and retain such a
> wonderful head of hair.

Einstein's lion's mane with its soft white volts aimed skyward seemed to defy gravity just like his theories. His electric hair plus his standing as one of the three most influential figures of the twentieth century (Freud and Picasso being the other two) made his visage perfect for gracing posters and T-shirts from his heyday until recently. Fewer Einstein memorabilia are seen today in our stubbornly anti-intellectual times. Just a few decades ago, students of all ages delighted in writing $E = mc^2$ on blackboards and as graffito on bathroom walls, but no more. The formula's profound meaning that all energy is equivalent to mass — now the basis for how nuclear reactors work and the sun itself — may not have been understood by those compelled to scribble it. But then, new generations were no worse off than their predecessors had been back in the 1920s when Einstein first eclipsed Newton.

BIBLIOGRAPHY

"Einstein's Own Story." *Literary Digest* 64 (January 31, 1920): 29-30.
"Is the Einstein Theory a Crazy Vagary?" *Literary Digest* 77 (June 2, 1923): 29-30.
Nichols, Joseph B. "You Have One Chance in a Hundred to Understand Einstein." *Scientific American* 150 (February 1934): 72 + .
"Relativity: The Winning Essay for the Eugene Higgins Five Thousand Dollar Prize." *Scientific American* 124 (February 5, 1921): 106-107.

The Emmanuel Movement

The Reverend Elwood Worcester, Rector of Emmanuel Church in Boston, wrote these words in an article for *Century Magazine* (July 1909):

> When we began this work, our only thought was to give relief to a few distressed persons. We did not dream of the notoriety this undertaking would achieve, and I will frankly say that if anything could have induced me to give up a work to which I believe I was called of God, it would be the painful publicity which from the beginning has attached itself to our undertaking.

Reverend Worcester's undertaking was to heal the sick using auto-suggestion, faith, and prayer. Under his direction, the Emmanuel Movement first began administering to tubercular patients. The rule was that each patient had to see a medical doctor before coming to the church clinic. The doctor determined whether or not the affliction was organic. Reverend Worcester treated functional disorders only, because organic disorders were beyond his ability to heal. This steadfast rule separated the Emmanuel Movement from Mary Baker Eddy's Christian Scientists, who believed faith in God alone cured functional and organic disorders. Reverend Worcester never promised to work miracles, nor did he expect faith and prayer to do any more than succor the patient. A Doctor of Divinity and Philosophy who spent long hours studying the emerging field of psychology, he simply mixed religion and medicine to achieve what he called, "the moral control of nervous disorders."

Early on, Reverend Worcester's success with tubercular patients made news far beyond Boston. No one really knew the degree of his triumph over the predominately "organic" disease of tuberculosis. And by his own admission, he treated just a few suffering souls, hardly enough to start a movement. But the public took him at his word and asked no questions, ensuring his fame would spread across America and the Atlantic. As the movement gained momentum and Reverend Worcester delved deeper into psychotherapeutic methods, the church clinic expanded its practice. Admitted for treatment were persons suffering from congestive and neuralgic disorders, anemic headaches, certain forms of paralysis, simulated epilepsy, neurasthenia, hypochondria, psychasthenia, hysteria, hysterical pains, insomnia, melancholia, nervous irritability, hallucinations, morbid fears, fixed ideas (the phobias), incipient insanities, stagefright, worry, stammering, abuse of tobacco, alcoholism, morphinism, cocainism, kleptomania, and suicidal tendencies. A psychiatric clinic in 1909 would have had its hands full dealing with such a list, but the church clinic didn't blink an eye. Bona fide psychiatrists in 1909 were more theory-bound than self-assured therapists, unlike the fearless Reverend Worcester and his staff who plunged right into treatment. Soon the good old days when only a handful of tubercular patients came forth were over. There was no charge for church clinic treatment, which explains in part why so many sick people begged admittance. In this respect, treating patients for free in a church setting with reports issued that miracles had happened brought Reverend Worcester his unwanted "notoriety." Some people thought he and Jesus Christ were one and the same.

The Emmanuel Movement used autosuggestion to get a patient to concentrate on positive thought. A person with tuberculosis would repeat that he was going to get well until he believed it. His chest did not hurt, his lungs were not full of painful lesions, and he was on his way to recovery. Next, the patient had to accept God as all-healing, to place complete trust in God's beneficence. The final step was for the patient to act on his own behalf and pray to God for strength to overcome weakness of the spirit. Reverend Worcester had read his psychology and was familiar with the underlying causes of neuroses:

> Since unhealthy self-centered thoughts, taken up by the brain mechanism, translate themselves into mischievous nervous effects, our aim is to teach the sufferer to remove these mental images from the focus of consciousness by substituting for

them thoughts of power and of inward harmony, by stirring up dormant interests, and by suggesting lines of unselfish activity. The majority of nervous patients are extremely emotional and suffer from lack of will power.

Thus, Reverend Worcester proceeded from some kind of knowledge base and avoided mystical incantations or strict reliance on divine intervention.

In full stride, the Emmanuel Movement lasted from 1908-1910. Several controversies retarded its growth. For one, the Christian Scientists felt personally attacked by it. If Reverend Worcester maintained that organic disease could not be cured by belief in Jesus Christ, then he was their enemy and an anti-Christ. Jesus Christ raised Lazarus from the dead and raised Himself after three days' burial. Death is certainly an organic disease, so Reverend Worcester was wrong. Then, theologians around the country renewed discussion about the veracity of Christ's miracles. The Emmanuel Movement's position was that only some of the miracles were truthful. Making a blind man see again was due to Christ talking the man into foregoing his functional disorder. He was blind because his mind willed it, not because disease had destroyed his eyes. On the other hand, curing a leper with prayer alone was hard to imagine. Other critics of Reverend Worcester argued that a theologian should not expend time doing work other than ministerial. A man who thought he was Christ would feel too self-important, and such a man's fame would harm his ministry by engendering in people a false belief in his superhuman ability to cure sickness. Reverend Worcester did not help himself when he wrote that the Emmanuel Movement would eventually "outdo the wonders of the Apostolic and post-Apostolic age" in healing the sick, words that made his critics really gasp.

A scant two years after beginning the Emmanuel Movement, Reverend Worcester decided to discontinue the church clinic. Although he and his staff would continue to receive a few referrals from Boston hospitals. Still, thousands of applications flooded in. Reverend Worcester had not capitulated to his critics; he simply came to the realization that the job was too big for one church with a small staff. The "tremendous pressure" he was under was very much the same Jesus Christ had faced. Just as after Christ's early success, a healing hysteria ensued, and peer healers not divine got jealous. He also worried that the Movement would not prosper at other church clinics without his guidance. Reverend Worcester died in 1940. During the 30 years after faddish interest in the Emmanuel Movement, he continued to work his magic on a few select cases that interested him.

BIBLIOGRAPHY

Buckley, James M. "Dangers of the Emmanuel Movement." *Century Magazine* 77 (February 1909): 631-635.

Flower, B. O. "Christ, the Sick and Modern Christianity." *The Arena* 39 (May 1908): 557-564.

McComb, Rev. Samuel. "Christianity and Health: An Experiment in Practical Religion." *Century Magazine* 75 (March 1908): 793-798.

Worcester, Rev. Elwood. "The Emmanuel Movement." *Century Magazine* 78 (July 1909): 421-429.

———, et al. *Religion and Medicine.* New York: Moffat, Yard & Company, 1908.

These suppliant Esalenites have become one with nature. Before them is the azure Pacific off the coast of Big Sur. As they meditate, ocean waves play a symphony and soft breezes tingle their flesh. Upon hearing about Esalen hedonism, people unable to escape the rat race either drowned in envy or condemned the nudist cult. (1968)

Esalen

During his twilight years, English author Aldous Huxley (1894-1963) lived in Big Sur, California. There, at the edge of the Pacific Ocean, with awe-inspiring nature all around him, Huxley espoused a belief in the perfectibility of humankind. Thirty years before, his most popular novel, *Brave New World* (1932), had described a nightmare world of automaton people bred by cold scientific calculation. But that dystopian reverie now gave way to what Huxley called "human potentialities," which meant that an individual could surpass normal limitations to personal growth given the proper environment and incentive. Huxley, a revered visionary who had tasted the Pierian Springs, believed such a renewal of the human spirit was imminent, if only someone would coax it along. Michael Murphy, a native of Salinas, California, and Richard Price, a student at Stanford, thought so too. Together they decided to buy Slate's Hot Springs in Big Sur and turn it into a center for exploring Huxley's human potentialities. Price would oversee the daily operations of Esalen (named for a tribe of Indians the Spanish decimated — the first in California to become totally extinct), and Murphy would line up seminar programs. The center would stimulate mind and body innovatively, holistically, and pleasurably. Esalen was to be the wished-for realization of Huxley's dream.

Begun in the early 1960s, Esalen's rise to fad stardom (wholly unwanted) was as leisurely as the daily Tai Chi classes taught on the swimming pool deck. Intellectuals such as the creator of Gestalt therapy Fritz Perls, architect and inventor Buckminster Fuller, self-actualization theorist Abraham Maslow, massage therapist Ida Rolf, and Zen philosopher Alan Watts infused Esalen with cerebral energy. Their seminars were full of fire and erudition. Visitors to the center listened intently to the persuasive intellectuals, either adopting their ideas or at least mulling them over. Between seminars, visitors participated in exercise classes, read good literature quietly to themselves, took naps outdoors, or indulged in the restful mineral baths. Once Esalen became known as the nerve center of the human potential movement, things just started happening spontaneously. For one, the Big Sur Folk Festival coordinated by Joan Baez turned into an annual event, featuring artists like Simon and Garfunkel, Judy Collins, and Bob Dylan. For another, people from as far away as Australia asked for reservations, along with investigative journalists. The latter novitiates were to become the fad mongers.

In their articles, the journalists explained Esalen's commitment to realizing human potential. But after a few words about the seminars and the peaceful setting, they told the reader the real truth. People went to Esalen to live like hedonists. The highbrow talk merely filled time; the big draw was nudity and sex. Of all the "awareness" classes — mind, energy, feeling — massage awareness was the most eagerly anticipated. Under the temperate sun of Northern California, to the placid sound of billowing waves, students removed their clothing and took turns stretching out on massage tables. An instructor taught the students (no one got bored) exactly how to ripple flesh to remove all vestiges of tense muscle. What made the classes even more zestful was group massage. Six masseurs/masseuses, three per side, twelve hands, sixty fingers, oiled and kneaded one heaven-bound person. Surely such an experience eclipsed any rays of wisdom emanating from Alan Watts or Buckminster Fuller. Next to massage awareness, the baths were too delicious for words. But let one of the lucky investigative reporters, Richard Atcheson, writing for *Holiday*, guide you through the sensation:

> . . . the baths were far and away my favorite spot at Esalen. They are, perhaps, a sort of symbol of the acceptance of awareness, of honesty, which seems to me to be at the center of the Esalen experience. It is good to walk down a path to a terrace, closed on three sides and roofed, but open to the sea and sky, to take off your clothes and sink into one of several wide, deep tubs full of the hot-spring water that flows ceaselessly out of the mountain and down to the sea. It is good to be able to do that with other people, alone with them or together

with them as you wish. I went to the baths many times, and it seemed to me that it was a uniquely private place.

Amy Gross, calling herself Pilgrim, wrote this account for *Mademoiselle:*

> Chatting in one of the tubs, Pilgrim realizes that she's in the ultimate conversation pit, the last word in icebreakers. The water seems to soften the skin, the muscles, maybe even the bones. She likes it, this night bath. The excitement of it. The sociableness. The exhibitionism — an antidote to a lifetime's training in inhibitionism. The sensuality of the water and the air, the bodies, the occasional brushing of one leg against another as someone shifts position. The nudity doesn't feel natural, but it doesn't feel bad either.

Visitors checked in for a weekend or for a month, if they had time. One of the unwritten rules of Esalen was to avoid small talk. Silence should predominate over nervous chatter. No one had to feel compelled to prove his or her existence by unrestrained verbiage, especially about inconsequential worldly matters. Esalen was a place where anyone could freely admit as a reason for coming, "I want to put myself together," or "I want to take a look at myself — I've always been too busy before." To the outside world, such a desire was conspicuous narcissism, and the only human potential in sight was to hop nude in a hot bath with an attractive person. From the late 1960s into the early 1970s, Esalen magnetized college professors interested in the seminars, Hollywood stars looking for novel stimulation, wealthy spa-goers seeking the unusual, followers of hip Californian trends, and an assortment of the plain curious. Visitors did their best to exploit Esalen for whatever reason brought them to the once sacred Indian grounds. Some of them tried hard to understand the original purpose of Esalen, i.e., as a center for calm reflection and the pursuit of bodily health. But not everyone did, and the fad passed on when ennui set in. To the disappointment of promiscuous visitors, Esalen was more a monastery than an open-air bordello. One of the most often heard comments about Big Sur and Esalen was that life there was too beautiful. The air was pristine, the sunrises and sunsets breathtaking, the people impossibly friendly, and the pressure to do anything unpleasant absent.

In 1987, Esalen celebrated its twenty-fifth anniversary. *Time* was the only news magazine to cover the event. The article written by Pico Iyer characterized Esalen as an anachronism hanging on at the end of an ultra-conservative decade that did little for anyone's human potential. No more hot flashes from reading about massage awareness or the baths, visitors to Esalen had dwindled down to those who genuinely wanted to "hang out" with their feelings. Iyer concluded, "And as the Gestaltifying days of old recede, the place seems to be settling into a comfortable calm—less a crisis center, perhaps, than an otherworldly spa where affluent mid-life professionals can come to chop vegetables, lose themselves in books, and enjoy a little quiet."

BIBLIOGRAPHY

Anderson, Walter Truett. *The Upstart Spring: Esalen and the American Awakening*. Reading, MA: Addison-Wesley Publishing Co., 1983.

Atcheson, Richard. "Big Sur: Coming to My Senses." *Holiday* 43 (March 1968): 18+.

Gross, Amy. "Pilgrim's Progress: The Path to Self-Awareness Is Littered with Naked Bodies." *Mademoiselle* 83 (April 1977): 202+.

Iyer, Pico. "In California: Being 25 and Following Your Bliss." *Time* 130 (September 14, 1987): 10+.

Esperanto

Of the many universal or artificial languages that have been proposed in the last 200 years, Esperanto seemed to be, in the early part of the twentieth century, on the verge of worldwide acceptance. Dr. L. L. Zamenhof of Warsaw created Esperanto in 1887, claiming that it offered "maximum internationality" because only a few hundred root words and a mere 16 rules of grammar had to be learned. Prior to Esperanto, the only universal language in use was French, but that was for conducting affairs of state. Travelers who did not speak French had to muddle along as usual with broken phrases and hand gestures. Zamenhof and his disciples were humanitarians; not only did they hope to unite all people through the bond of a common language, but they wanted to see an end to war. It was their belief that people who cannot communicate with, or who misunderstand, one another will invariably resort to suspicion and conflict. Worldwide use of Esperanto would cure that problem and also foster the sharing of ideas in every field of human endeavor.

By 1905, 15 international congresses demonstrated the strength of the movement. Five thousand Esperantists from 43 different countries marked the high point of attendance. At the congresses, everyone spoke Esperanto, from formal addresses to chance discussion. Even the entertainment was in Esperanto: plays, opera, vaudeville sketches, and the like. One tour de force was to stage a play with every actor chosen from a different country. The normal jarring of accents did not occur; instead, the Esperantist actors all spoke the same melodious language.

With such an auspicious beginning, what happened to Esperanto? And why can it be considered a fad? The two world wars, in addition to producing an unheard-of number of human casualties, also destroyed any number of social movements. Esperanto, the peacemaker, could not compete with Ares and Mars. After WWI, the conception of a League of Nations to provide world governance again thrust Esperanto into the limelight. But for Esperanto to work effectively, it had to be taught to every child in every nation, not on an optional basis. Since the League of Nations encountered resistance on many other matters, mandatory teaching of Esperanto as a covenant never came to pass. Between world wars, Esperanto fared worse and, sadly, became embroiled in political power moves. Adolph Hitler wrote in *Mein Kampf* that the spread of Esperanto throughout Europe was a Jewish plot to break down national differences so that Jews could more easily assume positions of authority. Taking a little heat off the Jews, some political reactionaries screamed that Esperanto was the language of communism. By getting all the people of the world to speak one common tongue, later conquest would be a cinch, much like the Jewish scheme. Thus, Esperanto, the language proposed to unify the world, made superb propaganda, allowing Hitler to persecute both Jews and Communists. After the Nazi's successful blitzkrieg of Poland, the Warsaw Gestapo received orders to "take care" of the Zamenhof family. The founder of Esperanto had died in 1917, leaving his heirs to continue his work. Zamenhof's son was shot and killed immediately; his two daughters were sent to the Treblinka death camp, where they eventually succumbed to its ravages. War hysteria also caused some people to fear that Esperanto was possibly a secret code used by spy rings. Miscomprehension and persecution of Esperantists continued unabated until the end of the war.

In the United States, Esperanto groups formed simultaneously with those in Europe and elsewhere, although they were not as numerous. Americans recognized the need for a flexible language vehicle. Emerging modes of rapid travel to every corner of the world sanctioned, if not mandated, a universal language. So study began here in earnest. The vocabulary of Esperanto is based on the Romance languages and Latin. Nouns end in *o*; adjectives, in *a*; and adverbs, in *e*. The plural form of nouns and adjectives ends in *j*. The present tense of a verb ends in *as*; the past tense, in *is*; the future tense, in *os*; the subjunctive mood, in *us*; the infinitive mood, in *i*. Every word is read exactly as written: there are no silent letters. The accent always falls on the penultimate syllable, pronunciation is phonetic, and so on, until the pupil mastered all 16 rules of grammar. These comparative texts will furnish an illustration:

English	Esperanto
Now all communication and propagation of science uses the means supplied by language, and so the internationality of science irresistibly demands the internationality of language.	Sed chiu komunikado kaj divastigado de la scienco uzas la helpilon de la lingvo kaj tial la internacieco de la scienco nerezisteble postulas la internacieco de la lingvo.

Now try this one without a translation:

Simpla, fleksebla, belsona, vere internacia en siajelementoj, la lingvo Esperanto prezentas al la mondo civilzita la sole veran solvon de lingvo internacia; char tre facila por homoj nemulte instruitaj, Esperanto estas komprenata sen peno de la personoj bone edukitaj.

Although the widest acclaim for Esperanto was pre-World War I, there are still Esperantists today who eagerly promote the universal language. The Esperanto League for North America, founded in 1952, currently has a membership of 825. The American Association of Teachers of Esperanto, founded in 1961, is not as large, but the 90 members continue to teach or have taught Esperanto. Therefore, World War II did not completely wipe out interest in one world tongue. What has relegated Esperanto to fad history is, first of all, that English has become the universal language. Even though Esperantists affirm that Esperanto is much easier to learn than English, they haven't made much headway in convincing others of the fact. Because Esperanto derives from the Romance languages and Latin, people in the Far East don't find it that simple to master. Italians, yes; Spaniards, yes; the French, yes; the Japanese and Chinese, no. National pride in one's language is, likewise, an imposing barrier, correct pronunciation another ticklish matter. In practice, speaking Esperanto leaves people as straining to listen as ever. Confused meaning occurs with regularity. None of these facts seem to support the early Esperanto congresses in saying that their plays were performed audibly perfect by actors from every clime.

BIBLIOGRAPHY

Durrant, E. D. *The Language Problem: Its History and Solution*. Heronsgate, Rickmansworth, Herts., England: Esperanto Publishing, 1943.

Hetzel, Henry W. "The International Language." *Education* 48 (January 1928): 325-330.

————. "The World Language, English or Esperanto?" *Education* 51 (June 1931): 629-634.

Large, Andrew. *The Artificial Language Movement*. London: Basil Blackwell, 1985.

Pei, Mario. *One Language for the World*. New York: Devin-Adair, 1958.

Privat, Edmond. *The Life of Zamenhof*. London: Allen & Unwin, 1931.

est

The brainchild of Werner Erhard, an ex-encyclopedia salesman with only a high school education, Erhard Seminars Training (est) held its first self-help sessions (1971) in a friend's borrowed apartment. The premise of est is to tear down and humiliate a group of individuals, then rebuild them like recruits in an Army boot camp. Mortification en masse worked, and in only a few years est weekends originated from spacious quarters in swank hotel conference rooms in over a dozen major American cities. The nouveau riche Erhard wore designer clothes, drove a Mercedes 450 SEL, and flew across the country in a private plane.

Born Jack Rosenberg near Philadelphia, the son of a small restauranteur, Erhard had come a long way. Prior to starting est he had worked at a variety of jobs: as a representative for a school that taught operation of construction equipment, as a used car salesman, as a correspondence school employee, as a *Great Books* salesman, as sales manager for the Parents Cultural Institute, and as a trainer of door-to-door salesmen for Grolier, Inc. Also, during his formative days, he studied hypnosis, Scientology, and Mind Dynamics, methods of which he incorporated into est. By the early 1970s, Erhard could recite hard-sell techniques in his sleep. All he had to do to cash in on the current rage for psychotherapy was to add ample servings of Zen, Gestalt, Transcendental Meditation, Transactional Analysis, Esalen, and other pop-psychology movements. Erhard's genius lay in drenching his adherents with a 2-weekend, 60-hour thunderstorm that washed them psychically clean. With est, no one had to endure months and years of standard psychotherapy at a clinic. For $250 apiece, each person got a quick-fix ultimate answer for whatever upset his or her mental equilibrium. Soon detractors called est "the McDonald's of Zen" because it was fast food for the mind and just about as nourishing.

Tearing down the individual began like this. He or she had to agree not to leave the training room for any reason: to stretch, eat, smoke, or go to the bathroom. Two breaks were allowed per 15-hour session. Inside the training room, no one could talk except to share an experience with the group, and definitely no squirming or bellyaching. An instructor came in and, without saying hello, began telling the group they were all worthless "assholes" and would remain so until they "got it." The instructor promised eventually everyone would "get it," but for the time being, they were "assholes" and their lives a wreck. The prepaid customers were also told they would have to go along with everything shoveled out to them. Since they were all worthless "assholes" anyway, they should be overjoyed to have someone tell them the truth at last. Adelaide Bry, a counseling psychologist, participated in est training and wrote about her experience in *est: 60 Hours That Transform Your Life:*

> The verbal flagellation continued: "You people are here today because all of your strategies, your smart-ass theories, and all the rest of your shit hasn't worked for you. In this training you're going to find out you've been acting like assholes. All of your fucking cleverness and self-deception have gotten you nowhere."

One woman questioned the profanity, and the instructor barked back: "'Spaghetti' and 'fuck' are the same. They're only words. The difference is the significance you add to them." A cadre of est trainers came and went, bending the audience's mind even more. The first apex of involvement occurred when everyone stood, after being coaxed into reverie by simple exercise and incantations, and listened to their leader of the moment read "the poem." It was a long creed full of personal affirmations and positive attitudes. Were the "assholes" about to emerge from the muck and mire of their sad existence? Not so fast. They had to pass through the "truth process" first. Each person was to select his or her biggest problem in life and concentrate on it, recalling every emotionally wrenching detail. After the unnerving harangues that had preceded the truth process and in the presence of a powerful est father confessor, many of the trainees writhed and gesticulated on the floor, whimpered, sobbed, and even vomited. The truth process provided a perfect example of crowd psychology at its best. But there was more to endure. A wave of unsparing est trainers stormed through the audience to stare and sneer at random trainees. Without uttering a word, the trainers drew tears from the hapless, mute victims. Other standard indoctrination tricks were played right up until the final payoff—"getting it."

Adelaide Bry relates what happened in the final hours of the last day:

> "Enlightenment," he [the est trainer] continued, "is knowing you are a machine. You are a machine!" He paused to let that sink in. "You thought"—he glared at us—"that the heavens would part and there would be visitations of angels. That ain't so. You're machines, machines, machines. Whether you accept this or not, it's so." . . . "I don't get it," the first protestor announced. "Good," came the reply. "There's nothing to get, so you got it."

For $250, the indignity of being called an "asshole" repeatedly, and having to suffer red eyes and a swollen bladder, the est climax left many trainees feeling cheated. Whatever they had learned about themselves during their 60-hour ordeal was all they would get—but was that enough? Yes, it seemed; only a few people screamed hoax. The rest returned home filled with a new sense of purpose in their lives and recommended est to their friends.

The psychiatric community felt compelled to respond. In an article published in the *American Journal of Psychiatry* (March 1977), three expert investigators reported five cases of mental disturbances associated with est. The five ex-est trainees had developed psychotic symptoms including "grandiosity, paranoia, uncontrollable mood swings, and delusions":

> [Case 1] jumped into his swimming pool at home nude and tried to breathe under the surface. He felt he was god-like and could survive without air and ignored his family's entreaties. He attempted increasingly hazardous feats to validate his grandiose self-image. After 2 days of manic activity his wife called local police and involuntary hospitalization was instituted.

[Case 3] began to feel estranged from himself, his wife, and his role in the dental clinic [where he was a student]. He developed ideas of reference and influence and became convinced he could read his son's mind. He spent hours pacing the city streets, afraid to let anyone see his face lest they control his mind.

The investigators concluded that est could not be held completely responsible for the psychotic symptoms, the seeds of which were probably already planted in the individuals. But the impetus of the article certainly implied that est should be carefully monitored.

The early 1980s brought about the downfall of Erhard's est empire. A major lawsuit claiming extreme emotional distress as the result of est training and an IRS demand for $2 million in back taxes injured Erhard. Declining enrollment in est (hard to believe that people got tired of being called "assholes"), the defection of his top-level aides, and his wife of 22 years filing for divorce were the final blows. But, like the good old days when he had watched sobbing and vomiting trainees survive the truth process, Erhard outlasted his personal trial by fire. By 1985 he had thought up a new seminar journey of self-discovery—the "Forum." This time around, he geared it toward already successful people, not confused, groping ones, who could pay $525 for four 16-hour sessions. The end product of the Forum (note use of the capital letter here, whereas est always began with a lowercase letter) was to teach its trainees how to achieve excellence. Erhard explained:

> Excellence in all cases is a matter of being excellent. When you take an honest, uncomplicated look at those you know who possess the qualities of excellence, creativity, competence and achievement, clearly they are simply being excellent, being creative, being competent, being able. It's really as simple as that.

From the ashes of one fad another was born.

BIBLIOGRAPHY

Brewer, Mark. "We're Gonna Tear You Down and Put You Back Together." *Psychology Today* 9 (August 1975): 35 + .

Bry, Adelaide. *est: 60 Hours That Transform Your Life*. New York: Harper & Row, 1976.

"Erhard's 'Forum': est Meets the Eighties." *Newsweek* 105 (April 1, 1985): 15.

Glass, Leonard L., et al. "Psychiatric Disturbances Associated with Erhard Seminars Training: I. A Report of Cases." *American Journal of Psychiatry* 134 (March 1977): 245-247.

"His Wife and Former Followers Question the Human Potential of est Guru Werner Erhard." *People Weekly* 22 (September 24, 1984): 41-42.

Eugenics

It is almost inconceivable today to think that civilized Americans ever endorsed eugenics, "an applied science that seeks to maintain or to improve the genetic potentialities of the human species." This definition sounds harmless enough and actually very modern, given that our genetic engineering is much the same. But the eugenics movement in this country in the 1920s verged on madness as extremists advocated racial purification measures akin to those in ancient Sparta and Hitler's Germany.

The Spartans were a dominant race that felt no remorse in abandoning a sickly child. The child died, but the race profited from not having an inferior being in its midst to produce more of its kind. The Spartans relied on economic incentives to promote eugenic marriage; they penalized celibacy and regularly killed large numbers of conquered subjects to prevent interracial dilution of their own stock. Later, Plato, revered for his wisdom concerning the ideal state, likewise sanctioned destroying birth-defective children, children of inferior parents, chronic invalids, and self-indulgent individuals (e.g., drunkards and lazy people). Moral degenerates would also forfeit their lives through state indifference to their fate. The last category was indeed dangerous. The state could deem anyone a moral degenerate who was perceived to be different from the status quo, thus granting the state supreme power over its cowering citizens.

After Sparta, eugenics went into a lengthy hibernation before the Englishman Francis Galton (1822-1911) resurrected the notion. Galton studied volumes of genealogical data, reaching the conclusion that degeneracy, no less than talent, is inherited. He and his associate, Karl Pearson (1857-1936), devised mathematical formulas for the determination of inherited characteristics which could then be applied to eugenic selection. The two became world famous. In the United States, Alexander Graham Bell saw merit in eugenics and began conducting his own research. The American Galton, however, was the geneticist Charles B. Davenport (1866-1944).

Harvard educated, Davenport rediscovered Mendel's laws of heredity and made them the basis of his own search for the key to improving humankind. In 1911, he published his most important work, *Heredity in Relation to Eugenics,* in which he postulated that all human characteristics are the product of immutable genes that appear in succeeding generations in simple Mendelian ratios. Now begins the monstrous side of eugenics that attests to how far fad and bigotry can obscure legitimate scientific aims. Davenport began a public crusade urging "the fit" to reproduce and "the unfit" to abstain. He told believing crowds that this was the only way to stamp out "imbecility, poverty, disease, and immorality." His cruel doctrine played well. With the help of a wealthy donor, he was able to establish a small research center at Cold Spring Harbor on Long Island. Ten years later, the fledgling center took wing as the Carnegie Institution's Department of Genetics (1920). At the center, Davenport and his colleagues gathered family data from asylums, reformatories, and other institutions that housed flawed humanity. Their research continued to underscore that the unfit passed on bad genes, ruining the social fabric. Proof in hand, Davenport began making more vehement and ridiculous public statements. He was positive that the dilution of Anglo-Saxon blood in the U.S. imperiled democracy, so he advocated stringent immigration restrictions and racial segregation. His research could not possibly have supported this extreme position, but he voiced it anyway, and because of his standing as an erudite geneticist few people challenged him.

Davenport's zeal to spread the word about eugenics naturally caused disciples outside the scientific fold to arise and fight by his side. The result might have been amusing if not for the malicious bigotry and rampant ignorance that ensued. From his book, *In the Name of Eugenics* (1985), Daniel J. Kevles describes the typical disciple:

Eugenics enthusiasts in the United States and Britain were largely middle to upper middle class, white, Anglo-Saxon, predominately Protestant, and educated. The movement's leaders tended to be well-to-do rather than rich, and many were professionals — physicians, social workers, clerics, writers, and numerous professors, notably in the biological and social sciences.

This holy band of WASPs lashed out at every vice. For example, they declared that nicotine in tobacco shrivels the sexual organs; too much sexual activity not directed toward procreation squanders the life principle; a man who has intercourse with a pregnant woman implants in the unborn child the seeds of sensuality; and divorcees live briefer lives, incur more mental disease, and usually become sterile outside of marriage. Therefore, smoking, lust, and broken marriage were disgracefully uneugenic. WASPs in American colleges and universities such as Harvard, Columbia, Cornell, Brown, and Berkeley offered courses in eugenics, both from a scientific and theoretical standpoint. Women's clubs hosted eugenic forums, featuring noted experts who advised on how to cleanse society of human detritus. Men of the cloth preached impassioned eugenics sermons. And fairs like the Topeka, Kansas, Fitter Families Eugenic Competition (1924) paraded human stock to exemplify proud lineage free of weak offspring.

Besides giving bigots and moralists an excuse to exercise their prerogative, eugenics was blind to societal change. All the "undesirable" flotsam and jetsam of humankind had been set adrift by the Industrial Revolution. The lower class labored piteously to keep the upper class fat and sassy, so naturally it produced some weak offspring. In turn, those of the lower class who made it to adulthood inherited the same mental and physical problems their parents had endured. The proverbial vicious circle was all too real for the human oil and grease that kept the machines of production going. For some eugenicists, it didn't matter that society demanded the ultimate of its members, including forfeiture of parenthood, and even death, for not living up to agreed upon standards. One social thinker, Alexander Johnson, made this candid suggestion:

I think neither restrictive marriage laws, elimination by a painless death, nor wholesale sterilization can be applied, at any rate within the next generation or two, so as to have any serious effect in the reduction of the number of the degenerate classes. . . . It is quite possible and practicable to establish, in every state in the union, orderly celibate communities, segregated from the body politic; set off by themselves on land selected for the purpose, in buildings constructed to some extent by their own hands, where the feeble-minded people, and the epileptic people, and the chronically insane people may be cared for permanently, and a large part of them made entirely self-supporting.

Out of sight, out of mind was somewhat more humane than "painless death." If the rabid eugenics movement of the 1920s were to resurface today, for starters, all of the homeless, AIDs patients, drug users, and welfare recipients would face state indifference or annihilation. One wonders if these same fanatical eugenicists felt any remorse two decades later when Stalin and Hitler purged people by the millions, referring to them as expendable vermin?

BIBLIOGRAPHY

Guyer, Michael F. *Being Well-Born: An Introduction to Eugenics*. Indianapolis, IN: Bobbs-Merrill, 1916.

Haller, Mark. *Eugenics: Hereditarian Attitudes in American Thought*. New Brunswick, NJ: Rutgers University Press, 1963.

Johnson, Alexander. "Race Improvement by Control of Defectives (Negative Eugenics)." *The Annals of the Academy of American Political and Social Science* 34 (July 1909): 22-29.

Kevles, Daniel J. *In the Name of Eugenics: Genetics and the Uses of Human Heredity*. New York: Alfred A. Knopf, 1985.

Wiggam, Albert E. *The New Decalogue of Science*. Indianapolis: Bobbs-Merrill, 1923.

Existentialism

This mid-twentieth-century philosophy was an amalgam of other belief systems before it (Descartes, Pascal, Kierkegaard), but did not come into its own until Jean Paul Sartre clarified its precepts. Sartre wrote: "Man can count on no one but himself; he is alone, abandoned on earth in the midst of his infinite responsibilities, without help, with no other aim than the one he sets himself, with no other destiny than the one he forges for himself on this earth." In a nutshell, this is what existentialism means. The key terms are alone, abandoned, and one not mentioned — absurd. By saying all human beings are alone on earth and abandoned, Sartre denied the helping hand of God. If there is a God, He remains aloof, and man must fend for himself. Existential absurdity relates to the meaninglessness of life: we are born, we live for a short time, then we die — all seemingly without purpose. A prolific writer, Sartre made existential thought his constant theme and influenced other writers and thinkers worldwide. Why this philosophy of despair seized the public's imagination owes much to the genius of Sartre and in no small way to perfect timing.

Already a literary lion in his native France and the leading exponent of existentialism in Europe, Sartre became well-known in this country during the tumultuous 1960s. His writings and those of another French existentialist, Albert Camus, were so unique and revolutionary that their appeal was hard to resist. American college students read every word of their novels, plays, and essays and couldn't get enough of the new — albeit dark — philosophy. Sartre and Camus seemed to know more about life than any other writers, living or dead. Their fictional heroes faced palpable dilemmas, and they grappled with the big questions of life: Why are we here on earth? Why is there so much suffering in the world? Why do men continue to kill one another senselessly? Both Tolstoy and Dostoyevsky had written better existential fiction, but not as lucidly as

Sartre and Camus. The two Frenchmen were superb stylists, and without their work, existentialism probably would have remained a minor European philosophy. For disgruntled spirits of the 1960s, existentialism mirrored their anger toward American society, a society they thought absurd and meaningless. The charismatic Kennedys and Martin Luther King, Jr. were assassinated; the Vietnam conflict raged on, taking American lives for no apparent reason; the United States and the Soviet Union continued to stockpile obscene numbers of nuclear warheads to deploy at any moment; and political leadership, indifferent to youth, just added to the absurdity of the decade.

Several distinctions made existentialism an intriguing intellectual fad. First, everyone had a different definition of it. Many ideas could be read into the philosophy, and people weren't really sure what it meant or, if they did understand it, how they could put it to use in their daily lives. Wasn't existentialism redressed German "angst"—a deep-set feeling of anxiety? But everyone already knew the twentieth century brimmed over with anxiety. So why construct a philosophy to describe the obvious? Because, said Sartre, "The majority of people have always been afraid to think." He wanted people to open their eyes and take a hard look at what they saw. If they were the least bit observant, they would notice that the world was clearly absurd. Right action, beauty, and altruism were chimeras, not reality. In essence, Sartre's message was "Don't just be there—do something! Exist!" Naturally, this battle cry appealed mightily to rebellious American college students. It infected them with hope for the future, even though they did not know how to begin to "Exist!" Sartre's existentialism was surely a conundrum: first, he told young people the world is a monstrous place, then he instructed them to get out there and fight; and in the end, he restated, life is absurd. So why make the effort to fight? Sartre's paradox perplexed his followers: the philosophy of despair was also a philosophy of hope. If nothing else, a human being who tried to exist (i.e., to do something in life that mattered) could for a time dispel some of life's absurdity. So college students joined the Peace Corps and VISTA (Volunteers in Service to America), got politically active, sought graduate degrees, and read more Sartre and Camus for enlightenment.

Nausea (1938; English translation, 1949) is the Sartre novel that best explains existentialism. Its plot is meager but its theme — everyman's eventual realization that he is alone in the world — is haunting. The hero, Antoine Roquentin, discovers this immutable fact of life when his handful of so-called friends act indifferently toward him. Either they have changed beyond his recognition or memory of them, or they could care less about his leaving their presence for good. A nagging nausea constricts Roquentin as he comes to understand that his friends' apathy is no less that of life's in general. He despises the constant feeling of alienation, yet he must deal with it or go mad. Given no other choice, Roquentin decides to go to Paris and write an important book — that will be his "raison d'etre." *The Stranger* (1942; English translation, 1946) is the Camus novel that, along with *Nausea*, defined existentialism for American audiences. Like *Nausea*, it is practically plotless. The hero, Meursault, awaits execution for murdering an Arab in self-defense. At first he meditates on how null and void life is; he has been a passionless man walking on a passionless earth. The prosecutor in his case uses his inability to cry at his mother's funeral to point out his remorselessness. It wasn't that he didn't love his mother; he was just unmoved by the absurdity of death. He, Meursault will die in a short time, and there won't be anyone around to shed tears on his behalf. This stark realization triggers a strong desire in him to want to live. But, alas, he must die: that is society's irrevocable sentence. So Meursault shrewdly pleads for a large crowd to watch his execution and scream insults at him. He will win in the end because they, the unfree crowd, will hoot at a free man who has lived without illusions.

Nausea and *The Stranger* still provoke thought and will always be literary classics. As mentioned earlier, the timing of the unveiling of existentialism in America was exquisite. So many absurd things happened in the 1960s that existentialism offered an explanation. In Europe, where two world wars had decimated the population, devastated the land, and produced the hellion Adolph Hitler, taking existentialism to heart seemed more natural. But in America, victorious in both world wars and unscarred by fighting on native soil, embracing the dark philosophy did not quite make sense. Even during the 1960s, Americans knew all bad things would one day change for the better. That has been our national experience and, if you will, our birthright. Perhaps intellectuals still endure existential pangs, but for today's college students, who are not engaged in the 1960s dialogue, Sartre and Camus are mumbling relics of the past.

Postscript: Sartre, who denied the existence of God and saw no need for one, returned to dust being called the most religious of men; for existentialism had given man back his soul and made him responsible for his own actions on earth. Sartre with his wry sense of humor would have liked the investiture.

BIBLIOGRAPHY

Barrett, William C. "What Is Existentialism?" *Saturday Evening Post* 232 (November 21, 1959): 44 + .

Capouya, Emile. "Free Self in a Captive Society." *Saturday Review* 48 (June 12, 1965): 40-41.

"Existentialism." *Life* 57 (November 6, 1964): 86-96.

Gray, J. Glenn. "Salvation on Campus: Why Existentialism Is Capturing the Students." *Harper's Magazine* 230 (May 1965): 53-59.

Krutch, Joseph W. "What I Learned About Existentialism." *Saturday Review* 45 (April 21, 1962): 10-12.

"The Prophet of Nevertheless." *Time* 84 (October 30, 1964): 44.

Feeling Therapy

In 1975, three young psychologists published a book, *Going Sane: An Introduction to Feeling Therapy*. Based at the University of California at Irvine, Joseph Hart served as the Clinical Director of the Center for Feeling Therapy; Richard Corriere, Research Director of the Center Foundation; and Jerry Binder, Director of Professional Training at the Center. Properly credentialed, the three enthusiastically promoted feeling therapy. Boldly they proclaimed they were both psychotherapist and patient, in a radical departure from accepted practice. They formed the first psychotherapeutic community in which therapist and patient lived together for extended periods of time. And they practiced a therapy that purportedly allowed patients to express their feelings without subterfuge or half-truth. In their words:

> To live truthfully is to live true to feelings. It took us several years to discover this truism, for it is not always easy to discover and understand the obvious. We know now that only "complete feelings" are therapeutic and that only the complete living through of feelings is transformative.

Explaining their new psychotherapy was not easy. Often they got enmeshed in a web of words that were vague and abstruse:

> When we talk about feeling we mean "integral feelings," consisting of sensations, meanings, and expressions which are completely matched. When expressions equal inner sensations and meanings, then there is full feeling. To attain a balanced feeling state is the aim of Feeling Therapy. It is the most difficult undertaking any individual can begin.

Or they bludgeoned already fragile egos with harsh terminology:

> Without being in an integral state, a person is insane. There
> are two states of being: balanced or unbalanced. There is no
> in-between. There is balanced feeling or disordered feeling.
> Because many people have such good answers about them-
> selves and their world, their insanity does not seem too insane.
> . . . What we do say to anyone who finds his answers unsatis-
> factory is that he must face his own insanity. Once answers
> begin to be given up, then personal insanity becomes visible.

A patient gained admittance to the Center for Feeling Therapy
only after filling out numerous questionnaires, taking a battery of
personality tests, and committing to at least a full year of intensive
therapy. In addition, the new patient had to show requisite strength
by beginning a program of self-discipline. A fat woman was told to
lose 30 pounds before she could start therapy. Likewise, a sex addict was instructed to abstain from any kind of sexual activity for
two months, and a drug addict had to stay clean for six months prior
to admittance. The first month of feeling therapy required daily
attendance and called for a regimen of individual sessions, feeling
groups, reality groups, and therapy activities. Then, for the next 11
months, the meetings were weekly, following much the same regimen. After a year, some patients were ready for co-therapy, which
meant they no longer needed the regimen and were on their own to
help other people. They acted as disciples of feeling therapy to
spread the word, but not without complication:

> What is frightening in doing co-therapy is that the patient be-
> gins to see other people just as they are. When a patient sees
> others clearly, he is forced to see himself more clearly. To
> move toward the core of the therapeutic community a patient
> must continue to sustain deeper levels of feeling.

What the patient learned in 12 months was how to break down
mental and emotional defenses. During formative years, people
carefully construct these defenses to protect themselves from external hurt. By doing so, they also lose the ability to feel wholly and

honestly. The objective, then, of feeling therapy was to recapture pre-defense-making innocence.

The therapy sessions achieved a high level of emotionalism, shaking a person to his or her foundation, drawing tears, and fomenting anger. The therapist encouraged the patient to delve deeper into locked psychic regions until all the doors had opened. Each barrier or defense was named such and unhinged. Behind each door stood a parent or parental figure, a searing childhood event, an uncontrollable need, or some other dark embodiment. Unleashing these demons over the course of a year affected everyone:

> There have been times when the therapists have wanted to quit, to run away and make a safe place — a place where insanity could hibernate, a place which would be neither too bad nor too good, just good enough to get by. But in moving through insanity to contact, we were able to find for ourselves a life that is constantly changing and expanding, a life in which we participate completely.

The Center for Feeling Therapy closed in 1980. Up until then, around 350 therapists and patients had formed a "core community," often sharing homes. Other ex-patients were on the outside, presumably living and feeling more completely. All those connected with feeling therapy believed themselves to be potential leaders in the war against insanity. So why did the Center fail? One investigator of the therapy likened it to brainwashing. The patients spent so much time in the core community that they became insulated. After several months of immersion, they "chose" to believe the therapy worked. Scientific studies conducted by the Center demonstrated that physiological change occurred in sleep patterns, body temperature, pulse, and blood pressure. But these indicators of change were the natural outcome of the patient recalling and acting out highly charged emotional scenes and did not necessarily prove the efficacy of the therapy. By contradicting basic principles of psychotherapy — loss of strict doctor-patient relationship, forming a dependent community, and instilling in patients the notion they were co-therapists — the naive founders thought they were on the road to success. In the end, they had forced their patients to expose the roots of conflict and forego defenses. But what then? As a matter of record, some ex-patients reported that they were harmed by feeling therapy. Uncured, they were left holding a bagful of raw memories with nowhere to put it, and their supposed "insanity" had only gotten worse. The most obvious problem with feeling therapy is trying to function in society without defenses. A person cannot blurt out true feelings about everything. It would be too chaotic. A slight twinge of hate, instead of being held calmly inside, might trigger a tongue-lashing. Love for a stranger, instead of being handled delicately, might cause instant repulsion.

BIBLIOGRAPHY

Hart, Joseph, et al. *Going Sane: An Introduction to Feeling Therapy*. New York: Jason Aronson, 1975.

Hochman, John. "Iatrogenic Symptoms Associated with a Therapy Cult: Examination of an Extinct 'New Psychotherapy' with Respect to Psychiatric Deterioration and 'Brainwashing.'" *Psychiatry* 47 (November 1984): 366-377.

Karle, Werner, et al. "Maintenance of Psychophysiological Changes in Feeling Therapy." *Psychological Reports* 39 (December 1976): 1143-1147.

_____, et al. "Preliminary Study of Psychological Changes in Feeling Therapy." *Psychological Reports* 43 (December 1978): 1327-1334.

Woldenberg, Lee, et al. "Psychophysical Changes in Feeling Therapy." *Psychological Reports* 39 (December 1976): 1059-1062.

Forteans

Charles Fort (1874-1932) wrote four of the most eccentric books ever published in any language: *The Book of the Damned* (1919), *New Lands* (1923), *Lo!* (1931), and *Wild Talents* (1932). Together the books are actually one long diatribe railing against what passed for conventional scientific wisdom. With one broad sweep of his hand, Fort dismissed science as "the accumulated lunacy of fifty centuries." To prove his point, he spent every working day for 20 years buried in research at the New York Public Library and the British Museum. What he searched so diligently for was any scrap of unexplained phenomenon that baffled science. Fort combed through scientific journals, popular scientific magazines, and newspapers to collect enigmatic tidbits such as this one in *New Lands*, Chapter Five:

> Birmingham *Daily Post*, May 31, 1867:
> Mr. Bird, the astronomer, writes that, about 11 a.m., May 30, he saw unknown forms in the sky. In his telescope, which was focused upon them and upon the planet Venus, they appeared to be twice the size of Venus. . . . My animation is the notion that it is better to think in tentative hysteria of pairs of vast things, travelling like a North and South America through the sky, perhaps one biting the other with its Gulf of Mexico, than to go on thinking that all things that so move in the sky are seeds, whereas all things that swim in the sea are not sardines.

This is a typical Fortean datum and, alas, also a typical Fortean commentary. What Fort uncovered in his reading might have been of more value if he had possessed a balanced mind. But his shrill denunciation of the scientific establishment and his disjointed way of presenting material destroyed what he wanted to accomplish.

The opening words of *The Book of the Damned* set the tone for every page thereafter:

A Procession of the damned. By the damned, I mean the excluded. We shall have a procession of data that Science has
excluded. Battalions of the accursed, captained by pallid data
that I have exhumed, will march. You'll read them—or they'll
march. Some of them livid and some of them fiery and some
of them rotten. . . . The power that has said to all these things
that they are damned, is Dogmatic Science.

And so on, maniacally, for another 12 pages before Fort opens his
Pandora's box of profound secrets.

Inside almost 1,100 pages of crowded text he chronicles such
"amazing" things as: space alien artifacts fallen from the sky to
land on earth; weird showers of blood, ice, stones, insects, mud,
and all-in-one shower—periwinkles and crabs; unknown airships
that swept the ground with searchlights; poltergeists, levitation, and
teleportation; inexplicable piles of slaughtered animals; uncon-
nected human murders; and water divining, witchcraft, and vam-
pires. Fort excited every occult nerve ending in the general reader.
Mirroring himself, he also addressed the cranks among his readers
by championing the flat earth theory and discrediting Copernicus:

In the system that was conceived by Copernicus I find nothing
that can be said to resemble foundation, nothing but the appeal
of greater simplicity. An earth that rotates and revolves is simpler to conceive of than is a stationary earth with a rigid composition of stars, swinging around it, stars kept apart by some
unknown substance, or inter-repulsion.

Fort's cosmology included the notion that the planets in our solar
system are much nearer than astronomers let on. Undetected planets
exist among the familiar ones, and beings from both visit earth regularly. The strange beings avoid scientists, preferring to communicate with simple folk who won't harm them. When Fort wrote this,
he had forgotten his own strong case for space alien mayhem.
Butchered beasts and jugulated earthlings might just be the work of
vicious Venusians.

Chapter 15 in *The Book of the Damned* further showcases Fort's
nonsensical ranting:

> If it is our acceptance that, out of the Negative Absolute, the positive Absolute is generating itself, recruiting, or maintaining itself, via a third state, or our own quasi-state, it would seem that we're trying to conceive of Universalness from Nothingness. Take that up yourself, if you're willing to run the risk of disappearing with such velocity that you'll leave an incandescent trail behind, and risk being infinitely happy forever . . .

From this quotation it's easy to see why a critic for *The New York Times* regarded Fort's books as "a quagmire of pseudo-science and queer speculation." But then another critic and well-wisher called Fort, "One of the most original and courageous thinkers in the world today." One year before Fort's death, American novelist Tiffany Thayer (1902-1959) founded the Fortean Society. Thayer agreed with Fort that orthodox science needed whittling down to the size of a toothpick and was more than happy to continue the work of collecting Fortean data, although being more of a bon vivant, Thayer did not blind himself in libraries like the master. Popular writers such as Booth Tarkington, Theodore Dreiser, Ben Hecht, and Alexander Wollcott joined the Fortean Society. Even for the iconoclastic 1930s, their approval of Fort is somewhat mystifying. A poor writer with meager intellectual skills, Fort could only claim to have amassed a large amount of interesting data. He was no belletrist. Science fiction writers ransacked his pages for plot ideas and their literary output sent readers scurrying back to Fort like an etymologist to the *Oxford English Dictionary*.

Fort's quartet sold well during his lifetime. His books became faddish reading for adolescents, agnostics, and skeptical inquirers. When the UFO craze blazed across the heavens in the 1950s, Fort rose again as the prophet of space invaders. The Fortean Society still exists today, having changed its name to the International Fortean Society with 1,500 members and a tiny budget of $25,000. The IFS studies all natural phenomena of a controversial nature that still marches in a procession of the damned. Fort spent his last year completing *Wild Talents* while suffering from enlargement of the heart. In keeping with his disdain for scientists, Fort distrusted doctors and would not see one for any reason, not even to ease his crippling pain. A figure of fad, in the *Encyclopedia of the Unexplained*, edited by Richard Cavendish (McGraw-Hill, 1974), Fort rates only one sentence placed at the end of an article on "Physical Powers." Fort, the father of the unexplained who toiled two decades so he could thumb his nose at science, should have had his portrait as the frontispiece.

BIBLIOGRAPHY

Fort, Charles. *The Complete Books of Charles Fort*. New York: Dover Publications, 1974.
Knight, Damon. *Charles Fort: Prophet of the Unexplained*. Garden City, NY: Doubleday, 1970.
Shepard, Leslie. *Encyclopedia of Occultism & Parapsychology*. 2 vols. Detroit, MI: Gale Research Co., 1978.

The Four Hundred

Not very long ago some one invented the assertion that there were only "Four Hundred" people in New York City who were really worth noticing. But a wiser man has arisen—the census taker—and his larger estimate of human interest has been preferred in marking out the field of these little stories of the "Four Million."

This spirited rejoinder prefaces O. Henry's masterpiece of American literature, *The Four Million*, published in 1903. Like most New Yorkers for the past 20 years, he had heard enough about the Astors, the Vanderbilts, Ward McAllister, and the rest of the hoity-toity Four Hundred. Kowtowing to America's self-proclaimed royalty sickened O. Henry. He settled the score for readers by writing his peak of perfection short stories.

The history of the Four Hundred begins with what *The New York Times* called "Festivity at Eastertide," but acknowledged the day after as "The Great Fancy Dress Ball." For the post-Lent party on March 26, 1883, Mrs. William K. Vanderbilt invited 1,000 friends—"everybody who amounts to anything." She requested that each guest come dressed in the costume of a fictional or historical personage, and she directed carriage drivers to bring the revelers to the Vanderbilt mansion at Fifth Avenue and Fifty-Third Street, a reproduction of a renaissance French chateau.

The guests, on arriving, found themselves in a grand hall about 65 feet long, 16 feet in height, and 20 feet in width. Under their feet was a floor of polished and luminous marble, and above them a ceiling richly paneled in oak, while over a high wainscoting of richly-carved Caen stone hung antique Italian tapestries. Over this hall, to the right, rose a grand stairway of the finest Caen stone, carved with superb delicacy and vigor, to the height of fifty feet.

Mrs. William K. Vanderbilt ordered so many flowers for the ball that some New York churches had to go without their usual sprays of Easter and calla lilies. In addition:

> A canopy of roses supporting a curtain of smilax [a vine with glossy foliage] will conceal the orchestra which is to be composed of 25 pieces, and throughout the house, the whole of which is to be thrown open, there will be disposed [arranged] palms, ferns, orchids, azaleas, and other ornamental plants; and rose, hyacinths, tulips, and other cut flowers in cones, vases, plateaus, and various designs.

The day after "The Great Fancy Dress Ball," those not invited got to read about the swell time had by all. The hostess, Mrs. W. K. Vanderbilt, impersonated a Venetian princess:

> The underskirt of her dress was white and yellow brocade, shading from the deepest orange to the lightest canary, while the figures of flowers and leaves were outlined in gold and white and iridescent beads; her white satin train was embroidered magnificently in gold, and lined with Roman red. The waist was of blue satin covered with gold embroidery, and on her head was a Venetian cap covered with magnificent jewels, among them a peacock in many-colored gems.

Mr. W. K. Vanderbilt looked very impressive himself as the famous French general and statesman, the Duke de Guise. Lady Mandeville wore a costume copied from a painting by Vandyke of the Princess Marie-Claire Decroy. Mr. Cornelius Vanderbilt arrived as Louis XVI, his wife, more creatively, as the Electric Light in white satin trimmed with diamonds. One group entered the grand hall dressed as nursery rhyme figures; there was Mother Goose, Jack and Jill, Bopeep, Miss Muffet, Mary Mary Quite Contrary, the Pieman, and more. The doorman announced each of the 1,000 guests by name and costume before photographers took individual portraits to commemorate the night. Just getting everyone inside the Vanderbilt mansion was a feat in itself; the clock struck midnight and beyond before everyone had arrived. The ball breezed on past dawn as Bluebeard danced with Joan of Arc, the Fairy Queen with a picador, and Marie Stuart with a Mexican ranchman.

"The Great Fancy Dress Ball" was an indubitable success. But there was one somber face among the nouveau riche of the Gilded Age who thought 1,000 guests lacked proper discrimination. Ward McAllister, born in Savannah, Georgia, a lawyer by profession, decided to prune the unweildly list. He had already won the attention of New York high society by affirming its purpose. In his book, *Society As I Have Found It* (1890), McAllister doted on his wealthy friends:

> The mistake made by the world at large is that fashionable people are selfish, frivolous, and indifferent to the welfare of their fellow-creatures; all of which is a popular error, arising simply from a want of knowledge of the true state of things. The elegancies of fashionable life nourish and benefit art and artists; they cause the expenditure of money and its distribution; and they really prevent our people and country from settling down into a humdrum rut and becoming merely a money-making and money-saving people, with nothing to brighten up and enliven life. . . . Fashionable people cultivate and refine themselves, for fashion demands this of them. Progress is fashion's watchword; it never stands still; it always advances, it values and appreciates beauty in woman and talent and genius in man. I know the general belief is that all fashionable people are hollow and heartless. My experience is quite the contrary. I have found as warm, sympathetic, loving hearts in the garb of fashion as out of it.

But of the "warm, sympathetic, loving hearts" it seemed only 400 were truly that way. McAllister made history in 1892 when he and Mrs. William Astor deliberated over the guest list for an upcoming ball. The archrival of Mrs. William K. Vanderbilt for the title of society doyenne, Mrs. William Astor would attract more notoriety by snubbing acquaintances. The 400 guests she and McAllister decided on were the fanciest of the fancy. Their lineage had to be flawless, their fortunes old money. Parvenus were not invited. Besides being a genius at natural selection, McAllister knew everything about how to entertain: the importance of soup for awakening the palate, which wine to serve with which course, the order of sauces so as not to cloy taste, and so on, through three hours of fine dining.

Until both died, the team of Astor and McAllister ruled New York high society with an iron fist enclosed in a vainglorious mauve glove. In 1904, another fop by the meretricious name of Charles Wilbur De Lyons Nichols tried to better McAllister. Nichols wrote *The Ultra-Fashionable Peerage of America*, listing only 150 people who qualified. He proclaimed, "Newport, not the White House, is the supreme court of social appeals in the United States; Mrs. Astor, and not the wife of the President of the United States, is the first lady of the land, in the realm of fashion." But 150 qualifiers reduced the circle of ultrafashionable by too many. With so few, how could one throw a good ball? And what if half of them were away in London or Paris? "Grand Dieu!"

BIBLIOGRAPHY

Morris, Lloyd. *Incredible New York*. New York: Arno Press, 1975. (reprint of 1951 ed.)

The New York Times. March 25, 1883, 14:6 & March 27, 1883, 1:7.

Nichols, Charles Wilbur De Lyons. *The Ultra-Fashionable Peerage of America*. New York: Arno Press, 1975. (reprint of 1904 ed.)

Smith, Henry Nash, ed. *Popular Culture and Industrialism, 1865-1890*. New York: New York University Press, 1967.

When Sigmund Freud unleashed his own psycho-sexual demons, people the world over thought him a genius. Resolution of the Oedipus complex became so real that Freudian interpretation of historical and literary figures took precedence over more verifiable interpretations.

Freudian Interpretation of Historical and Literary Figures

Often in his writing, Sigmund Freud warned against making faulty assumptions in lieu of having all the facts. For instance, it is wrong to interpret a dream without knowing the client's personal history. Misinterpretation results from not reviewing every shred of remembrance. Much of Freud's defense in the face of detractors was that they hadn't spent a lifetime talking with clients about their innermost secrets as he had. Firsthand knowledge of a client's psychic and behavioral makeup was essential before rendering diagnosis or constructing theory. Evident from his papers, Freud was a meticulous scientist who did not go out on a limb unless he knew his observations were correct. But twice he threw caution to the wind and engaged in speculative thinking: once when he psychoanalyzed the great Renaissance figure Leonardo Da Vinci, and for a second time when he delved into the psyche of President Woodrow Wilson.

Freud's study of Da Vinci appeared in 1910, the same year as his monumental *Five Lectures on Psycho-Analysis*. Freud was not the first to psychoanalyze a historical figure. At least three other studies were read during meetings of the Vienna Psycho-Analytical Society just prior to 1910. Da Vinci wrote in his notebook: "I recall as one of my very earliest memories that while I was in my cradle a vulture came down to me, and opened my mouth with its tail, and struck me many times with its tail against my lips." This is Da Vinci's only written recollection of his childhood. Freud interpreted the memory as a homosexual fantasy. In all likelihood, Da Vinci was a homosexual, although his biographers base their assumption on his having no recorded love affairs with women. Instead, Renaissance Italy offered him young male models, male art students, and male proteges, so the opportunity was there. Freud explains:

The translation is then seen to point to an erotic content. A tail, "coda," is one of the most familiar symbols and substitutive expressions for the male organ, in Italian no less than in other languages; the situation in the phantasy, of a vulture opening the child's mouth and beating about inside it vigorously with its tail, corresponds to the idea of an act of fellatio. . . . It is strange that this phantasy is so completely passive in character; moreover it resembles certain dreams and phantasies found in women and passive homosexuals.

Freud explicates the memory further. He reminds the reader that the most pleasurable first memory of infancy is sucking the mother's breast. Later, when the child sees a cow's udders that are for sucking and that dangle from the cow's belly like so many penises, the child forms a "repellent sexual phantasy," a la Da Vinci. Furthermore, ancient Egyptian hieroglyphs depict a Mother Goddess whose head is that of a vulture and who can reproduce without male sperm. Freud suggests that Da Vinci not only knew Egyptian mythology, but because he was born illegitimate, he thought of his mother as a self-sufficient vulture-woman and of himself as a vulture-child. Da Vinci painted the Blessed Virgin and Child to express his love for his vulture mother and to identify himself with Christ.

Certainly Freud possessed a vivid imagination and the requisite erudition to corroborate what he imagined. Yet, his interpretation of Da Vinci's memory is contradictory and, in the final analysis, not worth much. A bird of prey commits an act of aggression and Freud transforms the unpleasant memory into a messianic desire tinged with homosexual longings and breast-penis worship. In reality, the child Da Vinci may have been frightened by what seemed a large threatening bird. Every child experiences real fear when confronted by a fierce creature, whether it's a tiger at the zoo, a neighbor's big dog, or a squawking parrot in a cage (vulture). Painting the Blessed Virgin and Child was how an artist made a living during the Renaissance. And what if Da Vinci was a homosexual? In his milieu, homosexuality was more accepted than it is now. Whether Freud's interpretation of Da Vinci's memory is correct or not is beside the point. What is on point here is that Freud constructed a rather elaborate psychological profile of a man he never knew from a few sentences casually scrawled in a notebook. Freud berated lesser men for doing the same thing.

In 1966, the Boston firm of Houghton Mifflin published *Thomas Woodrow Wilson: A Psychological Study* by Sigmund Freud and William C. Bullitt. The manuscript was completed years before in 1932 (Freud died in 1939), but it was deemed appropriate not to publish the study until after Mrs. Wilson's death (1961). Bullitt had served on the American Peace Commission in Paris in 1919. He and Wilson had disagreed so bitterly about the terms of the Versailles Treaty that Bullitt resigned from the Commission. It was Bullitt who later interested Freud in writing a book that would explore Wilson's unconscious mind. What they came up with — the statesman and the psychoanalyst — is part vendetta and part specious hindsight. Freud, with Bullitt's approval, suggests that as a boy Tommy Wilson thought his minister father was God Almighty. Joseph Ruggles Wilson was the "incomparable father":

> Until he [Woodrow] was ten years old, he was the only beloved son of that God. His identification of himself with the Saviour of mankind, which became so important and obvious a feature of his character in the later years of his life, seems to have commenced as an inevitable conclusion in his unconscious during his first years: if his father was God, he himself was God's Only Beloved Son, Jesus Christ.

As an adult, Woodrow Wilson acted out his love-hate relationship with his father. He dealt with close friends and political associates as if each one were his father, at once admiring and rejecting them. Wilson's wanting to save the world for democracy, his Fourteen Points, and his intransigence regarding the Versailles Treaty were all manifestations of his unconscious identification with Christ. Bullitt added excerpts from speeches in which Wilson repeatedly makes references to sacrifice and the dignity of dying for a just cause. Anyone who betrayed him, like Bullitt, Wilson considered a Judas, and there were many Judases in his mind. From these meager suppositions, the whole of a prominent man's life stands in judgment. The psychoanalytic high court could not be swayed. For the second time, Freud broke his own rule not to psychoanalyze from an ivory tower.

Freudian interpretation of historical figures was short-lived. A few biographers tried it but left readers cold. Where Freudian interpretation did catch on was in literary criticism. Shakespeare's characters were especially amenable to psychoanalytic treatment. Freud wrote about Hamlet's Oedipus complex, as have other literary critics knowledgeable about or barely conversant with psychoanalysis. Before Freud, the world thought Hamlet wanted to avenge his father's murder and marry Ophelia; after Freud, it was good riddance to his father, and Hamlet really wanted to sleep with his mother. Ambivalent Oedipal feelings toward just about everyone at court leave Hamlet impotent at times. He acts manic in an effort to resolve his sexual malaise. Hamlet fits so neatly into the Freudian scheme of things that the Freudians say it's a mistake to view the play any other way. Freud's biographer, Ernest Jones, himself a psychoanalyst, at the end of his book, *Hamlet and Oedipus*, tells directors how to stage the play for full Freudian effect. Jones insists on certain ages for the characters and that an air of seething sensuality pervade Elsinore. Gertrude should act the wanton, as should Ophelia, although she is fated to die. In reality Shakespeare had three long hours to fill with dramatic invention. Therefore the cerebral Hamlet wanders Elsinore talking to himself to summon courage to kill his uncle. Since Hamlet was not a common thug, but a scholar, his father's command to commit murder was hard to carry out. It's ludicrous to think that Shakespeare had in mind a family love triangle. But then the Freudians say Shakespeare only wrote the play, and the literal interpretation of it is not the final word. Supposedly, great creative minds like Shakespeare can unknowingly speak sublime truth (Hamlet hot to diddle Gertrude) and their work include many levels of meaning (the tragedy heightened by Oedipal intrigue).

Freudian interpretation of literary figures has waned somewhat, even though the scholarly journal *Literature and Psychology* keeps this school of criticism alive. There is the ever-present impulse for these critics to discover an Oedipus complex in every story about a family, a Messiah complex in every story about personal sacrifice, and homosexuality in every story that refers to anything phallic-like. It disgraces Freud to have his theories treated with such ignorance. Few of these critics have studied psychoanalysis in depth, or early childhood development, or the etiology of neuroses. Yet they presume to know enough to engage in Freudian interpretation of literary figures. This fad will die hard because, as with *Hamlet*, it is very simple to pronounce a work of literature Oedipal or brimming over with Freudian implications. Human beings and literary characters are too complex for such a neat solution.

BIBLIOGRAPHY

Freud, Sigmund, and William C. Bullitt. *Thomas Woodrow Wilson: A Psychological Study*. Boston: Houghton Mifflin, 1966.

Hoffman, Frederick J. *Freudianism and the Literary Mind*. 2nd ed. Baton Rouge, LA: Louisiana State University Press, 1957.

Jones, Ernest. *Hamlet and Oedipus*. New York: W. W. Norton, 1976.

Strachey, James, ed. *The Standard Edition of the Complete Psychological Works of Sigmund Freud*. Volume XI. London: The Hogarth Press, 1957.

G Spot

In a 1950 article that appeared in the *International Journal of Sexology*, German obstetrician and gynecologist Ernst Grafenberg described an ultrasensitive area in the anterior wall of the vagina:

> [This erotic zone in females] seems to be surrounded by erectile tissue like the corpora cavernosa [of the penis]. . . . In the course of sexual stimulation, the female urethra begins to enlarge and can be easily felt. It swells out greatly at the end of orgasm. The most stimulating part is located at the posterior urethra, where it arises from the neck of the bladder.

At the time, Grafenberg's revelation that a woman can "get erect" like a man interested only a few sex therapists. The public hardly heard anything about it. In those pre-sexual revolution days, even if word had gotten out about the G spot, the news would have left people shrugging their shoulders. But three decades and many societal changes later, the G spot not only grabbed attention, it also sent thousands of women into their bedrooms to find their own delicious nub for orgasmic wavemaking.

Those pleasure seekers owed a debt of gratitude to Ladas, Whipple, and Perry who published *The G Spot and Other Recent Discoveries About Human Sexuality* (1982). One of the discoveries in their best-selling book was even more provocative than the G spot, if that can be imagined. According to Ladas et al., Aristotle was the first to write about female "gushing" of a fluid similar to semen. Yes, not only do women get erect, but they also ejaculate. Oh, brave new world, sex differences were shrinking away at a rapid pace. The reason why no one had written further about female ejaculation was due to modesty and also to the fact that most anatomists considered the notion apocryphal. So for over 2,000 years, medical researchers learned everything they could about the heart and lungs, while ignoring the body's capacity for erotic fulfillment. It just wasn't the polite thing to do.

Ladas et al., filled their book with personal testimony from women who either had known about the G spot and female ejaculation for years or had recently experienced the sensation. Other women, once shown by researchers where to locate the G spot, had no trouble rubbing it to an ecstatic peak. Here are some of their comments:

> I must tell you that you are dead right about the Grafenberg spot. I hadn't known what it was called, but it is definitely there.

> For me it [the clitoris] is a very poor place. My best orgasms come when the man enters me from behind. Then I can guide him to the right place and help him to touch the exact spot inside me.

> With Dan, we can lie facing each other and his penis reaches that spot in my vagina which feels so wonderful and which always brings me to orgasm. I think it's because of the way his penis lies when it is erect, flat against my tummy. It was never that way with my other partners.

The personal testimony, as convincing as it was, appeared to prove the existence of the G spot. So why had women been kept in the dark so long concerning their erotic potential?

The Grafenberg-gushing spot tantalized men and women alike to such a degree that other researchers delved into the unsolved matter. Most of their articles beseeched professionals to take the "neglected vagina" seriously. Moreover, the Freudian view of female sexual response centered in vaginal orgasm rather than in clitoral or some other erogenous zone was incorrect. Freud had obscured the true workings of a woman's body by insisting that she gets her deepest satisfaction from male intercourse. Another report post-Ladas et al., found other orgasm-inducing spots in the vaginal walls, not just the one discovered by Grafenberg. And in perhaps the most revealing study, the female ejaculate of those women who could get erect and gush was determined to be mostly urine. Which brings us full circle to Grafenberg's location of the spot near the neck of the bladder. It seems that G-spot sensitive women had been titillating their bladders to a swelling point, then pleasurably exuding urine mixed with vaginal secretions. Ladas et al., included a whole chapter in their book on the importance of healthy pelvic muscles. Those meshing-pinching muscles can also spurt out urine, which would normally cause embarrassment if the ejaculate were not thought to be semen-like. The G-spot fad promised more than it could deliver and, if it had been fact, would clearly have given women sexual supremacy over men — what with multiple orgasms already in their repertoire.

BIBLIOGRAPHY

Altschuler, Sandra. "The Hypothesis of Female Ejaculation: Too Little Interest, Too Little Research. *Journal of Social Work and Human Sexuality* 4 (Fall-Winter 1985-1986): 125-139.

Alzate, Heli, and Maria L. Londono. "Vaginal Erotic Sensitivity." *Journal of Sex and Marital Therapy* 10 (Spring 1984): 49-56.

Goldberg, Daniel C., et al. "The Grafenberg Spot and Female Ejaculation: A Review of Initial Hypotheses." *Journal of Sex and Marital Therapy* 9 (Spring 1983): 27-37.

Grafenberg, Ernst. "The Role of Urethra in Female Orgasm." *International Journal of Sexology* 3 (1950): 145-148.

Jayne, Cynthia. "Freud, Grafenberg, and the Neglected Vagina: Thoughts Concerning an Historical Omission in Sexology." *Journal of Sex Research* 20 (May 1984): 212-215.

Ladas, Alice K., Beverly Whipple, and John D. Perry. *The G Spot and Other Recent Discoveries About Human Sexuality*. New York: Holt, Rinehart and Winston, 1982.

Genius Sperm Bank

Retired physicist and millionaire Robert Graham founded the Repository for Germinal Choice (RGC) in 1979 in Escondido, California. One purpose in opening the nonprofit organization was to offer women "genetically superior sperm" for artificial insemination, hopefully to conceive precocious children. But Graham's main intention was to conduct an experiment in eugenics that went beyond the limits of animal breeding and would, he believed, corroborate his notion that 60 to 80 percent of intelligence is inherited. So Graham collected and froze the sperm of genius donors — men who had distinguished themselves mainly in the sciences, some of whom had won a Nobel prize. As expected, the RGC made the nightly news, and curious Americans wondered if the "Nobel Sperm Bank" could actually deliver a genius in swaddling clothes.

The first woman to give birth after an RGC implant, Joyce Kowalski, captured media attention three times: once when her 9-lb. baby, Victoria, was born; once when her ex-husband revealed to the *Chicago Tribune* that Mrs. Kowalski had abused their two children; and once when a reporter verified that the Kowalskis were federal felons out on parole. The details of the two criminal actions horrified the RGC, which immediately began screening its applicants better. The ex-husband claimed that the Kowalskis, who at one time had custody of his children, beat them with a strap. Moreover, the Kowalskis humiliated his son by sending him to school in pajamas with a sign hung around his neck proclaiming him a bed wetter, and in similar fashion pasted the word "Dummy" on his daughter's forehead. The federal offense the Kowalskis had been convicted of involved a scam using records of dead children to secure loans and credit cards. To prove their innocence in these matters and to establish themselves as capable parents, the Kowalskis told their side of the story to the *National Enquirer*. For a tidy sum of money, Jack Kowalski cheerfully announced, "We'll begin training Victoria on

computers when she's three, and we'll teach her words and numbers before she can walk.'' For the moment, all seemed right with
the world.

Afton Blake, a psychologist with a Ph.D., chose No. 28, the
sperm of a Northern European computer scientist and award-win-
ning classical pianist. In her case, artificial insemination was just
the ticket because she didn't like the idea of sleeping with a male
genius for personal gain. That would complicate things; a relationship would have to be nurtured, and there would be the possible
sharing of the child afterwards. Miss Blake was the first single-
parent client of the RGC. Once again, the sperm bank reeled from a
blow to the groin; it had wanted all its genius babies to be born to
couples. Doron (Greek for ''gift'') William Blake weighed in at 8
lbs. 11 ozs., and his mother, Afton, remarked, ''Most people see
me as something of a pioneer [but] I just felt it was time to have a
baby.'' About the RGC's meticulousness she remarked:

> They are careful to note every minor defect. It's almost too
> scientific for me. It put me off a bit to know how many diop-
> ters of myopia the donors have and if they have a history of
> hemorrhoids. But the point is the Repository's not trying to
> sell you a perfect person.

Joyce Kowalski and Afton Blake are certainly not representative
of women as a whole, yet they are representative of the types of
women who would pay approximately $500 (the 1982 price) for
genetically superior sperm. Surprisingly, the RGC has not done
hospital nursery business; as of 1985, only 17 children had been
born using the ''good stuff.'' This fact is intriguing. Everyday
women avail themselves of ''average stuff'' at regular sperm banks
or through the sadly uneugenic method of marriage. Why haven't
more women wanted to plant an oak in their loins rather than a
shrub? One would think that for progressive mothers, all roads lead
to Escondido. But that hasn't happened. Very few women are sold
on the idea of conceiving a genius child. What if he turns out to be a
Hitler? Or what if she is an intellectual giant but an emotional
wreck? Most likely, a genius child wouldn't be a loveable kid or
adult. And parents would have a difficult time communicating with

a genius child, who would probably look down on their ignorance. As one of her reasons for wanting a prodigy, Afton Blake said it was to give the world a superstar who might make all the difference in music, the arts, medicine, etc.

The time has come for follow-up studies on the 17 children born before 1985. So far, their display or lack of genius is known only to their parents and the RGC. Faddish interest in the sperm bank surely calls for periodic reports on Graham's experiment in applied eugenics. A lengthy report every five years on the children, complete with IQs, unusual abilities shown, and types of mastery demonstrated, would satisfy the public's need to know. Why the media ignores such a potentially big story is something of a mystery. A final note about the faddishness of genius sperm: Graham did not have an easy time collecting it. Most of the gifted men he contacted thought the idea of selling handpicked seeds ridiculous. Besides, the mother's gene pool, the learning environment, early disease, and any number of other factors also affect the child. Even in Escondido, producing genius remains a gamble.

BIBLIOGRAPHY

Bacon, Doris Klein. "When Unmarried Afton Blake Wanted a Baby, She Made a Withdrawal from Her Friendly Sperm Bank." *People Magazine* 18 (October 18, 1982): 63-64.

Mano, D. Keith. "The Nobel Sperm Bank." *National Review* 34 (November 12, 1982): 1429-1430.

"The Sperm-Bank Scandal." *Newsweek* 100 (July 26, 1982): 24.

Walmsley, Ann. "The 'Genius' Babies." *Macleans* 98 (September 2, 1985): 6.

Goldfish Swallowing

During a visit to Japan in 1878, Rear Admiral Daniel Amen of the United States Navy noticed that the Japanese kept a particularly attractive fish in aquarium bowls. The brassy creature showed up from across a room, and in the stark arrangement of a Japanese home or office looked all the more resplendent and cheerful. Thoroughly captivated, Amen brought some goldfish home and presented them to the United States Fish Commission. Fifty years later, in 1928, 770 U.S. commercial farms produced 21,500,000 goldfish—all descendants of Amen's original import. What had started as a nineteenth century pet fad in America had become big business with additional sales of glass bowls, underwater decor, and fish food. By 1937, Grassyforks Fisheries, Inc. in Martinsville, Indiana, laid claim to being the world's largest goldfish hatchery. Grassyforks and several other U.S. hatcheries met increasing domestic demands for goldfish and also shipped their surplus to markets in Europe, South America, and Africa. Pampered in water constantly aerated with pure oxygen pumped and filtered through charcoal, the brassy creatures arrived ready for sale in the best of health, whether in Boston or Stockholm.

Five-and-dime stores sold goldfish for 20 to 25 cents apiece. However, fancy varieties like Fantails, Telescopes, Veiltails, and Lionheads cost as much as $75 each. Earlier, for a World War I liberty bond drive, "Miss Liberty," a red, white, and blue goldfish, had fetched $5,000. Perhaps like nothing else, golden fish swimming happily in blue water brought a smile to wartime and later Depression-era Americans. Magazine articles reminded petless households that goldfish don't bark, soil the carpet, smell bad, or eat voraciously. For the home gardener, a tranquil goldfish pond could be constructed easily in the backyard in the Japanese manner. What about the Japanese manner? Weren't goldfish as American as apple pie? Yes, they were, to Harvard freshman Lothrop Withington, Jr., who was the first recorded gulper of a goldfish.

Withington performed his epicurean feat in 1939 after boasting he had done it once previously. A classmate slapped $10 on a table to see the proof. So, with a sure hand, Withington quickly netted one of his loyal pets and popped it into his mouth. Those present saw the young scholar carefully chew the squirming morsel and swallow every bit of it without regurgitating. Withington pocketed the sawbuck, and that was that until three weeks later, when an undergraduate at Franklin and Marshall, hearing about Withington's bold deed, salted and peppered three goldfish. Harvard's Irving Clark, Jr., wanting to regain the laurels for his university and not wanting to be outdone anytime in the near future, responded by downing 24 goldfish, sucking on an orange after each gulp. But sadly, Clark's glory lasted for less than a day, just long enough for University of Pennsylvania's Gilbert Hollandersky to eat 25 goldfish as an appetizer prior to consuming a steak dinner. Then University of Michigan's Julius Aisner answered with 28, followed by Boston College's Donald V. Mulcahy, who consumed 29 goldfish and 3 bottles of milk. Once the record stood at 36, held by Northeastern University's Jack Smookler, the absolutely ridiculous fad had to be stopped. State Senator George Krapf of Massachusetts introduced a bill ordering the State Conservation Department to "preserve the fish from cruel and wanton consumption." Boston's Animal Rescue League made it known that goldfish swallowing wasn't "a subject for levity" and that the League would prosecute any and all such deranged perpetrators.

Evidently, M.I.T.'s Albert E. Hayes, Jr. didn't fear the League. Three policemen and 100 cheering students watched him drink an afternoon cocktail of 42 goldfish mixed with 4 bottles of chocolate soda. While amazing the crowd, Hayes explained: "You lay the goldfish well back on the tongue, let it wiggle forward till it hits the top of the throat, then give one big gulp. Same effect as swallowing a raw oyster." Since legal threats had not worked to halt the gormandizing, the U.S. Public Health Service warned that goldfish might contain tapeworms which, lodging in the intestinal tract, would cause anemia. Of course none of the well-intentioned authorities realized that what was at stake here was no less than school honor. Chicago psychologist Robert N. McMurray called goldfish swallowing the most egregious of exhibitionist acts in which the eater delights in being repulsive. Further verification of McMurray's disdain had come to light several champions ago. In his quest to be Big Man on Campus, Harvard's Irving Clark, Jr. had offered to eat bugs, worms, or beetles for a wager. Shortly before the fad ended, the most repulsive individual was Clark University's Joe Deliberato, who consumed 89 goldfish.

BIBLIOGRAPHY

"Goldfish Derby." *Time* 33 (April 10, 1939): 33.
"Goldfish: Shipment of 40,000 Opens Export Trade for Year." *Newsweek* 9 (March 13, 1937): 25-26.

Harmonic Convergence

To save the planet Earth, more than 144,000 people "resonated in harmony" on August 16 and 17, 1987. They gathered at various "power points" around the globe: Mt. Shasta, California; Sedona, Arizona; Black Hills, South Dakota; Haleakala, Hawaii; Central Park, New York; Popocatepetl, Mexico; Machu Picchu, Peru; Great Pyramids, Egypt; Mt. Olympus, Greece; Ganges River, India; and Mt. Fuji, Japan. The participants held hands, danced, and engaged in "vibrational toning," i.e., repeating the chant "aaaahhhhh" until their minds achieved inner peace and their bodies shook with pleasure. The psychic actress Shirley MacLaine was there, as were folksinger John Denver and 1960s guru Timothy Leary. But the leader of the brave attempt to stave off certain destruction was Jose Arguelles, an artist/writer. Almost overnight, he convinced a receptive America that the upcoming dog days in August were "a turning point of historic magnitude exceeding anything we've ever known." The whole scenario of harmonic convergence and how it should be handled came to him one day as he drove through Beverly Hills.

Arguelles wrote in detail about the need to stage a happening to rescue Earth in his book, *The Mayan Factor*. He stated the facts clearly, so no one could say he had not warned them. However, understanding his explanation of harmonic convergence was not as easy as chanting "aaaahhhhh." First, Arguelles drew attention to the Aztec calendar; its 13 cycles of Heaven and 9 cycles of Hell were to end on August 16, 1987. That's one piece of the puzzle. Next, Hopi Indian legend said that 144,000 Sun-Dance-enlightened teachers would perform on a future date to awaken the rest of humanity. That date, as well as Arguelles could determine was August 16, 1987, when some of the mysteries of life would be revealed. Third, for the first time in 23,412 years, 9 of the planets in Earth's solar system would align to form a grand trine. This rarity would cause "an unprecedented amount of energy to converge in one place and harmonize with itself, creating an energy greater than any experienced on earth to date." But Arguelles had more to tell. The Mayan calendar's great cycle, running from 3113 B.C. to 2012 A.D., was about to elapse and pass into a different phase. Arguelles called it the "galactic synchronization phase." August 16 and 17 preceded the changeover by exactly 25 years. For the Earth's inhabitants to make the changeover a propitious and not a disastrous one, they had to show good faith in the cosmic powers that be. People everywhere had to encourage harmonic convergence by praying or humming for it to occur. Arguelles also promised that a signal from the heavens would tell earthlings how to attain full synchronization with the rest of the galaxy on or before 2012. He maintained that the ancient Mayans were actually extraterrestrials who left clues behind for us to decipher. But in our ignorance, we have not been able to read a word of what they wanted us to know. Otherwise, we would have already prepared for the imminent day of changeover. Arguelles told the faithful, "There will be anything from mass UFO sightings to actually receiving communications."

So, on August 16 and 17, 1987, over 144,000 dedicated saviors of the earth, exceeding the legend-prescribed number of Sun-Dance-enlightened teachers, met at the 11 power points around the world. And for two glorious days, they hummed and hummed until the earth vibrated with joy. And all the waters were still, and all the beasts of the land were tame, and all people loved one another. Their altruistic work done, the participants agreed that if nothing else they had experienced a lessening of hostility toward life's inequities. Moreover, they knew a peace greater than any they had ever known. Two *Newsweek* journalists, Bill Barol and Pamela Abramson, were not so impressed:

> Hostility may be in order when we consider the life of the planet—hostility toward earthbound miseries like disease and war and drug addiction, or any one of a million kinds of human problems that can't be solved by standing around in a circle and smiling. Making yourself feel good about the world is not the same thing as improving the world. Want to think a good thought? Think about 144,000 people volunteering an

hour a week to work in shelters for the homeless. That would be something to hum about.

Even though extraterrestrials did not fly by or etch the empyrean with formulas, everyone had a good time. But, oh, what nerve-racking suspense is building up. We won't know for sure if the hand-holding hummers saved the earth until the year 2012 is upon us. Or until another doomsday fad takes precedence over this one.

BIBLIOGRAPHY

Barol, Bill, and Pamela Abramson. "The End of the World (Again)." *Newsweek* 110 (August 17, 1987): 70-71.
Friedman, Jack. "Hum If You Love the Mayans." *People Weekly* 28 (August 31, 1987): 26-29.
Kemp, Mark. "Beam Us Up, Jose." *Discover* 9 (January 1988): 90.
Smilgis, M. "A New Age Dawning." *Time* 130 (August 31, 1987): 63.

Hippie communes promised safe harbor from the storms of life. People of like
mind could share meals, farm, make crafts, take drugs, and engage in free love
when and if they wanted to. But as in the establishment world outside, there had to
be some form of government to get things done, and with it, rankling set in.
(1969)

Hippie Communes

Newsweek called 1969 the year of the commune. By unofficial count, 500 or more collective settlements across America afforded peace, love, and shelter to some 10,000 hippies. The credo of one commune read:

> Getting out of the cities isn't hard, only concrete is. Get it together. This means on your own, all alone or with a few of your friends. Buy land. Don't rent. Money manifests. Trust. Plant a garden, create a center. Come together.

The terse credo demanded a simpler focus on life and made perfect sense to many young people harassed by urban living. Even if "money manifests" wasn't exactly clear, the exultant hippies found great comfort in repeating the words like a mantra. The Hindu holy syllable "Om," though, became the main chant, along with mystical stories told to outsiders:

> We are entering the time of the tribal dance as we go to live in tepees, celebrate our joys together, and learn to survive. We go to a virgin forest with no need for the previously expensive media of electronic technology. The energy we perceive within ourselves is beyond electric; it is atomic, it is cosmic, it is bliss.

To discover nature's bliss, the hippies settled in New Mexico's mesas and mountains, Oregon's lush valleys, California's Big Sur, and other choice spots. Mostly they built their own dwellings, grew their own crops, and lived as one big, happy family. Some communes went so far as to have an ordained minister marry all family members one to another. Sharing everything was gospel: food, drugs, books, tools, blankets, and sex. One hippie girl slept with three men until she got pregnant so she wouldn't know who the father was. The hippies also engaged in making crafts such as bead necklaces, furniture, moccasins, batik clothing, and other items for their own use or for sale. One of the best known hippie goods was the God's eye, a diamond-shaped mobile woven with yarn on a cross. The colorful eye symbolized different things, but in the main it represented an omniscient deity who watched over his favorite children. All seemed so idyllic in the communes: plenty of honest work; easy friendships; wholesome food from the good earth itself; ample supplies of marijuana, LSD, and peyote; and, last but not least, free love.

The 500-plus communes across America were similar in most respects—certainly ideologically bound—yet also varied. Some were more drug-oriented, some more religious, some more devoted to free love, and some more experimental. Robert Houriet, a freelance writer, visited Oz, a 130-acre hippie homestead situated in western Pennsylvania near the town of Meadville (population: 20,000). His purpose in going there was to describe the daily life of Oz for readers curious about communes. His report, published in the *The New York Times Magazine* (February 16, 1969), charts the life and death of Oz and is emblematic of what happened to other communes. Houriet observed the hippies' relaxed life-style. The family of 35 started waking up around 9:00 in the morning. One member coaxed wood to burn for a fire. Another member got a breakfast of coarse oatmeal, apples, and goat's milk ready. Over in a corner, a bearded youth strummed a guitar softly. Several of the family went out for nude bathing, then returned to warm their glistening flesh by the fire. As the family ate breakfast, they conversed in a light-hearted manner until Deja, a young girl with pigtails, spoke more seriously for the 35 homesteaders, telling why they lived in Oz:

> When people work for profit they deny their very brotherhood. The capitalist system forces people into boring activity and cuts them off from nature by forcing them to live in cities. It goes against the order of God.

This belief and others openly espoused by the Oz homesteaders infuriated the people of Meadville. To their mind the hippies were dirty loafers whose behavior was immoral. Civic groups in Mead-ville determined that some action had to be taken. First, the state police raided Oz and arrested family members for "maintaining a disorderly house" in violation of an 1860 statute. True, the commu-nal living quarters didn't look like grandmother's parlor; wild paint and figures covered the walls. Then the Juvenile Court charged the family with exposing children to "male" nudity and foul language. Snooping Meadville children had witnessed nude bathing at Oz and overheard four-letter words spoken. Then an undercover agent ob-tained more proof of the family's disorderliness: animals in the house, trash (biodegradable) in the yard, and more. Finally, two informers took pictures of the family posing nude in the woods and sold the "obscene" pictures to the local district attorney. With in-disputable evidence, the authorities nailed an injunction to the front of the farmhouse which prohibited the use of the premises for "for-nication, assignation, and lewdness." The authorities disregarded the fact that some locals had disturbed the peace of Oz by trying to solicit free love. Meadville's resentment and intolerance won out and after only four months' residence, the Oz homesteaders left as peacefully as they had come.

Oz failed because of Meadville, thereby putting other communes on the alert. But even if Meadville had left the Oz homesteaders alone, they probably wouldn't have made it. Daniel B. Reibel, cu-rator of Harmony Society, a successful communal experiment (1805-1905), lists the characteristics needed for a commune to pros-per. First, the commune must have a solid financial base so the members don't have to rely on the outside world for anything. Sec-ond, the commune members must subscribe to a fixed goal, usually religious. Third, strong leadership has to give the commune direc-tion. And fourth, every member of the commune must have a spe-cific job which he or she completes for the common good. The Oz homesteaders and 1960s hippies in general disdained such regimen-tation. At Oz, all their pooled money went for buying the land; their fixed goal was to live as they pleased; their leader, a student of philosophy, spoke of Oz as a "working anarchy"; and not all left their egos behind to join in and contribute.

The incentive to join a commune was too potent. Youth, gaiety, drugs, free love, and no care for tomorrow were powerful lures.

Life magazine ran one of its usual striking pictorials in 1969 entitled, "The Commune Comes to America." One full page shows a family of hippies posed in front of a tepee: in handmade dresses the plain women and three young girls wear flowers in their hair or hold flowers their hands; the men are bearded, some shirtless, all slender and virile; and the grass, bushes, and trees around them are seductively emerald. A two-page picture captures a family of long-haired blondes photographed inside a tepee; the sepia tint and their soulful looks are reminiscent of Victorian images, in particular the poet Tennyson and his family. Another two-page spread looks at a nude mother washing her daughter's hair in a lovely creek setting. What the pictures in *Life* don't reveal is the impossibility of achieving a perfect society. The 1960s hippies were no better at it than others before them, and less so because they found Reibel's principles hard to follow. "Do your own thing" was their one abiding truth.

Hippie communes were the natural result of the prevailing philosophy of the 1960s. Head guru of the counterculture, Timothy Leary, proclaimed, "Tune in, turn on, and drop out," which got him into trouble. At his California commune, a young girl drowned after taking too many drugs. California's equivalent of Meadville demanded that Leary, as head of the commune, go to prison for the accidental death. So Leary and his commune had to move on. And so, too, did the 1960s hippie movement until it and its throwback to collective settlements all but faded from memory.

BIBLIOGRAPHY

"The Commune Comes to America." *Life* 67 (July 18, 1969): 16B-23.

Houriet, Robert. "Life and Death of a Commune Called Oz." *The New York Times Magazine* (February 16, 1969): 30+; Discussion (March 9, 1969): 12+.

"Year of the Commune." *Newsweek* 74 (August 18, 1969): 89-90.

Hydropathy

Beginning in the 1840s and reaching their height of popularity in the 1850s, hydropathic centers provided Americans with the water cure. Highly restorative, the cure relieved backaches, subdued fever, quelled coughs, mastered arthritis, and humbled asthma, eczema, hepatitis, and high blood pressure. Or at least that's what the advertisements said. Three journals told the public all about it: *The Water-Cure Journal* published in New York from 1845 to 1861, was the longest lived — it carried the motto "Wash and be Healed"; the *Water Cure Monthly*, published in Yellow Springs, Ohio from 1859 to 1860; and *Water-Cure World, A Journal of Health, and Herald of Reform*, published in Brattleboro, Vermont from 1860 to 1861, which ceased publication due to the American Civil War. Even if there was nothing wrong with you, going to a hydropathic center was well worth the expense. It felt terrific to have a water therapist pamper you, and there were ample opportunities to meet a special friend.

The water-cure center in Brattleboro became a model establishment. Its daily regimen went like this:

Hours for bathing are from 5 to 7 o'clock in the morning; 10 to 12:30; 4 to 6 pm; and 8 to 9 pm.

After each bath fresh water should be drank, not much time be lost with dressing but out door exercise resorted to at once.

The baths to be used exactly according to the written prescription in regard to temperature or duration, no extra bathing allowed.

The hours for meals should be regularly observed, nothing eaten between meals . . . coffee, tea, spices, and warm or new bread are strictly forbidden . . . the same in regard to tobacco or other stimulants.

The patient should retire at ten o'clock or soon after, write or read as little as possible, and never after supper.

Brattleboro opened in 1845 with 15 patients. In less than a year, this number grew to 150. The next year, Brattleboro counted twice that number in its census, and by the end of the 1850s, 600 to 800 patients took the water-cure each year. Dozens of other hydropathic centers sprang up, from New England to the Mid-Atlantic to the Mid-Western states. Quite noticeably a lot of Americans wanted to wash and be healed. But why did simple bathing and the drinking of pure water that could be done at home engender such a craze for hydropathy? There are several reasons, the first of which was the most immediate.

One hundred and fifty years ago, medical science was not the competent healer it is today. Doctors then, no less than now, prescribed drugs to treat almost every ailment. But the drugs nineteenth century doctors used often overpowered and poisoned the body, such pollutants as mercurial drugs, calomel, quinine, strychnine, jalap, digitalis, and others in large doses. Patients who swooned, palpitated, and felt their nerves on fire from conventional medical treatment found welcome relief in hydropathy. If nothing else, the water cure cleansed their overmedicated systems and washed away the bad doctor's poisons. Another reason why mainly women went to the centers was to escape confinement at home. Expected to wear corsets and act proper all the time, many women in the 1840s and 1850s languished from boredom and silently stewed about female bondage. But at the centers everything changed. Off came the corset, down came the hair, and out popped the sweat from outdoor recreation. Joyously, the women took long walks with one another, talked for hours, laughed and giggled, and—best of all—children weren't allowed. The "no children" restriction gave birth to an auxiliary industry, that of boarding schools, which proliferated alongside the hydropathic centers. Not every night, of course, but often enough, amateur theatricals, musicals, and hydropathic balls entertained guests.

To further revivify women guests, the therapists discussed female problems with them. Long exploratory talks ensued about childbirth, menstruation, frequency of sexual intercourse, masturbation, abortion, and barrenness. At home, husbands and male doctors sidestepped these issues or refused to consider them seriously—that is, if they knew anything about the issues in the first place. But at the hydropathic centers, women could air their complaints and feel free to enjoy their femininity. This new freedom meant they could also frolic in the baths, regain their girlhood delight in living, and treat themselves to some sexual fun. The masturbatory cure, as it was called, was undertaken in or out of water (immersion versus directed flow) and with or without the use of water as the stimulus. The therapist might be present or need not be there once the guest knew how to produce the cure. Long sessions of water or digital massage of any erogenous zone effected the cure. When moral outcry condemned the blatant practice, it was pointed out that other approved methods did the same thing. Routinely, women not engaged in the masturbatory cure took sitz baths in a sitting position so flowing water massaged their vaginal area. In fact, the regular bath was called a douche because it cleansed the orifices and in doing its work titilated the whole body. Therapists, as well, gave women frequent vaginal injections to tone their interior walls and rubbed their pelvic areas daily. Not on record, it would be interesting to know how many women went to the centers to heal a physical ailment versus those who went for sensual pleasure. Perhaps the masturbatory cure in itself alleviated most complaints by settling the nerves in a friendly milieu.

The 1893 edition of the *Encyclopedia Britannica* says this about hydropathy: "Like many descriptive names, the word 'hydropathy' is defective and even misleading, the active agents in the treatment being heat and cold, of which water is little more than the vehicle." But what a vehicle it was for mid-nineteenth-century Americans who did not have the showers, hot tubs, and jacuzzis in which we linger. But not all of hydropathy was fun and games. Frequent enemas were one nose wrinkler. But, oh, to have a therapist wrap you (to produce copious sweat), massage you, bathe you, dry you, then send you off for a brisk walk before a meal—that was heaven on earth!

BIBLIOGRAPHY

Cayleff, Susan E., et al. *Wash and Be Healed: The Water-Cure Movement and Women's Health*. Philadelphia, PA: Temple University Press, 1987.

Donegan, Jane B., and Martha H. Verbrugge. *Hydropathic Highway to Health: Women and Water-Cure in Antebellum America*. Westport, CT: Greenwood Press, 1986.

Legan, Marshall Scott. "Hydropathy in America: A Nineteenth-Century Panacea." *Bulletin of the History of Medicine* 45 (1971): 267-280.

Sklar, Kathryn K. "All Hail to Pure Cold Water." *American Heritage* XXVI (December 1974): 64-69, 100-101.

Weiss, Harry B., and Howard R. Kemble. "The Forgotten Water-Cures of Brattleboro, Vermont." *Vermont History* 37 (1969): 164-176.

IQ and Genius

Psychologist Lewis M. Terman (1877-1956) devoted his working life to the study of mental measurement. Highly respected, he served as head of Stanford's psychology department and was elected President of the American Psychological Association and to the National Academy of Sciences. Throughout a long career, his achievements were many. Terman developed the Stanford-Binet test, which became the standard intelligence test in English-speaking countries. During World War I, he devised the Army Alpha and Beta tests to measure intelligence in military recruits. Terman undertook and almost completed a massive five-volume set (he died while writing the fifth volume) entitled *Genetic Studies of Genius*. He also devised measurement tools for determining male-female differences and degrees of marital happiness. All these pioneering efforts earned Terman a secure place in the history of psychology. But at one stage in his career, a book he inspired, but did not write, elicited considerable faddish interest.

For *The Early Mental Traits of Three Hundred Geniuses* (1926), Dr. Catharine M. Cox and two other researchers, under Dr. Terman's direction, spent two arduous years reading every available biography on the subjects selected. Cox and Terman intended the study (842 pages) to be an exploration of childhood precocity, but not the final word. They did state, however, that their research furnished evidence that genius was a trait inherited from intelligent parents, nourished by superior advantages in the child's early environment. This bit of historical presumption quickly caught public attention. If Cox and Terman were right, then genius could not be nurtured in the absence of facilitating genes, nor could it originate spontaneously under favorable conditions. Either a child got almost all the ingredients for genius from his or her parents, who then blessed the child with a rich environment, or there was no hope of ever achieving mental superiority. Cox and Terman assigned IQs to the 300 geniuses by interpreting the usual sketchy information found in biographies. Their analyses of mental development clicked because they already knew that each subject grew up to be a genius. Quite correctly, their study became a classic example of employing 20-20 hindsight to bolster a theory.

Cox and Terman began by using J. McKeen Cattell's "A Statistical Study of Eminent Men," in which Cattell listed 1,000 names. That number was reduced to 312; fewer than ten women made the list:

> The historical records of 312 eminent men and women selected for study, whether contained in collections of letters, histories, biographical dictionaries, or other works, were carefully searched, in so far as they were available, for material which would throw light on early mental development. . . . Eleven cases were then discarded for lack of data. For each of the remaining 301 an individual case history was prepared from the material furnished by upward of 1,500 biographical sources. . . . Each of the 301 case studies covers the following points:
>
> 1. Name, dates, field, and number indicating rank order of eminence in Cattell's list of 1,000
> 2. Bibliography
> 3. Chronology
> 4. Ancestry and family
> 5. Development to age 26
> 6. Characterization
> 7. The basis for eminence

From this information, Cox and Terman assigned two IQ ratings to each young genius. The first AI IQ averaged three independent estimates of intelligence to age 17; the AII IQ estimated intelligence to age 26. A person's IQ is obtained by dividing mental age by chronological age and multiplying the result by 100; thus a person of average intelligence would have an IQ of 100. Cox and Terman gave Miguel de Cervantes, author of *Don Quixote*, a paltry AI IQ of 105 and an AII IQ of 110. The astronomer Nicolaus Copernicus fared better, with 105 and 130 — he deserved the jump in AII IQ because at age 26 he became a Doctor of Philosophy and Medicine. Among composers, Johann Sebastian Bach rated 125 and 140; Ludwig van Beethoven, 135 and 140; and the boy wonder, Wolfgang Amadeus Mozart, 150 and 155. In the lofty 180 to 190 realm, 3 of the 6 were Jeremy Bentham, Blaise Pascal, and Johann Wolfgang Goethe. But way up in the clouds, with estimated IQs of 190 and 170, the British economist and philosopher John Stuart Mill stood alone. Cox and Terman attributed Mill's drop in AII IQ to a mental crisis he endured around age 20. On the other hand, Goethe, "One of the Greatest Poets of Any Age or Country," continued to advance mentally at an astonishing rate and by age 26 deserved the world record IQ of 200.

Another of the greatest poets, William Shakespeare, presented a problem. Not much is known about Shakespeare's early life, so Cox and Terman left him out. Or was it because Shakespeare's father was a simple country glover and not a man who could pass on soaring intellect? Or was it because Shakespeare disliked formal education and was not degreed like Christopher Marlowe? Or was it because Shakespeare's authorship of the plays is in question— aren't they too good for an unlettered rustic to have written? The inexplicable genius of Shakespeare conflicted with Cox and Terman's notions of inherited genius and a childhood record of rapid mental development.

Another example, that of Leonardo Da Vinci, also deviated from the study's "supported" conclusions. Leonardo's father was a fifth-generation notary "who rose to be a wealthy and much respected personage" — nevertheless a civil servant of unknown intelligence. As a boy, Leonardo was interested in everything and "mastered mathematical theory so quickly that soon he was able to propose questions which his master himself was unable to resolve." Furthermore, Leonardo studied music and "soon arrived at such perfection in playing the lute as to compose extemporaneous accompaniments to his own poetical effusions." These early accomplishments and others, of course, are not verifiable; they are the attributions of hero-worshiping biographers. It was not until the early part of the twentieth century that the critical biography came into being. Before that, biographers tended to enshrine their subjects (some still do) rather than scrutinize them. Again, all-seeing hindsight was at work; it made perfect sense to say Leonardo exhibited precosity, since he turned out to be a genius. How else can one explain it? Diligence and a stubborn will to succeed are too unlikely.

But the greatest inventor of all time, Thomas Alva Edison, possessed that kind of genius. His father was a shingle manufacturer, whether highly intelligent or not no one knows. Cox and Terman relied on social station to indicate braininess, which is always a mistake. After an abusive teacher told young Tom he was a dimwit, the disheartened boy learned his three Rs from his mother and read scientific journals by the armload. There is nothing in Edison's early development to show that he was a gifted child. Edison is an American icon because he made the best of what slender talents he had. Cox and Terman accepted every word of the hagiographic biographies they perused, a practice scholars today warn against. Mystery shrouds the early years of any person and what reminiscences remain are subjective.

Cox and Terman's assigned IQs were reprinted in textbooks and encyclopedia articles, discussed, and marveled at. Cervantes and Copernicus were not mentioned — IQ-wise they were too much like the rest of us — but Mill and Goethe were. Then the fad of debating the value of genius took over. Wasn't *Don Quixote* a greater contribution to human enlightenment than all of Mill's musings on the dismal science? But few Americans awed by the unattainable IQs asked the question Cox and Terman feared most. If genius is inherited, why didn't some of the 300 pass it on to their children? Anthony Burgess gave his view of the nature-nurture controversy when he wrote in his biography of Shakespeare, "The times were propitious for the birth of a great English poet."

BIBLIOGRAPHY

Cox, Catharine Morris. *The Early Mental Traits of Three Hundred Geniuses.* Volume II of *Genetic Studies of Genius.* Stanford, CA: Stanford University Press, 1926.

"Intelligence Ratings of Historical Characters." *Current History* 25 (January 1927): 544-545.

Seagoe, May V. *Terman and the Gifted.* Los Altos, CA: William Kaufmann, Inc., 1975.

"Kilroy Was Here"

Throughout World War II, reports came in from every corner of the world that a mysterious figure known only by last name had arrived at destinations before anyone else. It was uncanny how this "Kilroy" got around. He or she scrawled, "Kilroy Was Here," on just about everything — the Statue of Liberty's torch, the tomb of the Unknown Soldier, beneath the Arc de Triomphe, on the *Queen Elizabeth*, at Normandy invasion sites, on Okinawa beachheads, in New Guinea, Potsdam, and a thousand other places. Kilroy's playground was vast indeed, a fact that perturbed and delighted U.S. Armed Forces personnel. How did this Kilroy always get there first? And how long ago had Kilroy been there? For foot-weary soldiers to see the scrawl deep inside enemy territory was especially disturbing. Why hadn't Kilroy made it easier for them? Then again, it was great to know that an American had already been there and left a calling card. The assumption that Kilroy was an American went without saying. Who else but an American could keep up such a hectic pace, infiltrate enemy lines, and laugh at all attempts to catch him or her?

The Kilroy fad added much-needed comic relief to what was hell on earth. World War II was a barbaric experience for combatant and citizen alike. At an airfield on Canton Island in the Pacific, some wag had scrawled, "I Was Here Before Kilroy!," only to have scrawled underneath a short time later, "Like Hell You Were. I Was Here When This Was Only a Gleam in the C.O.'s Eye. Kilroy." On Kwajalein Atoll in the Marshall Islands, a sign read: "No Grass Atoll, No Trees Atoll, No Water Atoll, No Women Atoll, No Liquor Atoll, No Fun Atoll." To which had been added, "And No Kilroy Atoll!" But that wasn't the final word. A dashed-off rebuttal appeared, "I Just Didn't Pause Atoll. Kilroy." Once the war was over, Americans wanted to know who the phantom soldier was. He or she had lifted their spirits for five long years and should be given a medal, or maybe two. In response to overwhelming curiosity, the American Transit Association (ATA) sponsored a radio contest to learn the true identity of Kilroy, or at least to get a plausible explanation of who might have been the war's most indefatigable traveler and graffitist. The ATA declared a Halifax, Massachusetts man by the name of James J. Kilroy the winner. Here is his story:

> On December 5, 1941 I started to work for Bethlehem Steel Company, Fore River Ship Yard, Quincy Mass., as a ratesetter. . . . I started my new job with enthusiasm, carefully surveying every innerbottom and tank before issuing a contract. I was thoroughly upset to find that practically every test leader I met wanted me to go down and look over his job with him, and when I explained to him that I had seen the job and could not spare the time to crawl through one of these tanks again with him, he would accuse me of not having looked the job over. I was getting sick of being accused of not looking the jobs over and one day, as I came through the manhole of a tank I had just surveyed, I angrily marked with yellow crayon on the tank top, where the testers could see it, "Kilroy Was Here." The following day a test gang leader approached me with a grin on his face and said, "I see you looked my job over."

The other claimants to being the real Kilroy were an equally interesting lot. One Kilroy was a downed Irish-American RAF pilot who told the British after Dunkirk to keep the faith by writing his name everywhere. Another Kilroy was a young man who promised to marry his sweetheart, then disappeared to join a branch of the Armed Forces. Not knowing which branch, his sweetheart began searching for him, and people hearing of her frenzied quest scrawled "Kilroy Was Here" to tell her she was on the right track. A third highly imaginative, though ridiculous, entry was this one: hundreds of years ago a Viking named Yorlik explored the entire world which he called "Ereh"; at the end of his extensive journey, he allowed his countrymen to inscribe a plaque with the words, "Yorlik Saw Ereh," but only if they spelled the words in reverse.

Not everyone laughed when they saw, "Kilroy Was Here." The scrawl irritated the Nazis and Japanese, which caused American soldiers to write the graffiti even larger. Then there were the 62 soldiers actually named Kilroy for whom the scrawl was a migraine headache. Those Kilroys were wrongly accused of being practical jokers or impostors or of going AWOL. They hardly got a minute's rest from kidding and having to see their superior officer. The apotheosis of the Kilroy fad came when the American Transit Association presented James Kilroy of Quincy, Massachusetts with an award. He was the most likely candidate they had, so the ATA gave him a 22-ton streetcar minus the engine as his prize. Undaunted, James Kilroy graciously accepted the impractical gift and converted it into a dormitory for six of his nine children.

BIBLIOGRAPHY

"Kilroy Was in Quincy." *Newsweek* 29 (January 6, 1947): 21.
"Who Is 'Kilroy?'" *The New York Times Magazine* (January 12, 1947): 30.
"Who Is Kilroy?" *Saturday Evening Post* 218 (October 6, 1945): 6.

Language

Discovering the origin of faddish language is about as easy as tracing a joke back to its source. At best, only time periods can be ascertained. Because language is spoken, it travels rapidly, and the more attractive or faddish it is, the quicker it enters common usage. At the beginning of the eighteenth century in America, "ain't" was a perfectly good contraction for "am not." When used in the next century to mean "is not" and "are not," ain't lost its acceptability. Then English teachers sallied forth on a crusade to vanquish the hated contraction, but out of earshot defiant students said ain't all the more. Ain't really came into its own in the twentieth century with faddish phrases like: "Ain't it the limit?" (1908), "Ain't it the truth?" (1915), "Ain't we got fun?" (1920), and "Ain't that a laugh?" (1930). But the epitome of improper usage that brought smiles to beleaguered students everywhere and tears to the teaching profession was "Ain't ain't grammar" (1920).

Known for its gay abandon, the 1920s also produced some other wonderfully faddish expressions. "The cat's pajamas" meant the ultimate, as in remarking about a shapely young flapper who could Charleston all night long, "She's the cat's pajamas." Probably the expression came from the fact that pajamas for women were new in the 1920s, daring in style, and showed off more of the luscious female form. Most likely, the cat part derived from the old English expression to be like a Cheshire cat — to laugh or smile broadly. Then again, who knows? The cat's pajamas might just have been a piece of whimsy devoid of heritage. One thing is certain, though, the cat's pajamas gave birth to a whole litter of associated expressions zanier than the original. There was "the duck's quack," "the bee's knees," "the clam's garters," "the gnat's elbows," "the sardines whiskers," "the bullfrog's beard," "the leopard's stripes," and "the snake's hips" — all meaning the ultimate. By the 1930s and the onset of the Great Depression, "copacetic" — meaning satisfactory—had replaced the cat's pajamas. Copacetic was about all anyone could expect from an America run aground economically. But there was a substratum below copacetic populated by the unemployed and dispossessed living in shantytowns. They blamed their troubles on President Herbert Hoover (1929-1933), so their makeshift communities were "Hoovervilles"; the newspapers they slept under, "Hoover blankets"; the rabbits they killed for food, "Hoover hogs"; their one pair of soleless footwear, "Hoover shoes"; and their conveyances drawn by mules, "Hoover cars."

Harriet Beecher Stowe's extremely popular novel, *Uncle Tom's Cabin* (1852), contained colorful language that Americans liked to repeat. Topsy, a little black girl brought into the home of the wealthy southern St. Clare family, spoke two of the most memorable lines. About her becoming a big girl overnight, she said, "I 'spect I growed"; and when ater she replied, "I's wicked, —I is. I's mighty wicked," fans of the novel parroted her innocent admission. Even people who had never read a word of *Uncle Tom's Cabin*, but who had heard others mimic Topsy, said, "I's wicked, —I is. I's mighty wicked." Interestingly, the faddish epithet of calling a subservient black an "Uncle Tom" misrepresents the fictional character. Stowe portrayed Uncle Tom as a stalwart man of dignity who maintains a kind heart and helpful hand toward blacks and whites alike, no matter how much injustice he suffers. Uncle Tom is America's closest literary relation to the tragic hero in a Greek play. His only subservience occurs when he tries to get along with the cruel Simon Legree to avoid Legree's whipping the other slaves. In the 1960s and 1970s, militant blacks who called their unmilitant brothers Uncle Toms did great disservice to Stowe's proud creation. Another novel that provided a popular epithet—this time correctly termed derogatory—was Sinclair Lewis' *Babbitt* (1923). The central character, George F. Babbitt, is the very model of middle-class complacency and provincialism. The world revolves around Babbitt, and his notion of the way things work is infallible. Lewis' novel struck a responsive cord, and Americans in the 1920s chattered about all the Babbitts they knew (of course, discounting themselves).

When boy meets girl, faddish language arises. In the 1830s, a young man went courting "to spark a girl," hopefully out of sight of her father, on a "sparking bench" or "sparking sofa." In the 1850s, a beau sought "to spoon" with his girl, i.e., to nestle against her like two spoons in a drawer. In the 1860s, a lovesick youth wanted "to lollygag" with his girl, i.e., to kiss and caress her. In the 1890s, if an impetuous young man hadn't yet been introduced to the object of his attention, he made "goo-goo eyes" at her to let her know his interest. In the 1930s, a girl with sex appeal had a lot of "oomph"; she was in the eyes of her admirers an "oomph girl." Also in the 1930s, a sexually attractive but underaged girl was called a "San Quentin quail." Later, when Vladimir Nabokov wrote *Lolita* (1955) about an intoxicating nymphet, the "San Quentin quail" became a "Lolita." In the 1960s, black slang produced "fox" for a delicious girl and "foxy" for her inticing moves. Today, chaste courtship seems to have gone the way of the dinosaurs. The latest faddish expression, "Do the wild thing," from a rap song is obviously sexual and has American youth chanting it from coast to coast.

"Meanwhile back at the ranch" slipped into American conversation during the nickelodeon days (c. 1900-1913). Its overuse as a subtitle to allow scene changes in silent Westerns made it a favorite cliché. Any tedious story or speech or harangue by the boss could be deflated by someone whispering, "Meanwhile, back at the ranch." Cuss words have followed a certain faddish progression. "Zounds!" for God's wounds and "Gadzooks!" for God's hooks (the nails in the crucifixion cross) were popular sayings in seventeenth-century America. "Criminy!," "My Stars!," "Golly!," and "Gosh!" heated tempers in the eighteenth century. "What the deuce!," "Hell fire!," and "What the blazes!" sounded positively devilish in the nineteenth century. "Botheration!," "Ye Gods!," "I'll be jiggered!," "Land o' goshen!," and "Dad-burned!" also embellished the last century. "Jeez!" and "Jeepers!" got the twentieth century off to a mild start, followed by "Jesus H. Christ!" and "Holy Cow!" From that point on, modern Americans were less creative and resorted to almost exclusive use of four-letter words.

Saying hello in jive talk during the 1920s was a simple affair. "How's tricks?" and "Long time, no see" were faddish salutations. The latter 1930s produced "What's cookin', good lookin'?" and "Hello Joe, whata-ya know?" Switching over to World War II lingo, "snafu" (situation normal all fucked up) became such a celebrated acronym that it seemed everything military suffered from snafus. But America won the war anyway, and snafu, like the cat's pajamas, bred imitators. Servicemen not always pleased with military inefficiency said things were "fubar" (fucked up beyond all recognition) or "fubb" (fucked up beyond belief). If the whole world appeared ready to crash in, they said "tarfu" (things are really fucked up). The 1950s gave America cool jazz and hip talk. If the music was good, it was "real cool," "far out," "real gone," "out of sight," and "weird." The 1960s kept up the pace with "right on," "groovy," and "mellow" for the good things in life. "Fantastic" demonstrated excited approval in the 1970s, and in the 1980s "awesome" served the purpose.

Faddish language is shorthand communication. Once a word or expression is established, people instantly understand what the speaker means. It can become so truncated that one word can stand for many sentences of explanation. For example:

> "How was the beach yesterday?"
> Full reply: "The waves were perfect tubes for surfing. There were no clouds in the sky. Girls in string bikinis kept passing by me and smiling. My team won five straight volleyball matches. I ate three chili dogs, then got a date with one of the girls for that night. And I found a $50 bill buried in the sand."
> Abbreviated reply: "Awesome!"

Note: This brief entry cannot do justice to the plethora of faddish language. For sheer reading enjoyment, please obtain copies of the following books—they are the cat's pajamas.

BIBLIOGRAPHY

Flexner, Stuart Berg. *I Hear America Talking*. New York: Van Nostrand Reinhold Company, 1976.
———. *Listening to America*. New York: Simon and Schuster, 1982.

LSD

Dr. Albert Hofmann, a Swiss chemist working for Sandoz Pharmaceuticals in Basle, first discovered the hallucinogenic properties of lysergic acid diethylamide, or LSD. As the legendary story goes, on the afternoon of April 19, 1943, Dr. Hofmann drank 250 millionths of a gram of LSD-25 which he had synthesized in his lab. Before an hour had elapsed, he began to feel dizzy and asked an assistant to accompany him home. The two pedaled their bicycles at a rapid pace. Dr. Hofmann was already seeing visions and needed to lie down. By the time they arrived at his house, Dr. Hofmann couldn't speak. Nervously, the assistant summoned a physician, who declared there was nothing physically wrong with the patient. But the senior chemist who had ingested a speck of hell thought his whole body had been poisoned and his mind permanently damaged. Dr. Hofmann's initial experience with LSD had indeed been harrowing, though not so terrible as to prevent him from conducting more experiments under controlled conditions. *LSD: My Problem Child* (1983) relates what he learned about the drug and, as the title indicates, how society misused it.

Before Timothy Leary advised everyone in the 1960s to "turn on, tune in, drop out," the psychologist William James had indulged in some hallucinogenic experimentation of his own. In *The Varieties of Religious Experience* (1902), James described the effects of nitrous oxide and ether on the human brain. He found that laughing gas and the volatile liquid, when mixed with sufficient oxygen, "stimulate the mystical consciousness in an extraordinary degree." As if that recommendation from an eminent thinker weren't enough to excite the public, James added, "Our normal waking consciousness, rational consciousness as we call it, is but one special type of consciousness, whilst all about it, parted from it by the filmiest of screens, there lie potential forms of consciousness entirely different." That was the go-ahead for Americans to indulge in "ether frolics." Brave souls inhaled nitrous oxide and ether and got very light-headed. Because they did it more for play than for spiritual enlightenment, no pervasive cult formed. At the turn of the century, these innocent frolickers in no way resembled those to come who ate LSD like candy and did create a cult.

With James as godfather to the psychedelic movement, Timothy Leary, a respected Harvard psychologist, became a tireless advocate for mind exploration. Leary read Hofmann, synthesized LSD in the lab, and studied the effects of the drug on himself, colleagues, priests, criminals, and students. Another Harvard psychologist, Richard Alpert, worked with Leary to chart "acid" trips. For them, LSD had unlimited potential to reveal worlds of hidden thought, or as Aldous Huxley phrased it — open the doors of perception, that for the time being nothing else mattered. Leary and Alpert dropped acid day and night, assured that they were on the verge of liberating the brain from its mundane shackles. Not so impressed, Harvard released the increasingly dangerous Leary from his job. Thus began a phenomenal journey that drew adherents to the cause from every corner of America.

No longer bound to academe, Timothy Leary saw himself as a Catholic priest placing the sacrament of LSD on everyone's tongue. Swallowing acid heightened awareness of all things beautiful and made one feel that peace on earth was possible. Taking LSD was a love feast, and the evils of life subsided into nothingness. In 1963, Leary organized the International Federation for Internal Freedom and the Castalia Foundation and, in 1966, the League for Spiritual Discovery. He established headquarters for his movement in Mexico and in Millbrook, New York. The Tibetan *Book of the Dead* served as sacred scripture, "a manual for recognizing and utilizing altered states of consciousness and applying the ecstatic experience in the postsession life." To make the book more accessible to lay readers, Leary translated it into "psychedelic English." Then, for his followers to wrestle with before and after taking LSD, he posed seven spiritual questions: the Power Question, the Life Question, the Human Being Question, the Awareness Question, the Ego

Question, the Emotional Question, and the Escape Question. Aided
by LSD and ample prompting from Leary, it was left to each person
to attempt to answer the all-encompassing queries. These philo-
sophical/religious trappings demonstrated that acid eaters weren't
mindless dopeheads. At least that's how Leary explained it to his
enemies, who rejoiced when the LSD guru got 30 years in prison on
a marijuana charge, followed by two 10-year terms also for possession of marijuana.

Flashbacks: An Autobiography (1983) is Leary's own account of
the LSD years—a thoroughly fascinating time. How one man convinced a whole generation to drop acid in hope of escaping responsibility is a saga not so improbable, given the times. More honest
than Leary, Richard Alpert later admitted the psychedelic experience failed to open the longed-for doors of perception. At one
point, Alpert and 5 other people had locked themselves in a building for 3 weeks and taken 400 milligrams of LSD every 4 hours. All
they got was very high, drained themselves of energy, and afterwards fell into severe depression.

What kind of highs did LSD give? Trippers reported six basic
experiences:

1. The freak-out: nightmarish, individual may lose emotional
   control and suffer paranoid delusions, see hallucinations, have
   catatonic seizures, in some cases for a prolonged time.
2. The nonpsychotic adverse reaction: not as intense as the freak-
   out, the individual passes through varying degrees of tension,
   anxiety and fear, depression and despair.
3. The psychodynamic: unconscious ideas and strong emotional
   feelings surface so that the individual relives past conflicts in a
   symbolic way.
4. The cognitive: former confused thought becomes crystal clear,
   the individual sees the interrelationship and meaning of many
   things.
5. The aesthetic: the senses intensify and intermingle, the individual may see sounds and hear colors, everything becomes
   more alive and vivid.
6. The mystical: the individual feels a oneness with the universe,

great joy, blessedness and tranquility, all too wonderful to put
into words.

Of the six kinds of LSD experiences, the first three were undesirable and the last three the much ballyhooed reasons for taking the
drug. Not on the list but a potent incentive for tripping, Timothy
Leary told *Playboy* magazine, "There is no question that LSD is the
most powerful aphrodisiac ever discovered by man." Even if that
were true, what happened when one amorous tripper freaked out or
started to relive a childhood trauma while making love? *LSD, Man
& Society* (1967), edited by Richard C. DeBold and Russell C.
Leaf, presented the facts surrounding the LSD controversy. The
collected essays attempted to deglamorize the drug before its usage
became widespread, but sane arguments could not compete with all
the allurements of popular culture. Tripping on LSD was the chic
thing to do, and like all fads, it had to run its course. Some trippers
freaked out completely and committed suicide, which LSD advocates chalked up to their already having a death wish.

Twenty years later, *Storming Heaven: LSD and the American
Dream* (1987) by Jay Stevens assessed the craziness of it all. Two
examples from the book illuminate part of the mania. In spring
1967, six college students in Pennsylvania took LSD and then went
out to a grassy knoll near campus and supposedly stared wide-eyed
into the sun for hours. Their retinas badly burned, all six became
totally blind. Norman M. Yoder, Commissioner of the Office for
the Blind in Pennsylvania's Department of Public Welfare, released
the report to the media. Several ophthalmologists questioned the
incident, saying that even LSD couldn't shut down the eye-closing
reflexes so completely. The state attorney general, upon investigat-
ing Yoder's report, got at the truth. Yoder, who himself was 90
percent blind, had fabricated the story to frighten people away from
taking LSD. The false tale stuck, and parents across America worried their children might come home blind. Next, two researchers in
Los Angeles gave 30 acid-trippers marked maps to follow to measure their spatial orientation. None of the subjects was on LSD during testing. The befuddled bunch turned east instead of west, north
instead of south, and got lost. When given braille maps to feel di-

rections, the trippers did better. The researchers concluded that prolonged use of LSD resulted in perceptual change. Like young children, the trippers spun around aimlessly more than they should have.

BIBLIOGRAPHY

DeBold, Richard C., and Russell C. Leaf, eds. *LSD, Man & Society*. Middletown, CT: Wesleyan University Press, 1967.

Eliade, Mircea, ed. *The Encyclopedia of Religion*. Vol. 12. New York: Macmillan, 1987.

Hofmann, Albert. *LSD: My Problem Child*. Los Angeles, CA: J. P. Tarcher, Inc., 1983.

Leary, Timothy. *Flashbacks: An Autobiography*. Los Angeles, CA: J. P. Tarcher, Inc., 1983.

Masters, R. E. L. and Jean Houston. *The Varieties of Psychedelic Experience*. New York: Holt, Rinehart & Winston, 1966.

Stevens, Jay. *Storming Heaven: LSD and the American Dream*. New York: The Atlantic Monthly Press, 1987.

Marxian Socialism

After a "terror" had seized him, novelist Jack London (1876-1916) converted to socialism around 1895:

> The woman of the streets and the man of the gutter drew very close to me. I saw the picture of the Social Pit as vividly as though it were a concrete thing, and at the bottom of the Pit I saw them, myself above them, not far, and hanging on to the slippery wall by main strength and sweat. . . . Since that day I have opened many books, but no economic argument, no lucid demonstration of the logic and inevitableness of Socialism affects me as profoundly and convincingly as I was affected on the day when I first saw the walls of the Social Pit rise around me and felt myself slipping down, down, into the shambles at the bottom. (*How I Became a Socialist*)

London's terror afflicted other Americans mired in the Social Pit or sympathetic to those who were. At the dawn of the twentieth-century, the great capitalists weren't just rich, they were filthy rich. Without a pang of conscience, they displayed their wealth ostentatiously. The American proletariat toiled long hours under deplorable conditions to supply the haves with their many mansions. Anyone who moved about a city saw the flagrant exploitation of workers forced to endure poverty. European workers were in the same plight, as were brethren throughout the world. The proles far outnumbered the capitalists but were powerless to help themselves. Or were they? At the end of the nineteenth-century, on behalf of workers everywhere, intellectuals and anarchists banded together in an unholy alliance to remake society. Their goal was to topple capitalism and replace it with a classless society in which the workers owned the means of production and lived on equal footing with one another.

Marxian socialism seemed the answer. Force the rich to work for a living, or kill them off, and redistribute the wealth. Then everyone would labor for the Mother State. No more exploitation or poverty, no more Social Pit. It made perfect sense to Jack London and his fellow socialists, who began addressing each other as Comrade. However, the glorious cause dimmed shortly, so that by 1920, most Americans thought Marxian Socialism a faddish solution incongruent with democracy. Voter preference in Presidential elections from 1900 to 1968 shows its faint appeal:

1900 Socialist candidate Eugene V. Debs received .62% of the vote in the election won by the Republican William McKinley.

1904 Eugene V. Debs, 2.98%, won by the Republican Theodore Roosevelt.

1908 Eugene V. Debs, 2.82%, won by the Republican William H. Taft.

1912 Eugene V. Debs, 5.99%, won by the Democrat Woodrow Wilson.

1916 Socialist candidate Allan L. Benson, 3.18%, won by the Democrat Woodrow Wilson.

1920 Eugene V. Debs, 3.42%, won by the Republican Warren G. Harding.

1924 Progressive Party candidate Robert M. La Follette (included some socialism in the platform), 16.56%, won by the Republican Calvin Coolidge.

1928 Socialist candidate Norman M. Thomas, .72%, won by the Republican Herbert Hoover.

1932 Norman M. Thomas, 2.22%, won by the Democrat Franklin D. Roosevelt.

1936 Norman M. Thomas, .41%, won by the Democrat Franklin D. Roosevelt.

1940 Norman M. Thomas, .23%, won by the Democrat Franklin D. Roosevelt.

1944 Norman M. Thomas, .16%, won by the Democrat Franklin D. Roosevelt.

1948 no socialist candidate

1952 no socialist candidate

1956 Socialist-Labor candidate Eric Hass, .07%, won by the Republican Dwight D. Eisenhower.

1960 Eric Hass, .07%, won by the Democrat John F. Kennedy.

1964 Eric Hass, .06%, and Socialist-Workers candidate Clifton DeBerry, .05%, won by the Democrat Lyndon B. Johnson.

1968 Socialist-Labor candidate Henning A. Blomen, .07%, won by the Republican Richard M. Nixon.

At first, American socialism resembled European in its strict adherence to Karl Marx's tenets. But then, as various factions fought for political control, socialism branched out tenuously. In 1900, Eugene V. Debs ran as the candidate for two socialist groups, the Social Democratic Party and the more moderate Socialist Labor Party. In succeeding presidential elections, compromise and agreement were not the norm. Extremists in the Communist Party saw to that. For instance, the Debs-type socialists considered religion a private matter that the state shouldn't restrict, whereas the communists demanded the abolition of religion since it enslaved people no less than capitalism. Closing all churches was unthinkable to Americans, as was relinquishing all property to the State. On every issue, the communists sought radical change immediately; they were not interested in winning power through an orderly process. Anarchy was the key to success—blood in the street! Another socialist group, the Industrial Workers of the World (I.W.W.), used sabotage and strikes as its main weapons. In addition to internal bickering, the common worker for whom all the machinations were intended didn't understand what was told him. A letter in *The New Republic*, April 7, 1917, pointed this out:

Think of clubbing a sweatshop worker's brain with the shibboleths of Marxian dogma, "emancipation of the worker," "surplus value," "economic determinism," and all the rest of them. It is like teaching a schoolboy arithmetic in terms of the differential calculus. No wonder the victims edge away and cry: "If this be the litany of salvation, we'll stick to the good old tunes of the prince of this world of trusts."

Open revolution failed in America for the reasons given and because the agitators — mainly European zealots — didn't know how to galvanize American workers. The atrocities of the Russian Revolution practically ended what remaining sympathy there was for the workers' movement. In 1916, just before communism became a fact in Russia, Jack London resigned from the American Socialist Party. He disliked "its lack of fire and fight, and its loss of emphasis on the class struggle." Another noted writer of the day, Gustavus Myers, stated in *The Nation*, February 15, 1917:

> Most of the idealists who have quit the Socialist party were altruists. . . . Their vision was of a state of society in which, if guarantees of good subsistence were afforded to everybody, the human race, relieved of its sordid worries and conflicts, would ascend to noble heights of attainment and brotherhood.

When that vision faded, all the altruists had left was the memento of an intellectual fad. Like London, they had believed wholeheartedly in the concept of Marxian socialism, but the reality of it — the murderous grappling for power among the Russian leaders, the workers worse off than before, loss of individual freedom, one tyranny exchanged for another, the institution of a police state — sickened them. Even the Socialist party candidate in 1916, Allan L. Benson, resigned with these words:

> Pursuing their policy of rule or ruin, the syndicalists [I.W.W.] began work within the party to capture or to destroy it. By persistent wrangling and quarreling at party meetings they discouraged and disgusted enough Socialists to bring the dues-paying membership down to 65,000 [from 125,000] . . . the syndicalists have contaminated Socialist doctrine by foisting anarchist ideas upon the country as Socialist ideas.

Patience paid off, though, for those altruists who believed "the best place to work for socialism is outside the Socialist party." Deb's 1904 platform included reforms asked for by the Populists and other agrarian-labor movements. Later enacted, the "radical" reforms were: referendum and recall, women's suffrage, the graduated income tax, and higher wages and shorter hours. State ownership of transportation, communication, and exchange have yet to be realized, if ever.

BIBLIOGRAPHY

Benson, Allan L. "What the War Has Done to Socialism in America." *Current Opinion* 65 (August 1918): 82-85.

Congressional Quarterly's Guide to U.S. Elections. 2nd ed. Washington, DC: Congressional Quarterly, Inc., 1985.

Egbert, Donald Drew, and Stow Persons, eds. *Socialism and American Life.* 2 vols. Princeton, NJ: Princeton University Press, 1952.

Grendon, Felix. "In Defense of Socialism." *New Republic* 10 (April 7, 1917): 297-298.

Myers, Gustavus. "Why Idealists Quit the Social Party." *The Nation* 104 (February 15, 1917): 181-182.

Watkins, Gordon S. "The Present Status of Socialism in the United States." *Atlantic Monthly* 124 (December 1919): 821-830.

Mensa

Founded in 1960, American Mensa has 53,000 members distributed among 144 local groups. Worldwide, there are many thousand more Ms, as they like to be called. To join Mensa, a person must score higher than 98 percent of the population on a standard intelligence test. The aim of this elite group is "to identify and foster human intelligence and to provide a stimulating intellectual and social environment for its members." Mensa got its start directly after World War II, when two British barristers, Roland Berrill and Dr. L. L. Ware, gathered a select panel of highly intelligent people to discuss means for attaining world peace. Latin for "table," Mensa connotes a roundtable society of equals, i.e., equals on the highest plane of human intelligence. Meeting and talking for hours about anything is what Mensans like to do. Since 1960, articles in American magazines have informed the public about the group, and from the masses have come new Mensans. In the 1980s, four Mensa books appeared, and with them a fad emerged.

The *Mensa Genius Quiz Book* (1981), *Mensa Genius Quiz Book Two* (1983), *Mensa Think Smart Book* (1985), and *Mensa Book of Words, Word Games, Puzzles & Oddities* (1988) test the average person's intelligence for comparison with the lofty Mensans. Being able to remain anonymous while taking the sample tests is an attractive feature, lest the test taker display too much ignorance. If the test taker does well, the next step is to write Mensa for information on how to take a valid intelligence test leading to membership. Mensa contends that one out of every 50 people qualifies for membership, which means a lot of people are ignorant of the fact that they are smart. Otherwise, Mensa membership would be much larger. Could Mensa have miscalculated the number of elite brains in the general population? Perish the thought.

Divorce rate is high among Mensans. Often they remarry to one another for a more compatible union. Once they learn their current

192

spouse isn't up to Mensa standards, it's "ave atque vale" (Hail and farewell!). If hereditary transmission of intelligence is true, Mensans are dying out because they have few or no children. The original purpose of forming Mensa—to discuss ways to achieve world peace—is no longer a burning issue. In fact, many commentators note that Mensa appears to be purposeless. It devotes itself to intellectual Ping-Pong and not much else. But, then, it's very comforting to be a Mensan, as one member relates:

> You don't have to prove anything in Mensa. You've already proven it by qualifying for membership. So you don't have to hold back for fear of showing up or antagonizing a superior on the job, or a friend or relative . . . You don't have to be afraid to show your ignorance or make a mistake, either. Everyone knows you're not stupid.

Perhaps faddish interest in Mensa will really take off in the 1990s, if belonging to the society grants immunity from ignorance. Besides, what could be more fun than playing cerebral one-upsmanship with a roomful of geniuses—yourself included—and not having to fret about blowing hot air?

BIBLIOGRAPHY

Alexander, Shana. "High I.Q. Frat." *Life* 55 (August 16, 1963): 11+.

Callum, M. "Are You a Superbrain?" *Saturday Evening Post* 249 (January 1977): 43-44.

Grosswirth, Marvin. "Mensa: It's a State of Mind—But a Mind Finely Tuned." *Science Digest* 87 (February 1980): 74-79.

At the turn of the century, progressive education demanded that children leave the fetid air of the classroom and go outdoors to learn from nature. In the sunshine they would be more alert and could observe earthly wonders firsthand. But few teachers knew the natural world well enough to explain it to the kids, who mostly got dirty and bug-bitten.

Nature Study

At the dawn of the twentieth century, educators rallied around the flag of nature study for elementary school students. In Germany, teachers had taught directly from nature for years to good advantage. So it was high time for American schools to adopt nature study. Ever since the Greek philosophers had endorsed going outdoors to look at trees, flowers, and leaves, men and women of intellect considered observing nature in the raw a powerful stimulant for the soul. Walter E. Ranger, Superintendent of Education of the State of Vermont, agreed:

> Nature-study tends to correct an error of traditional school education by opening, in response to the needs of the child, the door of the schoolroom to the truth and beauty of Nature, the child's dear companion and teacher. . . . It restores the pupil to a true relation and sympathy with his own life, and brings the school into harmony with other educative influences. (1904)

The child's curiosity determined what was taught. Wherever little feet led the child to stare at one of nature's creations, that was the lesson for the day. Advocates of nature study believed so strongly in their mission that their words rang with urgency:

> The aim of nature-study is to put the child in sympathy with his surroundings—with his own life. . . . Nature-study contributes much to right civic and moral training. It inspires kindness to God's creatures, gentle manners and a fine regard for the rights and well-being of others. It gives a larger love of home and familiar scenes and a deep interest in men and things, which are at the heart of good citizenship.

Nature study began with animal pets. A child could hardly fail to love puppies, kittens, and bunnies. Next, insects—because children

find great delight in their odd variety, followed by plants "which
are admired for their beauty and peculiarities, yet they do not appeal
to the awakened mind with the same force that is aroused by a living
animal." Then came garden study, which was more advanced as
one learned about propagation of plants by seed, layering, cutting,
grafting and budding, and transplantation. After this came garden
insects — children buzz over bees and butterflies. Then, the toad,
frog, and salamander — funny creatures children held in their hands.
Lastly, the teachers devoted ample time to bird life, forestry, nut
trees, aquaria, miscellaneous animals (bats, squirrels, spiders,
snakes, etc.), and flowerless plants (ferns, mosses, mushrooms,
mildews, etc.). Needless to say, the curriculum was full.

Most of the articles commending nature study appeared in the
journal *Education* from 1900 to 1908. Coincidental with the movement to teach children about nature was the outdoor life movement
(sleeping under the stars, hiking, canoeing, etc.), which enthralled
parents. Both were a reaction to the change from a rural to an urban
population, rampant industrialization, and unsalutary city living.
People were losing touch with nature, and that was a terrible shame.
Not that long ago, children learned about nature while growing up
on a farm. Nature was their first teacher, and a good one she was,
probably better than book knowledge. The crying need, then, was
to expose urban children to the many wonders of nature, and the
only way to accomplish that was to pack them up and go outside.
But the nature study movement withered away quickly. By 1908, a
decline in interest was evident.

Unlike the Germans, American teachers — good as they might
have been in the classroom — were not naturalists. They lacked the
skills to turn the great outdoors into a veritable feast of discovery.
They wandered around flipping over rocks and poking their fingers
inside flower blooms to no avail. Some teachers were too pedantic,
snuffing out the mystery of nature. But most were simply superficial and perfunctory because they hadn't learned how to enliven
nature study. At least some teachers were honest about their inade-
quacies. In a survey, 37% reported that securing materials from
nature was their biggest problem; 30% admitted they lacked the
knowledge to teach nature study adequately; and 18% complained
they didn't have enough time outdoors to do a good job. However,

not part of the survey, teachers disliked having to live by assessment measures. Administrators demanded accountability, i.e., hard-and-fast proof that nature study brought results. Did the children actually learn anything, or was nature study just extra recess? Moreover, the teachers who already felt somewhat incompetent had to deal with supervisors breathing down their necks. Outdoors the children darted off in different directions as if on an Easter egg hunt or squirted frogs at each other—all of which looked like undisciplined chaos to a stiff-backed supervisor. Yet, proponents stressed the importance of "spontaneity and vitality which lies at the heart of nature study." Either frog-squirting stayed or nature study had to go. By 1910, it was the three Rs again.

BIBLIOGRAPHY

Dewing, Arthur S. "Some Reasons for Decrease of Interest in Nature Study." *Education* 29 (January 1909): 291-293.

Long, W. J. "School of Nature-Study and Its Critics." *North American Review* 176 (May 1903): 688-698.

Ranger, Walter E. "The Nature-Study Movement." *Education* 24 (April 1904): 501-503.

Waldo, Frank. "Proper Guidance in Nature Study." *Education* 23 (September 1902): 36-40.

Orgonomy

Wilhelm Reich (1897-1957) began his professional career as a psychoanalyst in Vienna—a respected colleague of Sigmund Freud's with a brilliant future ahead of him—and ended it ignominiously in an American prison, convicted of quackery. During his Vienna years, Reich saw hundreds of patients who were afflicted with a variety of neuroses. He conferred with the best psychoanalytic minds of his time on what might be causing their afflictions. Reich, like the others, sought a basic explanation—there had to be some imminent cause, which once understood, would permit better treatment of neuroses. After years of being immersed in the etiology of neuroses, Reich declared "that all patients, without exception, are severely disturbed in the genital function. Most disturbed of all were those men who liked to boast and make a big show of their masculinity, men who possessed or conquered as many women as possible, who could 'do it' again and again in one night." Reich did not consider orgasm easy to obtain:

> Orgasmic potency is the capacity to surrender to the streaming of biological energy, free of any inhibitions; the capacity to discharge completely the dammed-up sexual excitation through involuntary, pleasurable convulsions of the body. Not a single neurotic is orgastically potent, and the character structures of the overwhelming majority of men and women are neurotic.

Reich's strong indictment of the whole human race as being sexually inadequate, or at least not enjoying the full potential of sexual relations, is mainly what got him in trouble. He became obsessed with sex and in this regard far outdistanced Freud, who many thought the archsexologist. Reich's insistence that impeded orgasm was the primary cause of neuroses, and his unwillingness to accept any other explanation chilled his fellow psychoanalysts. Furthermore, he believed that dammed-up sexual excitation is due to "body armoring," i.e., inflexible muscles that retard full orgasmic release. Body armor has to be removed to permit the "streaming of biological energy," or orgone energy, to flow freely. With armoring gone, the individual will experience complete, earth-shaking orgasms, and love will conquer all. By 1934, the International Psychoanalytic Association had ousted him for his extreme views and intransigence.

Reich was not after small miracles; he wanted to usher in a new age of libido satisfaction such as the world had never seen. To achieve his majestic goal, he began treating patients in a very physical manner to purge the armor. Not only did he touch his patients — then verboten in psychoanalysis — but he used considerable force to break through their stubborn armor. His intimate massaging and pounding of patients went too far. He poked and prodded them, making their bodies black and blue, all in an attempt to destress their muscles. Reich's eccentric treatment marked him as imprudent and dangerous. One day soon, his estranged colleagues warned, he would embarrass the entire field of psychoanalysis.

But World War II intervened, and the controversial Reich left what he surely thought was a heavily-armored Germany (in both senses of the word) for a safe haven in America. He settled in Maine and after a time began conducting experiments with boxes that would collect orgone energy — the stuff of vibrant life. His orgone accumulators, which where large enough for a patient to stand in, could then be used for beneficial purposes: to recharge a human sexually for one, on up to curing cancer. Orgonon, his research center, oversaw the development and sale of orgone accumulators to the public. However, the Federal Drug Administration would have none of Reich and his fraudulent boxes. The FDA stopped the sale of what it condemned as outright quackery and ordered Reich to desist from further sales unless he wanted to go to court. By this time, Reich was ready to die for the just cause of orgonomy, the vernal science he had created. There was no turning back now. Reich succumbed to the FDA, was sentenced, and died a martyr in prison in Lewisburg, Pennsylvania.

His martyrdom is what is of interest to fad history. Because the FDA burned Reich's books, hoping orgonomy would disappear in flames, illicit copies of his writing began selling for a reported $80 a volume on New York's black market. Intellectuals like Norman Mailer—more concerned with Reich's mystique than his apparent pseudoscience—rallied behind the memory of the great thinker. Their common bond was the notion that sexual blockage caused all neuroses, a fact puritanical America did not want to accept. That alone was enough to prompt some rebels to become neo-Reichians. The villain in all this, the FDA, had never disputed the orgone theory; the federal agency simply wanted to protect the public from believing a trumped-up outhouse could cure impotence, cancer, and the common cold.

Foremost among Reich's admirers was Dr. Elsworth Baker, who continued dearmoring neurotics the Reichian way and wrote a book about it, *Man in the Trap: The Causes of Blocked Sexual Energy* (1967). Baker's book *Wilhelm Reich Selected Writings: An Introduction to Orgonomy* (1960) and *Me and the Orgone* (1971) by Orson Bean added to the popular Reichian literature. An actor, Orson Bean describes how Dr. Baker treated his neurosis by actually "gouging" his armored flesh, so that he felt like he had been placed inside a cement mixer. Bean responded well to the rough treatment and survived to praise Reich, Baker, and orgonomy in his amusing, though idolatrous, book. As late as 1982, a group of Reichian therapists in California had modified the forceful bludgeoning of armored flesh. They advocated a more docile series of breathing exercises to limber up the armor. Their neo-Reichian credo is not so accusatory:

> Male ejaculation is not orgasm as we see it from a Reichian perspective. Orgasm is a total body response—two lovers melting and merging into each other's bioenergetic fields. . . . Actually sex is an act of honor and physical aliveness and integrity. Sex is a virtue. A cross-cultural study reveals that other peoples that participate in healthy sexual and emotional expression do not have cancer, rape, pornography, war or any of the other miseries that we do.

It was Reich's mistake to maintain that sex was the underlying cause of all neuroses, and his orgone accumulators were pure folly.

Too often when a once-respected scientist espouses a personal obsession, people tend to believe every word. Then faddish thinking takes root, only to die out quickly once critical analysis commences.

BIBLIOGRAPHY

Baker, Elsworth F. *Man in the Trap: The Causes of Blocked Sexual Energy*. New York: Macmillan Company, 1967.
Bean, Orson. *Me and the Orgone*. New York: St. Martin's Press, 1971.
"Boxed-In." *Newsweek* 56 (September 5, 1960): 66-67.
Reich, Wilhelm. *Wilhelm Reich Selected Writings: An Introduction to Orgonomy*. New York: Farrar, Straus, and Giroux, 1960, 1973.
Wright, Bond. "Demystifying Reichian Therapy." *Issues in Radical Therapy* 10 (Fall 1982): 32-39.

Personal Names

When the Puritans broke from the Church of England and came to America, they left behind religious differences and their personal names. In the new land, they named their girls after virtues, e.g., Grace, Hope, Charity, Constance, Mercy, and Faith. Their male children received sterner appellations, e.g., Fear-Not, Increase, Sin-Deny, The-Lord-is-Near, and Praise-God. Also, the Puritans chose esoteric Old Testament names in a departure from reliance on the usual New Testament ones. Here their zeal for independent thinking went a bit too far. Instead of Matthew, Mark, Luke, and John, there was Zerubbabel, Zaphenathpanead, and Mahershalalhashbaz. Those truly God-fearing names must have taken a saint's patience to spell or pronounce. Of course, the Puritans did not regard their proclivity for lofty christenings as faddish, but succeeding generations of Americans have.

At the time of the Revolutionary War and the Continental Congress, the most popular names were, quite naturally, George Washington and John Hancock. Since Smith and Johnson were among the top five surnames (and still are), a significant number of babies born in the late 1700s bore the names George Washington Smith and John Hancock Johnson. Of record in 1775, Alexander Anderson of New York, whose wife had twins, named his boy child George Washington and his girl child Martha Dandridge, after the Commander-in-Chief's wife. Anderson's patriotism was unassailable. Other pre-1800 popular male names which were not the product of patriotism were Chauncey, Clinton, Eliot, Dwight, Cotton, Bradford, Endicott, Leverett, and Winthrop. All had a distinctive patrician ring. In the case of Cotton, the name indicated sizeable land holdings in that commodity. However, patriotic names have continued in vogue up to now, only changing as new heroes have emerged. After a while, George Washington Smith was no longer a great name, not when one could be called Benjamin Franklin Smith or Thomas Jefferson Smith or John Adams Smith. Then came John Marshall Smith, Andrew Jackson Smith, and Abraham Lincoln Smith. Closer to the present, there was Grover Cleveland Smith, Theodore Roosevelt Smith, and Franklin Delano Smith. John F. Kennedy has been the last president whose name Americans proudly attached to their own.

After the American Civil War, Elmer—today associated with a country bumpkin—was a well-liked name. The first hero of the war was Colonel Ephraim Elmer Ellsworth, killed at Alexandria, Virginia, May 24, 1861. The name stood for nobility and renown and was bestowed in that light. No one even thought about kidding Elmers back then. Elmer is a good example of a once-respected name that peaked quickly then fell into disuse because of its proliferation.

At present, most parents automatically select a middle name for their offspring. Yet in the nineteenth century, doing so was thought faddish. Lower-class Americans did not name their babies Thomas Jefferson Jones like the voguish upper class did. A baby born to them was simply Tom Jones. But having a sonorous middle name did seem to add stature, e.g., John Quincy Adams, James Fenimore Cooper, Francis Scott Key, and Charles Brockden Brown. A *Harper's Magazine* editorial suggested (December 1859):

> We might very easily, and perhaps wisely, revive the Roman usage, and give children, beside their proper name and that of the family, a middle name, taken from the most important ancestor or the most characteristic branch that has been grafted onto the family tree. . . . Such a custom does good by cherishing a proper family feeling, and suggesting the important truth that a man's blood is a fact significant enough to be looked after, whether to correct failings or to encourage virtues that run in its arteries.

After that the fad took hold, and besides, acquiring a middle name cost nothing and gave the child a second name to be called by. So it became popular for lower-class parents to mimic their betters and argue over a middle name. Half a century later the reverse was true, and Tom Jones sounded more congenial and less stuffy. The apex of informality arose when James Earl Carter, Jr. became the thirty-ninth President of the United States. He grinned and said, "Call me Jimmy." A later mid-twentieth-century fad that also encouraged informality was to take Jr., which normally follows the surname, and use it as a middle name, e.g., John Junior Jones.

During the nineteenth century, female names held a fairly steady course, with Ann, Dorothy, Elizabeth, Helen, Jane, Katharine, Margaret, and Mary the mainstays. But plain Jane got boring. Then romantic inventions etched birth certificates: Aletta, Blandina, Dovinda, Irista, Levantia, and Wealthena (wishful thinking?). Mothers steeped in gothic novels and chivalric poetry could not resist having a little Parnethia or Luzertta underfoot to remind them of knights and castles in the days of yore. In the late 1800s, diminutives attracted male attention, e.g., Lovie, Dolly, Hattie, and Nellie. Some men liked their come-hither appeal, while other, more self-righteous males considered such female ploys too obvious. A girl named Lovie was doubtless a frivolous creature intent on quick marriage and control of the purse strings. In the twentieth century, the silver screen substituted for romantic literature, and girl babies were named after such female stars as Theda Bara, Jean Harlow, Ava Gardner, Marilyn Monroe, and Raquel Welch. A recent development is for the disenchanted owner of a standard name to change its spelling. Jane becomes Jayn; Susan becomes not Suzan but Soosan; Mary becomes Mari or Marri; even Gigi, which already has a casual look to it, becomes Gygi. All these newly styled names are pure Hollywood and faint attempts on the part of plain people to appear different, exotic, or somehow mysterious.

In 1898, among the plain names, Mary and John were the most popular. Fifty years later, Linda and Robert were favorites. In 1964, Lisa and Michael topped the list. In 1973, Jennifer beat out Lisa, but Michael held on. Other current favorites for girls are: Jessica, Nicole, Melissa, Michelle (after the Beatles' song), Maria, Lisa, Elizabeth, and Christine; and for boys: David, Christopher, Joseph, Anthony, Robert, Jason, James, and Daniel. It's anyone's guess how long these serviceable names will remain in vogue. As we approach the twenty-first century, who knows what science fictional dubbings we'll hear? Perhaps one-word names taken from the end of the alphabet like Xenon, Ytterbia, and Zardok.

Black names have also followed faddish dictates. During slave days, white masters conferred on their male property easy-to-remember names like Tom, Joe, John, Henry, and Jim. Black women were called Mary, Nancy, Eliza, Jane, and Ann. Their African names were not used, for the obvious reason that as slaves they had no choice but to assimilate. A faddish exception to the rule of doling out sturdy English names was to bestow the now detested Sambo. According to Maryland birth records, the first instance of naming a black male Sambo occurred in 1692 and thereafter slipped into common usage. Over time, Sambo came to apply generically to all black males, which was a humiliation hard to live down. When the Emancipation Proclamation freed the slaves, blacks also liberated their names. They delighted in calling one another by faddish pet names that eventually obscured what was on their birth certificates. Alligator, Buckshot, Doodle Bug, Frog, Ivory, Monkeydo, Possum, Sausage, and Two-Bits were just some of their happy monikers. With freedom, blacks also embraced names of great classical heroes such as Hannibal, Caesar, Cato, and Ulysses. Black women preferred more ethereal names like Wind, Hail, Storm, Freeze, Morning, Cotton, Easter, and Harvest. Given a choice, blacks did not pick Sambo.

A hundred years after the Emancipation Proclamation, the Civil Rights Act was passed and brought with it a new awareness of black heritage. To demonstrate their racial pride, Afro-Americans looked back to Africa for their names. Black Muslims encouraged followers to replace their slave surnames with Xs. Given names were to be purely African or Arabic, e.g., Satonya, Nadra, Luhema, and Muhammad Sharieff. Appropriating names of famous people continued as usual, but in lieu of paying respect to white leaders, African leaders got the nod, e.g., Patrice Lumumba Jones and Jomo Kenyatta Brown. Black pride also concocted such a name as Kwame Nyerere Bongodiea, a combination of two African statesmen and a Jamaican holiday drink.

In naming their children, parents draw inspiration from one of these categories:

1. In honor of another person, usually a relative
2. In admiration of a famous person (Dante Gabriel Rossetti after Dante Alighieri)
3. Because it harmonizes with the surname (Clark Gable, rather than Sylvester Gable)
4. After some circumstance of birth (place born: Atlanta; having triplets: Faith, Hope, and Charity)
5. To show strength of purpose (Grace, Luther)
6. Descriptive of the child (Blanche, Rufus)
7. For an object (Daisy, Pearl)
8. Because of association with the surname (Lily White, Peter Streeter)
9. From error (Vagina instead of Virginia)
10. To be eccentric (completely made up names or calling a boy Sybil, and a girl Frederick)
11. As a result of chance (first name seen after opening a book, first name mentioned by a visitor, drawing the name from a hat)
12. From invention (Ethyle for Ethel)

The tenth category was strained to its limits during the "Do your own thing" 1960s and 1970s. The radical activist Abbie Hoffman named his son "america" with a small "a." Rock musician Frank Zappa liked the sound of "Moon Unit Zappa" for his baby girl. The flamboyant and unchaste Cher decided on "Chastity" for her little girl. And falsetto singer Tiny Tim, whose most famous song was "Tiptoe Through the Tulips," picked for his daughter, what else — "Tulip." Some other fanciful appellations were: Twila Delilah Blonigan, Sividious Stark, and Luther Orange Lemon; some amusing appellations: a father of 11 who lived up to his name, Peter Rabbit, and a millionaire oilman named Carbon Petroleum Dubbs; and some downright embarrassing appellations: Harry Ball, Dick Head, and Ima Hogg. Parents who delight in silly names spawn a good deal of mischief. Somewhere a poor child has to stand up in class on the first day and say in a clear voice, "I'm Harry Ball," only to hear later in the hall, "Where's your twin brother, just hanging around?"

BIBLIOGRAPHY

Andersen, Christopher P. *The Name Game*. New York: Simon and Schuster, 1977.

"Black Names." *Newsweek* 72 (July 29, 1968): 88.

Mencken, H. L. *The American Language, Supplement II*. New York: A. Knopf, 1948.

Smith, Edison C. *The Story of Our Names*. New York: Harper & Brothers, 1950.

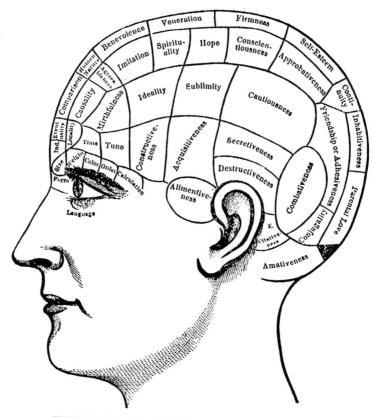

NUMBERING AND DEFINITION OF THE ORGANS.

1. AMATIVENESS, Love between the sexes.
A. CONJUGALITY, Matrimony—love of one. [etc.
2. PARENTAL LOVE, Regard for offspring, pets,
3. FRIENDSHIP, Adhesiveness—sociability.
4. INHABITIVENESS, Love of home.
5. CONTINUITY, One thing at a time.
E. VITATIVENESS, Love of life.
6. COMBATIVENESS, Resistance—defense.
7. DESTRUCTIVENESS, Executiveness—force.
8. ALIMENTIVENESS, Appetite—hunger.
9. ACQUISITIVENESS, Accumulation.
10. SECRETIVENESS, Policy—management.
11. CAUTIOUSNESS, Prudence—provision.
12. APPROBATIVENESS, Ambition—display.
13. SELF-ESTEEM, Self-respect—dignity.
14. FIRMNESS, Decision—perseverance.
15. CONSCIENTIOUSNESS, Justice equity.
16. HOPE, Expectation - enterprise.
17. SPIRITUALITY, Intuition—faith—credulity.
18. VENERATION, Devotion—respect.
19. BENEVOLENCE, Kindness—goodness.

20. CONSTRUCTIVENESS, Mechanical ingenuity
21. IDEALITY, Refinement—taste—purity.
B. SUBLIMITY, Love of grandeur—infinitude.
22. IMITATION, Copying—patterning.
23. MIRTHFULNESS, Jocoseness—wit—fun.
24. INDIVIDUALITY, Observation.
25. FORM, Recollection of shape.
26. SIZE, Measuring by the eye.
27. WEIGHT, Balancing—climbing.
28. COLOR, Judgment of colors.
29. ORDER, Method · system - arrangement.
30. CALCULATION, Mental arithmetic.
31. LOCALITY, Recollection of places.
32. EVENTUALITY, Memory of facts.
33. TIME, Cognizance of duration.
34. TUNE, Sense of harmony and melody.
35. LANGUAGE, Expression of ideas.
36. CAUSALITY, Applying causes to effect. [tion.
37. COMPARISON, Inductive reasoning—illustra-
C. HUMAN NATURE, Perception of motives.
D. AGREEABLENESS, Pleasantness—suavity.

Phrenologists claimed they could read a person's character just by rubbing his or her head. A little bump here signified amativeness, a little bump there indicated mirth, and so on. Phrenology was a harmless pursuit until practitioners used it to sort out the mentally-ill for confinement and suspected criminals for hanging. (1840s)

Phrenology

Franz Joseph Gall (1758-1828), a Viennese physician-anatomist, in collecting human skulls noticed that they displayed a wide variety of "prominences." From further study of the skulls, Gall deduced that the assortment of prominences could be categorized, each with a meaning. In fact, they gave evidence of an individual's personality and mental powers. An enlarged prominence on the back of the skull meant something entirely different from one on the front or side. Slowly, over a period of years, Gall propounded what he called the new science of craniology to tell the world what he had learned about skull contours. Gall's pupil, Johann Spurzheim (1776-1832), assisted his mentor by publicizing craniology through a series of lectures. Spurzheim added his own observations about skull contours and renamed the new science phrenology (mind + study). Phrenology was the apter term, since the prominences revealed brain functioning and not just insignificant bony excrescences. Spurzheim enthralled audiences when he asserted the new science could detect good and bad modes of thinking and even better, could modify the modes.

Not long after Gall and Spurzheim had died, Americans began to hear more about phrenology from articles in national journals. This one from *The New England Magazine* (November 1834) reported the pros and cons of what had already captivated Europe:

> Dr. Spurzheim maintained that the brain is the organ of the mind; that the several parts or convolutions of the brain are organs of the several powers and dispositions of the mind; that the strength of the power or disposition depends mainly on the size of the convolution, and the particular temperament of body, with which it is connected; and so that, to the Phrenologist, it is a mere work of observation to determine the charac-

ter of any man's mind, his weak and prevailing propensities, his excellences and defects.

Evidently, people caught up in the ensuing rage for phrenology did not flinch at its preposterous claim. They read authoritative texts, attended astute lectures, and believed wholeheartedly that a phrenologist could "determine the character of any man's mind" by rubbing the man's head. But luckily, in the same article, good sense prevailed:

> He [the phrenologist] will observe objects, as suits his convenience, through either end of the telescope. And he will be more likely to do this, because he compares what is visible with what is invisible. . . . There is great danger that the Phrenologist will adapt the head to the character, and the character to the head; that, in support of his favorite theory, he will, unintentionally, perhaps, exaggerate or depreciate facts, which he learns by moral observation, so as to suit them to mechanical development.

As it turned out, "moral observation" was really at the heart of the matter. It was simply uncanny how a phrenologist found abnormal prominences in, say, a confessed thief that proved he was a thief, or in a repentant adulterer that proved she was an adulterer.

Of the many popular phrenology texts published a decade later in the 1840s, one by L. N. Fowler, *The Principles of Phrenology and Physiology Applied to Man's Social Relations; Together with an Analysis of the Domestic Feelings* (1842), shows just how far the new science had advanced in America. Building on Gall and Spurzheim, Fowler discusses the four mental faculties most requisite to achieving a solid marriage. The first faculty is amativeness, which is "situated in the cerebellum, giving width between and behind the ears." Prominences in this skull area signify that a person is more susceptible to love and more loveable. Large amativeness, however, can indicate overdeveloped passion and even licentiousness. The next faculty is philoprogenitiveness, "located immediately above the middle of the cerebellum, from which it is separated by a small membrane, called the tentorium, directly under the centre of the occipital bone." Prominences in this skull area denote instinctive love for children, and pronounced philogenitiveness means the person will feel deeply for a weak and destitute offspring. Adhesiveness is the third faculty: "It is located upon both sides of Philoprogenitiveness, outward and above." Noticeable development in this skull area discloses that the person will be loyal to his or her object of affection. The final faculty essential for a lasting marriage is inhabitiveness: "It is located directly over Philoprogenitiveness, being supported upon both sides by Adhesiveness." Rises in this skull area assert that the person isn't a rolling stone, but one who will remain content at home.

Of the four mental faculties, amativeness most concerned another Fowler. O. S. Fowler, L. N.'s brother, penned an essay entitled, "Amativeness, Embracing the Evils and Remedies of Excessive and Perverted Sexuality, Including Warning and Advice to the Married and Single," in which he took to the pulpit. According to O. S., a person with prominent amativeness should abstain from all sexual relations and pray daily for restraint; should take lots of cold baths, wear wet bandages, and shave the organ (the pubic region, not the head); should avoid all stimulants and irritants and "keep doing"; and should get married at the first opportunity.

In the 1840s, phrenological diagrams sold at a rapid rate. The standard diagram illustrated the location of the 37 faculties or organs of thought, so that the skull resembled a butcher's meat chart. In addition to Fowler's four faculties, there were vitativeness—"love of life"; secretiveness—"management policy"; ideality—"refinement and taste"; mirthfulness—"wit and sense of fun," and tune—"sense of harmony and melody," to name a few. Phrenological examination of a person's skull to determine suitability for marriage was a less harmful fad than employing the new science to assess criminality. A book such as Marmaduke B. Sampson's *Criminal Jurisprudence Considered in Relation to Cerebral Organization* went through three editions (1841, 1842, 1846) and was declared a valuable contribution to American penology. Again, this treatise insisted that the inner workings of the mind were an open book for the phrenologist to read by tracing the contours of the skull. But this time the psuedoscientific fad threatened society in two ways: first, proponents of phrenology advocated executing all mentally ill persons who "might" commit a crime; and second, even though the chance of an incorrect reading was so great as to render the effort worthless, phrenologists could bully anyone they so desired. To his credit, Sampson said:

> Above all things we should remember mitigation of the evil tendencies of the lowest mind is never impossible, so long as lesion of the brain has not taken place. . . . To destroy the life of a fellow-creature, in whom any improvement may be effected, must be an act of wickedness and brutality.

But Sampson's sensitivity to the capital punishment question did not preclude phrenologically typing a "fellow-creature" as one who should be watched like a hawk.

BIBLIOGRAPHY

Davies, John Dunn. *Phrenology Fad and Science: A 19th Century American Crusade*. New Haven: Yale University Press, 1955.
"Phrenology." *The New England Magazine* 7 (November 1834): 467-479.
"Phrenology Vindicated." *The New England Magazine* 7 (December 1834): 433-444.
Rosenberg, Charles, and Carroll Smith-Rosenberg, eds. *Sex and Science: Phrenological Reflections on Sex and Marriage in Nineteenth Century America*. New York: Arno Press, 1974. (Contains the two Fowler studies.)
Sampson, Marmaduke B. *Rationale of Crime; Criminal Jurisprudence Considered in Relation to Cerebral Organization*. Montclair, NJ: Patterson Smith, 1973. (Reprint of 1846 edition.)

Politically Correct

In the 1990s, being politically correct (PC) requires that a person watch what he or she says so that no one is offended. Part of being PC has to do with manners and sensitivity toward the feelings of others. All racial slurs should be eliminated: don't call a black an Oreo; an Asian, a banana; a Mexican, a coconut; an Italian, a grease ball; and so on. Only ill-bred people do that. Renouncing racial slurs is a precondition for being PC. The rest of the requirements are more demanding.

The Multicultural Management Program Fellows have compiled a reference guide, *Dictionary of Cautionary Words and Phrases*, to foster politically correct journalism, and for society at large, politically correct communication. Unpublished, though highlighted in numerous articles, the dictionary immediately raised eyebrows because its contents seemed to be satirical when in fact they were serious. According to the dictionary, if these words are in your vocabulary you had better banish them:

Articulate: Can be considered offensive when referring to a minority, particularly a black person, and his or her ability to handle the English language.

Beauty: Avoid descriptive terms of beauty when not absolutely necessary. For instance, do not use "blond and blue-eyed" unless you would also use "brown-haired and brown-eyed" as a natural measure of attractiveness.

Leader: Use with caution. Be more specific: black politician, black activist. Implies person has approval of an entire group of people.

Soulful: Can be objectionable adjective when applied strictly to blacks.

Sweetie: Objectionable term of endearment. Do not use.

Without rhythm: A stereotype about whites. Implies that others have rhythm, also a stereotype.

Woman: The preferred term for a female adult. Girl is appropriate only for those 17 years old and under. Avoid gal and lady. Also avoid derogatory terms for women, such as skirt, broad, chick, bimbo, babe, and little woman. Also avoid adjectives describing female physical attributes such as pert, petite, foxy, buxom, fragile, feminine, stunning, gorgeous, statuesque, or full-figured.

Verbal self-censorship got its start in the early 1970s with the Women's Liberation Movement. Two decades ago, feminists insisted that man was not the measure of all things and demanded parity. Forerunners of the *Dictionary of Cautionary Words and Phrases* focused on nonsexist language like woman in the above example. These guides proliferated and made some impact on common usage. Not only were women given their due, but other minorities as well. Occasionally, an absurd use occurred such as the construction s/he for he and she, though mostly newfound respect resulted from the use of nonsexist language. Humorous dispute between the sexes peaked when feminists spoke of God as She.

Being politically correct today assumes the use of nonsexist language, but goes far beyond that. PC calls for revision of history. In Academe, where it flourishes sporadically, PC has taken on these dimensions. At Georgetown, a literature class, White Male Writers, examines the works of Hawthorne, Melville, and Faulkner. The notion here is to label the class correctly and to deemphasize any importance it might have over Black Male Writers or White Female Writers. A Stanford professor won't discuss manifest destiny and American Imperialism because minority people were crushed in the onslaught; to do so would be "morally distortive." At Kenyon College, a class on the biology of female sexuality taught in the biology department does not stick to pure science, but centers more on ethics, social status, and "women's realities." Being PC polarizes campuses. The PC professor is thought to be either a crusader or eccentric. To illustrate eccentricity, a team-taught course, "Introduction to Women's Studies," at the University of Washington brought to light that the nuclear family is dysfunctional, that masturbation is preferable to male dominance, and that lesbians make the best parents. When a male student asked for proof of the assertions, the feminist professor retorted, "Why are you challenging me?"

Charles J. Sykes, author of *ProfScam: Professors and the Demise of Higher Education*, and Brad Miner, literary editor for *National Review*, reported in a cover story for *National Review:*

> Across the country, teachers and students are directed to avoid giving offense to any individual or group officially designated as oppressed. What's more, teachers and students are asked to accept a new kind of scholarship, a "scholarship of advocacy" designed to both enhance the self-esteem of the oppressed and to upset the oppressor's monopoly on power.

On face value, scholarship of advocacy has merit, if not for the zealots who abuse it. Dialogues, not diatribes, on lesbianism have their place in Academe; the hateful opinion that masturbation should replace male companionship and the unfounded declaration that lesbians make better parents.

Being PC in all its manifestations becomes very problematic. Texas has a large, ever-growing Mexican-American population. The State requires that Texas history be taught to every student. To be PC in a San Antonio classroom means to play down or forget that Texas settlers despised Mexicans enough to fight a War of Independence and thereafter to punish Mexicans for any attempted reencroachment. The same can be said for every state in the union and its disputatious people; history is one long chronicle of hate. Taken further, what if the American Civil War was made PC? Jefferson Davis would become the equal of Abraham Lincoln and a speech of his engraved next to the Gettysburg Address. Both the North and South would have equally good reasons for going to war. And instead of viewing the war as wanton fratricide, the idea that it was a gallant error would prevail.

Should history placate every sensibility? Can human nature accept equality among races? In a positive vein, these are the questions PC addresses. Negatively, PC creates the same dissension it tries to shun. At New York's City College, a professor teaches that blacks are "sun people"—warm, communal, and intuitive, and that whites are "ice people"—cold, individualistic, and brutal. The outcome of such teaching is, of course, reverse discrimination.

Note: The Multicultural Management Program Fellows whose dictionary will become a fad classic is politically incorrect. The dictionary's chief editor, Sandra Coombes, is not a fellow; she is a woman.

BIBLIOGRAPHY

Coleman, James S. "A Quiet Threat to Academic Freedom." *National Review* 43 (March 18, 1991): 28 + .

Coombes, Sandra, et al. *Dictionary of Cautionary Words and Phrases*. Consortium of Newspaper Journalists: Multicultural Management Program Fellows, 1989. Unpublished.

Goodman, Walter. "Decreasing Our Word Power: The New Newspeak." *New York Times Book Review* 96 (January 27, 1991): 14.

Henry, William A. "Upside Down in the Groves of Academe." *Time* 137 (April 1, 1991): 66-69.

Taylor, John. "Are You Politically Correct?" *New York* 24 (January 21, 1991): 32-40.

Primal Therapy

Psychologist Arthur Janov wrote *The Primal Scream* (1970) and *The Anatomy of Mental Illness* (1971) to announce a revolutionary psychotherapy. His first book explains the genesis of primal therapy and how it works in practice, while his second book establishes the "scientific" basis for it. Together the books contain over 650 pages of brisk reading that seem to unveil the cure for all types of neuroses. Both books became bestsellers, and soon celebrities like John Lennon and the actor James Earl Jones underwent primal therapy. Janov had already opened the Primal Institute in Los Angeles with high hopes that it would be successful. He did not have to wait long to realize his goal. Patients kept coming for treatment — more than he could handle, requiring the Institute to expand into larger quarters. Shortly thereafter, Janov cut the ribbon on a second institute in New York. He trained his clinicians himself, one of whom was his wife, Vivian, and discredited anyone who attempted to practice primal therapy without a certificate from the Primal Institute.

Dr. Janov fondly relates how he discovered the primal scream — the orgasmic high point of primal therapy — in the introduction to his first book. During standard therapy, a patient told of seeing a comedian in London. The comedian, a full-grown man, waddled around on stage dressed only in a diaper as he gulped milk from a bottle. Once the laughs died down, he shouted at the top of his lungs, "Mommy! Daddy! Mommy! Daddy!" After a few minutes of this childish humor, the comedian bent over and vomited. He passed out plastic bags and requested that the audience do the same — end of the act. Janov quickly discerned that what his patient had seen on the London stage must have been unforgettable for some reason. So Janov asked his patient to call out like the comedian, "Mommy! Daddy! Mommy! Daddy!" Reluctantly, the patient did and immediately fell into a fit. He writhed on the floor in agony, and his breathing became spasmodic as he screeched,

"Mommy! Daddy! Mommy! Daddy!" over and over. At last, a final "deathlike" scream issued from his trembling lips, which Janov said, "rattled the walls of my office." Somehow the scream liberated years of emotional frustration bound up inside the patient, who rejoiced, "I made it! I don't know what, but I can feel!" A few months later, another patient sat in Janov's office and complained that his parents habitually criticized him and did not love him like they should. Remembering his earlier idiosyncratic patient, Janov seized the opportunity to observe a repeat performance and asked his current patient to call out for his Mommy and Daddy. Breathing faster and deeper each time he did, the patient writhed until his near-convulsions culminated in a lung-bursting scream. Upon returning to normal the patient said his whole life suddenly became clear, and he now understood many troubling things in his past. Later, Janov, who had taped both sessions, replayed them, noting the unmistakable similarities from the onset of the fit to the ear-splitting scream to the great relief felt afterwards. From that point on, he asked other patients to call out for their parents until he had enough proof of the efficacy of the technique. Each time the results were nearly the same, so that Dr. Janov could state:

> I have come to regard that scream as the product of central and universal pains which reside in all neurotics. I call them Primal Pains because they are original, early hurts upon which all later neurosis is built. It is my contention that these pains exist in every neurotic each minute of his later life, irrespective of the form of his neurosis. These pains often are not consciously felt because they are diffused throughout the entire system where they affect body organs, muscles, the blood and lymph system and, finally, the distorted way we believe.

Thus, the primal scream saw light of day. In practice, it took several sessions to open up the patient before the big moment came. The primal therapist coaxed the patient into recalling the earliest memories of his or her parents, ranging back to infancy. Bad memories triggered the need to scream. Dr. Janov describes the event:

The Primal Scream is not a scream for its own sake. Nor is it used as a tension release. When it results from deep, wracking feeling, I believe it is a curative process, rather than simply a release of tension. It is not the scream that is curative, in any case; it is the Pain. . . . The real Primal Scream is unmistakable. It has its own quality of something deep, rattling, and involuntary. What comes out when the person screams is a single feeling that may underlie thousands of previous experiences: "Daddy, don't hurt me anymore!"; "Mama, I'm afraid!"

In 1978, the cost for a year of primal therapy was $6,600. Competing psychotherapists considered Janov's use of teddy bears, cribs, and other baby props to hasten remembrance of infant hurt unscientific foolishness. But his critics really shook their fingers at his hiring uncredentialed workers and making them therapists. So the props went, and Janov's therapists got their graduate degrees. But even with these moves toward credibility, there still remained considerable doubt whether one could cure neuroses through the sole expedient of reliving early pain. Over half a century before Janov, Sigmund Freud had reflected on the notion and discarded it. That must have been difficult for Freud, a man whose more controversial theories are based on childhood fixations. Yet, Freud did abandon the notion as too simplistic and lacking in therapeutic value. Janov claimed primal therapy worked because his patients experienced decreased levels of adrenalin. Less adrenalin to overstimulate the body means reduced stress, and reduced stress pacifies the debilitating effect of neuroses.

Some followers of Janov have taken primal therapy even further. One theorist believes that emotional distress begins in the fetus, transmitted to the developing child by a neurotic mother. In this case, the patient would have to relive life in the womb before uttering a primal scream. And there are those theologians who maintain that primal neurotic disorders are generational, which hark back to the fall of man from grace; therefore, when the primal scream breaks loose, it calls out to Adam and all his begets. Freud or no Freud, Janov's primal therapy made its way to the Federal Republic of Germany, where two legal cases questioned the validity of the therapy. The German courts decided that insurance companies did not have to pay for primal therapy because it scarcely appeared in the professional literature, signifying rejection. Furthermore, testimony in court revealed that most German psychotherapists perceived primal therapy as dangerous and theoretically unsound. A number of American psychotherapists likewise concurred. Considered a fad and an embarrassment in profession circles, primal therapy continues to this day. Janov's original Primal Institute in Los Angeles still treats patients intent on rattling office walls.

BIBLIOGRAPHY

Janov, Arthur. *The Anatomy of Mental Illness: The Scientific Basis of Primal Therapy*. New York: G. P. Putnam's Sons, 1971.

————. *The Primal Scream*. New York: G. P. Putnam's Sons, 1970.

Moss, Roger C. "Frank Lake's Maternal-Fetus Distress Syndrome and Primal Integration Workshops." *Pre-and-Peri-Natal-Psychology Journal* 1 (Fall 1986): 52-68.

"The 'Screaming Cure.'" *Newsweek* 92 (July 10, 1978): 12.

Torrey, E. Fuller. "Primal Therapy Trip: Medicine or Religion?" *Psychology Today* 10 (December 1976): 62 +.

Van-Rooy, Gordon. "Treating Infected Sin Through Primal Therapy." *Journal of Psychology and Christianity* 5 (Fall 1986): 32-36.

Psychoanalysis

As soon as Americans heard of Sigmund Freud's theories of how the mind works, they began to ponder the immense implications. Do all human beings actually live two separate lives: a conscious one known through daily living and an unconscious one — hidden, mysterious, turbulent, the key to waking life? Boni and Liveright published Freud's *A General Introduction to Psychoanalysis* in 1920, reprinting it in 1921, 1925, 1926, 1927, and 1935. The book consists of 28 lectures divided into three parts: "The Psychology of Errors," "The Dream," and "General Theory of the Neuroses." Glued to the pages, readers blanched at the thought that they made errors every day because their subconscious willed them to do so. More unnerving, readers learned that their dreams were really wish fulfillments and, in the sexual realm, often animalistic. But globes of sweat broke out when readers discovered that thwarted desires at the subconscious level — mainly sexual ones — ruled their lives and made them do obsessive things. Freud explained that to cure a neurosis, one has to determine what is behind the symptoms, then reveal the truth to the patient, which in turn unties the emotional knot causing the neurosis. Simple as that, reading *A General Introduction* was like talking to God. The good doctor knew everything there was to know about a person's psyche.

Even in translation, Freud's prose charmed his captive audience. He wrote more like a poet than a scientist. For example, his concept of the different working parts of the mind:

> We will compare the system of the unconscious to a large ante-chamber, in which the psychic impulses rub elbows with one another, as separate beings. There opens out of this ante-chamber another, a smaller room, a sort of parlor, which consciousness occupies. But on the threshold between the two rooms there stands a watchman; he passes on the individual

psychic impulses, censors them, and will not let them into the parlor if they do not meet with his approval.

Considerable enchantment enlivened Freud's pages, although sex talk in other parts of the book turned some readers away in disgust. The prudish blushed scarlet at the notion that sexual longing inspires most human acts — even in infancy! The supposition was just too shocking to bear, and Freud was surely a pervert. Was beautiful Vienna on the Danube, where Freud practiced psychoanalysis, Sodom and Gomorrah? How could an intelligent man spew out such filth? Whether one believed Freud a great thinker or a crank, during his ascendancy in the 1920s there was no denying his impact. A writer for *Current Opinion* made this observation (September 1920):

> One can hardly pick up a newspaper or a magazine without finding psychoanalytic terms. The "conflicts" from which we all suffer; the "ambivalent" attitude which we feel toward so many people and things; the "suppressed desires" which poison our lives, are becoming subjects of daily conversation.

Not all Americans were impressed with Freud. Dr. Frederick Peterson wrote in the *Journal of the American Medical Association* that Freud twisted dream content to fit his theories and that sublimation of sex was no more responsible for the creation of civilization than sublimation of hunger or other human drives. Dr. George Matheson Cullen stated in the *Dublin Review* that Freud had erected a "monstrous system" dependent on a bogus "psychic reality." And worse, psychoanalysis in practice resulted in transference of libidinal desire. The patient became emotionally bound to the analyst and instead of being cured, faced an additional problem more perilous than the first.

Faddish interest in psychoanalysis ballooned during the 1920s, so by decade's end, respected psychiatrist Dr. Karl Menninger felt compelled to regain perspective on Freud's theories. Dr. Menninger disliked the rampant misinformation circulating about psychoanalysis, a form of gossip he called "pseudoanalysis." With their brows furrowed, Americans discussed Freud, but few understood him:

I have seen a bantamweight Italian laborer pause a moment in his toil, lean a pick over a sweaty shoulder, and tell his brawny fellow worker that he had an inferiority complex. I have heard a little girl implore her mother to throw away her inhibitions and take her to the circus. As Freud, himself, points out in a recent article, the popularity of psychoanalysis in the United States is no real evidence either of a friendly attitude or a profound understanding on the part of its adherents.

People who read Freud casually or got their knowledge of his theories from a telephone conversation or party talk suddenly began dissecting one another. Relatives, friends, business associates, anyone and everyone exhibited Freudian complexes and hid behind Freudian defense mechanisms. Before Freud, these objects of scrutiny were ordinary human beings doing ordinary things. But after Freud, they became dramatis personae in an unending tragic play. So quickly did Freudian terminology enter American vocabulary that there was no doubt what it all meant. People knew their Freud. Dr. Menninger suspected otherwise:

To say a man has a complex, particularly one of the pristine pair, the Oedipus and the Inferiority, is to say exactly nothing at all. Every one has an Oedipus complex — an occasional desire for release from mature existence, and a return to the peace of the womb or the crib. And until evolution grants to the human another metamorphosis, we will, all of us, have inferiority feelings — complexes — about something or other. It is just about as relevant to say that so-and-so has a complex as to say he has a nose.

Dr. Menninger on defense mechanisms:

To indicate that a defense mechanism is abnormal is to admit the abnormality of the race. There is no one who does not use protective poses — however well or mistakenly — to lessen hurt, or avoid admission of disadvantageous positions.

And so on, for the entire Freudian lexicon. It's a good thing Dr. Menninger spoke out because no one would have listened to Freud.

BIBLIOGRAPHY

"Is Freudism Destined to Live?" *Current Opinion* 69 (September 1920): 355-358.

Menninger, Karl. "Pseudoanalysis: Perils of Freudian Verbalisms." *Outlook and Independent* 155 (July 9, 1930): 363 + .

"A Physician's Warning Against Psycho-Analysis." *Current Opinion* 71 (August 1921): 222-224.

Pyramid Power

The notion that a pyramid can harness psychic or some other power comes from the book, *Psychic Discoveries Behind the Iron Curtain* (1970), by Shelia Ostrander and Lynn Schroeder. The authors report a story they heard about a Frenchman, Monsieur Bovis (no first name given), who visited the Great Pyramid of Cheops in Egypt (no date when Bovis was there). Inside the King's Chamber, the Frenchman noticed a trash can full of dead cats. The curious felines had wandered into the Chamber, became lost, and died without food. Clean-up crews deposited the cats in the trash can. It was all very routine except for the fact the cats were perfectly mummified. Bovis rushed home and constructed a scale model of the Great Pyramid, complete with King's Chamber one-third of the way up between the base and apex. When he placed a dead cat on the platform, it mummified (no indication how long it took), as did other organic matter.

Before Ostrander and Schroeder introduced Monsieur Bovis to America, he was already something of a celebrity in Europe. A Czech radio engineer, Karel Drbal, read Bovis' published findings and applied pyramid power to solving an everyday problem. Drbal conducted several experiments before announcing that razor blades placed inside a scale model Cheops pyramid maintained their sharpness for a much longer period than normal. Elated, Drbal patented his "Cheops Pyramid Razor-Blade Sharpener" in 1959. Now the news excited people because previously there was no market for mummified cats. But keeping razor blades sharp for weeks grabbed attention. In America, pyramid power acquired an air of legitimacy when G. Patrick Flanagan, a child prodigy and physicist, looked into the matter. He discovered the pyramid shape is an effective resonator of randomly polarized microwave signals which can be converted into electrical power. Soon Dr. Flanagan marketed the "Pat Flanagan Experimental Sensor" for $12.95. The consumer

Due to their shape and imposing grandeur, the Egyptian pyramids have long been thought to house occult powers. Consumers in the 1970s bought pyramid products to do everything from tenderize meat to increase sexual potency. However, the original claim that a model pyramid could resharpen razor blades was never proven.

also needed to buy his book, *Pyramid Power*, for $6.95 to use the sensor properly. His weren't the only pyramid products available during the mid-1970s. There were many other sources of pyramidabilia. Pyramids came in all sizes and prices, from tabletop models to large-size tents.

But then why would anyone want to own a pyramid of any size except for a conversation piece? As claimed in books on the subject, pyramid power works miracles right before your eyes. It preserves food, removes bitterness from coffee, enhances the taste of wine, tenderizes meat, keeps milk fresh, purifies polluted water, relieves headaches, promotes restful sleep, aids meditation, accelerates bodily healing, speeds plant growth, polishes tarnished jewelry, keeps razor blades sharp (Drbal would be proud), and improves sexual performance. Making rump steak taste like filet mignon or turning a dull bedroom into a passion pit agitated consumers. By the end of 1975, Pyramid Products in Glendale, California, had sold 238,000 of its "Cheops Pyramid Tent," the standard model priced at $29.95 and the deluxe model with double zippers priced at $37.50. Ostensibly, the tent revitalized the person who merely sat inside it, and for anyone who slept there, heightened sensuality and ESP. Other pyramid products sold just as well and were very ingenious in design. Also by Pyramid Products, the "Pyramid Energy Generator" looked like a muffin tin turned upside down displaying twenty pyramids painted gold, each one inch high. The generator attracted and dispensed power throughout the consumer's living quarters for a variety of unseen uses. The next year, in 1976, Len Sausen, an executive with Ralen Marketing on Fifth Avenue in New York City, made a quick fortune with pyramid power. He had seen a physicist (Dr. Flanagan?) on a TV talk show explaining the basics about the mysterious power. Sausen hung on every word, and overnight thousands of plastic pyramids with little King's Chambers rolled down his assembly line. That Christmas, Ralen Marketing grossed $1 million selling plastic pyramids on a total investment of $150,000. Selling them was a snap since Napoleon had already talked up pyramid power. More than a century earlier, the French emperor had spent a night in the Great Pyramid of Cheops and upon exiting the next morning told his retinue he had experienced the supernatural. What happened to him he wouldn't say because no one would believe him. After such a promo and other hints of the occult, consumers had to have one of Sausen's pyramids (retail $5; manufacturing cost $.47).

The fad makers and faddists who saturated themselves in pyramid power forgot a few things in their headlong lust. Originally, Monsieur Bovis duplicated the Great Pyramid of Cheops as best he could. That meant he built a scale model with each side sloping precisely 51 degrees and the base fixed on exact east-west, north-south axes. He carefully attached the King's Chamber one-third of the way up from the base to the apex. And most crucial of all, he set his scale model in an area free of electrical disturbance. Monsieur Bovis' exacting specifications weren't followed to the letter on the assembly line. Even though pyramid power is a classic fad, there seems to be some truth to it, at least if one can put any faith in home experimentation. *Science Digest* received reports from readers that placing a razor blade inside a pyramid did indeed keep it sharp — for 40 to 50 shaves! In another report, a banana left under a pyramid for ten days remained golden yellow and tasted better than usual. Plants greened up faster and meditators experienced greater bliss inside pyramids. A few killjoys like Bill D. Miller, writing in *Mechanix Illustrated*, did not have such good luck. Miller tried the famous Drbal test and got a bloodletting blade for his trouble. Later, he was told his pyramid and the blade inside were not correctly aligned and there were too many electrical disturbances in his house. A fluorescent light, a radiator, and a television obstructed the generation of pyramid power. His only recourse was to move his family to the Sahara.

BIBLIOGRAPHY

"A Christmas Merchandising Story." *Forbes* 118 (December 15, 1976): 31.

Grosswirth, Marvin. "Pyramid Power." *Science Digest* 79 (February 1976): 26-33.

Miller, Bill D. "The Crack in the Pyramid." *Mechanix Illustrated* 73 (September 1977): 32-33.

Newman, Edwin. "O Great Cheops, What Hath Thy Offspring Wrought?" *The New York Times Magazine* (August 29, 1976): 24 + .

Smith, Warren. *The Secret Forces of the Pyramids.* New York: Zebra, 1975.

Tompkins, Peter. *Secrets of the Great Pyramid.* New York: Harper & Row, 1978.

Reconstructionism

Theodore Brameld best expressed the tenets of reconstructionism in his book, *Toward a Reconstructed Philosophy of Education* (1956). Before him, in the early 1930s, George C. Counts and Harold O. Rugg, both prominent teacher educators, had espoused a similar philosophy. Quite simply, reconstructionism was an attempt to teach students the imperativeness of social reform to avoid global destruction. The reconstructionist engaged students in lengthy debates on social problems and viewed them from every vantage point. A fuller understanding of the problems led to an awareness of the interrelatedness of the world's people and cultures. A social problem halfway around the globe, say in India, also affected Americans and vice versa. The ultimate goal was "to reconstruct" the world so that optimum cooperation prevailed. By addressing social problems in the classroom, young people, upon becoming adults, would be better equipped to solve them. Reconstructionism would promote a caring attitude, greater insight, and a social conscience.

Theodore Brameld campaigned for reconstructionism because he truly considered the new way of teaching an antidote for the ills of the world. Never before had humankind been so close to the brink of destruction as it was in the 1950s. The deadliest war in history had just ended with two hellish nuclear bomb blasts, and another war had already begun in Korea. The threat of deployment of more nuclear bombs by the Soviets against the United States and American retaliation promised doomsday, or at least the annihilation of a great many people. The writing was on the wall, or so it seemed to Brameld, whose angst forced him to action. Brameld hoped to establish "Schools of the People" in every land so students could congregate in "general assemblies." In assembly, the students would tackle a year-long "wheel curriculum." The hub of each wheel represented a central theme for inquiry and debate. Such a hub might be ending world poverty, overcrowding, or illiteracy. The spokes radiating from the hub took the form of discussion groups, content and skill studies, and vocational training in relation to the central theme. Four wheels, "all rolling forward together," would move the "carriage" of the entire curriculum — "a carriage built sturdily for exploration and adventure over a rough terrain."

Brameld included the teaching of basic skills in his plan, but the main emphasis was on the wheel curriculum of social problems. If young people were not taught altruism while in their teens, they might never learn it. For Brameld, reconstructionism was the only hope left for a sick world. It might take several generations of re-constructioned students to make a difference, but what other choice was there?

Timely and visionary, Brameld's philosophy of education was also faddish. Most educators believed that students must be drilled in basic skills. Even after 12 years of mandatory schooling, some students still had trouble with the three Rs. Higher education complained that entering freshmen are not prepared for college work. Several years of the wheel curriculum would only add to that deficiency. One of Brameld's shortcomings was his assumption that students and teachers alike could make the mental leap from working with spelling primers to establishing a mini-United Nations. Without much experience of the world, students were ill-equipped to conceptualize solutions to international problems. They sensed how bad things were, but had difficulty knowing what to do next. Either confusion or false confidence in their ability to right every wrong set in. The greatest shortcoming of reconstructionism was the impossibility of having every country in the world adopt the wheel curriculum. In third-world countries, learning basic skills meant the difference between life and death. These people knew firsthand how poverty, overcrowding, and illiteracy retarded their growth. And lastly, social problems are such a complex knot of political, sociological, and economic strands that it was beyond secondary school students to untie them. Brameld's noble fad was no less a quest than that of Don Quixote.

BIBLIOGRAPHY

Brameld, Theodore. *Toward a Reconstructed Philosophy of Education*. New York: Dryden Press, 1956.

Kneller, George. *Introduction to the Philosophy of Education*. 2nd ed. New York: John Wiley and Sons, 1971.

Morris, Van Cleve. *Philosophy and the American School: An Introduction to the Philosophy of Education*. Boston, MA: Houghton Mifflin, 1961.

Reincarnation

In just three months, from January to March 1956, *The Search for Bridey Murphy* sold 120,500 copies and topped the best-seller list. Morey Bernstein, a graduate of the Wharton School of Finance, wrote the book. A self-taught hypnotist, he liked dabbling in altered states of consciousness. When a 33-year-old housewife, Mrs. Ruth Simmons, came to his Colorado home, Bernstein had no idea where it would lead. Instantly, Mrs. Simmons fell into a deep trance. Then, minutes later it happened. Bernstein commanded:

> You are going back . . . back . . . back, way back into time and space . . . I want you to keep on going back and back and back in your mind. And, surprising as it may seem, strange as it may seem, you will find that there are other scenes in your memory.
> What is your name?
> [Mrs. Simmons] . . . Uh . . . Friday.
> Don't you have any other name?
> Uh . . . Friday Murphy.
> And where do you live?
> . . . I live in Cork . . . Cork
> [About midway through the session] All right. Now see yourself in that lifetime, and see yourself up to the time of your death. And tell me, tell me as an observer so that it won't disturb you, tell me how you died.
> Fell down . . . fell down on the stairs, and . . . seems I broke some bones in my hip too, and I was a terrible burden.
> Were you old?
> Sixty-six.

Friday Murphy recalled more each time Bernstein hypnotized her. First of all, she had made a mistake: her real name was Bridey.

She talked about her parents and husband and remembered the correct denomination of coins used in Ireland circa 1850, the names of retail stores in Belfast, and the name of her school and church. Bridey sprinkled her conversation with nineteenth-century Irish brogue and reminisced about dancing the Irish Morning Jig. In one especially intriguing session, Mrs. Simmons retreated even farther back into time — a good hundred years before Bridey — recalling her life in New Amsterdam as a sickly infant. Bernstein made six Bridey tapes, each one covering previous ground but also adding more to the tale of reincarnation. When he spoke to Mrs. Simmons out of hypnosis about Bridey, she gasped, then settled into acceptance of her former self: "I know there has got to be something to Bridey Murphy, but it has in no way affected my outlook in this lifetime."

Unlike Mrs. Simmons, people who either read or heard about Bridey Murphy could hardly restrain themselves. *The Search* was not fictional; it was real! The public perceived that a normal woman had discovered one of her relatives — and that person was herself! Forget about the other momentous news stories of 1956 — the Suez Canal Crisis, the FBI solving the $2.7 million Brink's robbery, or Grace Kelly marrying Prince Rainier III in Monaco — the mystery of Bridey Murphy screamed for attention. Accounts of reincarnation had appeared before without causing such notice. A clever writer, Bernstein captivated his audience with a hundred page introduction called, "The First Step on the Long Bridge." These pages concerned the reliability of hypnosis and what of the occult sciences the public should believe. Bernstein's prelude breezed along, establishing credence or at least a willing suspension of disbelief in things supernatural. On page 108 the taped sessions began, ending eerily on page 208. The middle portion of the book moved even faster than the introduction; the dialogue between Bridey and Bernstein was clipped, puzzling, and wondrous. However, several critics who reviewed the book thought the opposite; the tedious dialogue bored them to tears. But the halting, repetitious words Bridey spoke in answer to Bernstein's clinical questions ensured verisimilitude for many readers. Twelve appendices ended the book. Each one added credence to the promising new science of parapsychology. Without impugning Bernstein's motive in writing *The Search for Bridey Murphy*, one can say the book serves as a model for how to write a best-seller.

Across America the Bridey fad occasioned wonder but also some fun. If one newspaper serialized the book, its competitor ran editorials pooh-poohing reincarnation. A "Come As You Were" party made national headlines. At a Chicago bookstore, a passerby walked in and inexplicably bought all 166 copies of *Bridey* stacked in the window. And for readers who wanted to hear the actual voices, Bernstein talking to Bridey on an LP record turned a nice profit. Eventually, skeptics came forth to demystify the strange tale of Bridey Murphy. Their consensus was Mrs. Simmons had probably read accounts of Ireland in the 1850s or had absorbed family history told to her as a girl. Under hypnosis, what had been locked away in her subconscious spilled out, and she indeed became the colleen Bridey Murphy. Hardly reincarnation, Mrs. Simmons had simply reconstructed a former life for herself from fragments of memory. In this way anyone could experience residing in another time and place.

Once again, tales of reincarnation loom over America, but not with the same startling impact of *Bridey*. Actress Shirley MacLaine, in her third autobiography, *Out on a Limb* (1983), tells how she came to believe in rebirth. Not yet a major theme, MacLaine in her next autobiography, *Dancing in the Light* (1985), opened the floodgates of memory. To prick her remembrance, she used acupuncture. In other lives, she had been a princess who communicated telepathically with elephants, a Buddhist monk, a pirate, and a harem dancer (notice nothing dull like a fishmonger's wife). But most imaginatively, she had lived as a Mongolian nomad brutally murdered by a rejected suitor whom today she recognizes as an incarnation of her ex-husband. New York critics grudgingly reviewed *Dancing in the Light*. Since then, MacLaine has written two more reincarnation-occult-paranormal autobiographies, *Don't Fall Off the Mountain* (1987) and *It's All in the Playing* (1987), which the critics have ignored. Perhaps her forthcoming installment, *Many Happy Returns*, will win their favor, although it's doubtful that MacLaine's foolishness will ever transcend Bernstein's realistic documentation.

BIBLIOGRAPHY

Bernstein, Morey. *The Search for Bridey Murphy*. New York: Doubleday, 1956.

Keenan, Charles. "Riddle of Bridey Murphy." *America* 94 (March 31, 1956): 716.

Luccock, H.E. "Meet Bridey Murphy." *Christian Century* 73 (June 6, 1956): 692.

Mandel, Siegfried. "The Story Behind 'The Search for Bridey Murphy'." *Saturday Review* 39 (March 10, 1956): 18-19.

Rejuvenation

Director of Experimental Surgery at the College de France, Dr. Serge Voronoff intrigued Americans in the 1920s when he stated that the sex gland "pours into the stream of the blood a species of vital fluid which restores the energy of all the cells, and spreads happiness and a feeling of well-being and the plentitude of life throughout our organism." Earlier in his career, Voronoff had had the good fortune to study Egyptian eunuchs. While surgeon to the Khedive of Egypt, he had noted the 60 eunuchs about the palace had neither beard nor mustaches, had droopy cheeks, were obese, and were victims of premature senility. Voronoff had deduced that their missing sex glands made them that way, and more revelatory, the absent glands robbed them of elan vital. A man without sex glands, therefore, was doomed to rapid physical decay. His next deduction built on the first. Then, couldn't a normal man's sexual vitality be restored by grafting new sex glands onto the worn-out one?

To test his theory, Voronoff proceeded like the man of science he was — tentatively. He experimented with goats: on normal and castrated males and on exhausted and enfeebled males. A resounding success, "greffes testiculaires" restored sexual potency in the goats and improved their overall health. Next came the real test, in Voronoff's own words:

> After one hundred and twenty operations upon animals, all helping to establish the efficacy of "greffes testiculaires," I performed the first similar operation upon a man. The subject was forty-five years of age and had been deprived of his glands because they were tubercular. He had the appearance of an eunuch. The soil was unfavorable to the grafted gland, owing to the effects of previous disease, and I decided to remove the grafts, but I found them well united to the surrounding

tissues. I used the glands of monkeys in this and subsequent "greffes testiculaires" on men because the securing of human glands presents serious obstacles, and because the glands of monkeys, and especially those of the anthropoid apes, are the only ones that can furnish grafts which will find among human tissues the same conditions of life that they had originally.

Voronoff's second patient possessed favorable soil, and the graft took. The patient's beard grew back, even though he had not shaved in 20 years. A 74-year-old man who came to Voronoff for the highly experimental treatment became completely rejuvenated within eight months of the operation:

> His aspect was jovial, his movements vigorous, his eye clear and twinkling as he enjoyed our surprise [at seeing him thus restored]. The fat had disappeared, the muscles were firm, his body had straightened, and hair was growing on his head, covering an area where there had been none before. He had been climbing mountains in Switzerland and enjoying sports dear to the English. He had in effect become fifteen to twenty years younger.

More grafting of monkey glands onto humans convinced Dr. Voronoff that he had discovered a viable method of restoring youth. Slowly but surely, he gained the respect of the medical establishment, and other surgeons began to copy his technique. At the end of a distinguished career, Dr. Voronoff enjoyed the plaudits of his peers and the recognition that he was a great scientist.

An ocean apart both ethically and morally, the American opportunist John R. Brinkley made a fortune from Dr. Voronoff's work. Brinkley fabricated stories about almost everything in life and said he got the idea for rejuvenating men from a patient of his. Seeing a billy goat kicking up his hooves, the patient remarked, "I wish I had that much energy again." Brinkley mulled over the remark and the rest was a matter of deduction. Holding a meritless diploma from the soon-to-be defunct Eclectic Medical University of Kansas City, Missouri, Dr. Brinkley could legally perform surgery. In 1926, he initiated a saturation ad campaign in which he combined old-time religion and goat gland science. Throughout his medical career, Dr. Brinkley never mentioned Dr. Voronoff or the fact that monkey sex glands were more compatible with human ones for grafting. He used goats because they were simple to breed, whereas monkeys had to be obtained from overseas and were less plentiful. Money motivated Dr. Brinkley, and goat gland science was his ticket to riches; therefore, a young goat fix for an old goat human was good enough. He set up his medical gospel farm in Milford, Kansas, and purchased a radio station—KFKB ("Kansas First, Kansas Best")—to tell America about his wondrous cure for "impotency, high blood pressure, and enlarged prostate, sterility, neurasthenia, dementia praecox or any disease that is not malignant of the prostate."

Dr. Brinkley's come-on was one of the oddest during a time of pitchman oddities. He promised his patients a double rebirth. For $750, he would restore them in the eyes of God and no less in the eyes of a desirable woman. For $1,500 he would select the youngest, friskiest kid available and make satyrs out of tired men—but God-fearing satyrs, of course. By 1930, Dr. Brinkley claimed he received 3,000 letters of inquiry a day. He had built a sanatorium, an apartment house, and several bungalows for his staff. He owned four automobiles and humbly gave to Milford the Brinkley Methodist Memorial Church. Another interest, the Brinkley Pharmaceutical Association, got him in trouble. He used the airwaves to sell medical preparations prepared according to his secret formulas. Without examining the ailing person who had sent in a letter, Dr. Brinkley or one of his druggists prescribed a particular tonic. The Federal Communications Commission investigated the matter and later refused to renew his broadcasting license. This momentary setback hardly phased Dr. Brinkley. As if he had had a goat gland operation himself, he ran three times for governor of Kansas, promising such amenities as free textbooks for students, free motor licenses, and a lake in every county "of the driest state in the Union."

The remainder of Dr. Brinkley's story is even more fantastic than the first part. Leaving Kansas behind, mainly because he wanted to start radio broadcasting again, he moved to Del Rio, Texas. Just across the border in Villa Acuna, Mexico, he erected station XERA with an official 350,000 watts of power. On the sly, Dr. Brinkley increased the wattage to 1,000,000 to drown out every other radio broadcast for hundreds of miles, to sell whatever he thought the public wanted, including the "Doctor's Book." For $1, the customer learned about Dr. Brinkley's medical practice and saw pictures of the great man himself; his wife, Minnie Telitha; and son, Johnny Boy; their white stucco home, and the Brinkley six-story brick hospital. Other legal defeats followed the FCC suit, notably from patients who derived no benefit from tacked on goat glands. But Dr. Brinkley, Minnie Telitha, and Johnny Boy lived the good life on their Del Rio estate named "Palm Drive on Hudson Gardens." Sitting at night beside their splashing fountain and swimming pool over which "Dr. Brinkley" glowed in neon lights, the family rested happily. The great man dreamed of one day becoming president of the United States — according to himself he had already received 500,000 unsolicited letters urging him to run in 1940. Only crickets and naying goats broke the reverential silence.

BIBLIOGRAPHY

"Brinkley's Trial." *Time* 46 (April 10, 1939): 46-48.
Carson, Gerald. *The Roguish World of Doctor Brinkley*. New York: Rinehart, 1960.
Fishbein, Morris. "Modern Medical Charlatans: II." *Hygeia* 172 (February 1938): 172 + .
Perry, Armstrong. "The Renewal of Youth by Surgery." *The Forum* 71 (May 1924): 639-646.
"Voronoff's Own Account of His Operation to Restore Lost Youth." *Current Opinion* 69 (December 1920): 836-838.

Sea Serpents

The first faddish outbreak of sea serpent watching along American shores occurred in 1817. On August 21 of that year, Solomon Allen, a shipmaster, swore he had seen a strange marine animal "between eighty and ninety feet in length" with a rattlesnake-like head as large as the head of a horse. Solomon wasn't alone; 11 other people saw it too — a fantastic sea creature basking in the Atlantic off Gloucester, Massachusetts. The strange beast moved up and down in the water like a caterpillar, its neck erect it feared nothing. Pretty soon, other Gloucester inhabitants (not under oath) reported the monster also had ridges on its back, changed direction in the water with lightning speed, could drop out of sight in a flash, and stared at people with frightful, glaring eyes. Moreover, its horrible two-foot tongue could wrap around a man's arm and pull him into its ravenous mouth with ease.

Enough people saw the Gloucester sea serpent for the Linnaean Society of New England, a group of Boston intellectuals passionately interested in natural history, to investigate the sightings. The Linnaeans compiled a list of 25 questions to ask the eyewitnesses, hoping to obtain specific, comparative information. In the meantime, Gloucester fishermen searched the coastal waters for the undulant enemy that threatened to devour all the fish and thereby deprive them of their livelihood. Ten days after the sighting of the first sea serpent, a second one invaded Gloucester waters, or so reported several people who had seen it. How the lookouts determined the difference, or if the two beasts swam together, remains a historical mystery. Now the fishermen really chewed their nails because rumor had it the two sea serpents were male and female come to Gloucester to mate! Wasting no time, the fishermen festooned the harbor with nets and hung baited shark hooks from buoys to capture the reptilian lovers. Whalers came from nearby Marblehead to lend support. It seemed everyone wanted to stop the creatures from

The young man second from the left can't hold back a smile at the obviously faked sea serpent. Beginning in 1817 with the famous Gloucester sighting, Americans watched the coastal waters for sea serpents, from Maine to the tip of Florida and from California to Washington State. Some unscrupulous innkeepers reported false sightings to fill their seaside resorts.

sparking except the Linnaean Society, which prayed for babies to study and classify.

The Society got its wish in October (evidently sea serpents reproduce themselves with alacrity). An old salt had pitchforked a three-foot long, dark brown sea creature with "bunches" on its back. It was triumphantly removed to Boston, and the Linnaeans dissected what they thought was a baby sea serpent, naming it *Scoliophus atlanticus* (*scolio* = flexible; *ophis* = snake). The Society wrote a scientific paper describing its find and added to it the 12 eyewitness depositions and a complete dissection report. Copies were sent to various natural historians around the world. But across the very ocean which *Scoliophus atlanticus* patrolled, the English Linnaean Society doubted the baby sea serpent was real. And in skeptical France, a noted zoologist rejected the find completely, stating the little one was a full-grown black snake with a spinal deformity (the "bunches"). The American Linnaeans had done such a good job of illustrating their dissection that it was apparent to the Frenchman and, later on to most everyone else in the global scientific community, that *Scoliophus atlanticus* was a chimera. A foolish fancy or not, hornswaggled observers continued to believe what they wished.

Sightings of the Gloucester sea serpent and others of its ilk animated New Englanders. Seaside resorts were booked to capacity; managers posted new sightings of the creature hourly. The steamship *Connecticut* took quivering passengers out into once friendly waters to chance an encounter with the beast. The stories were chilling: mariners saw the beast battle with whales and win, landlubbers gawked at slimy trails left by the thing on beaches where a Rhode Island child had disappeared—gobbled up by the beast. Sighting mania lasted two more decades. Then, in October 1845, German-born Professor Albert Koch proclaimed he had found the fossil remains of a 114-foot-long sea serpent in Alabama. The news stunned the world and paved the way for a global tour. Professor Koch named his find *Hydrargos sillimanii*, or Silliman's Master-of-the-Seas, after Benjamin Silliman, professor of chemistry at Yale and editor of the *American Journal of Science*. There was a good deal of money to be made in exhibiting rarities, as P. T. Barnum had already demonstrated. Well into the tour, Jeffries Wyman, a member of the Boston Society of Natural History, revealed that *Hydrargos sillimanii* was a fake. Wyman insisted that the immense skeletal form — a clever conception of what people thought a sea serpent might look like — was in fact the bones of several primitive whales pieced together. The ruse fooled the public because it wanted to be fooled and because scientists were thought to be above such flim-flam. Professor Koch shrugged his shoulders at Wyman's accusation and continued raking in admission receipts. Disgruntled, Benjamin Silliman asked Professor Koch to remove his name from the spurious bag of bones.

For most of the nineteenth century, the sea serpent fad acted like a barometer of public fancy. Just when it seemed Americans were about to forget the fabled monster, another flurry of sightings made them believers once again. Even if honest scientists told the public that such phenomena as a thick ribbon of giant seaweed or the close flight of birds over the water's surface could be mistaken for a sea serpent, not everyone listened. That a row of leaping dolphins or the whale shark, rorqual, or a sea elephant might be their beast, failed to dampen public curiosity. Henry David Thoreau relates that the great orator, Daniel Webster, upon seeing what he thought was a sea serpent, begged those with him not to tell anyone about his sighting. Otherwise, he, the clear-headed rationalist, would be laughed out of politics and his career irreparably damaged. Likewise, some sea captains sealed their own lips for fear of losing command of their ships.

In 1864, a prominent artist, Elihu Vedder, exhibited a striking portrait entitled "Lair of the Sea Serpent." Finally captured if only on canvas, Vedder's monster slumbers lazily across several sand dunes. Its repose allowed awestruck viewers to examine the beast without chancing reprisal. The image was one of Vedder's finest and achieved rapid popularity. During the same time, other artists profited by making engravings of sea serpents to spread the fad far and wide. Satirists included sea serpents in their cartoons to epitomize deception and humbug. In fact, picturing the beast soon came to mean that pretense, dissimulation, and mendacity were afoot. First sighted in 1817, the Gloucester sea serpent lived another 80 years or so and cruised both American coasts. Floridians as well as

Californians saw it, and there is no telling how many little children the beast devoured.

BIBLIOGRAPHY

Erickson, Evarts. "When New England Saw the Serpent." *American Heritage* 7 (April 1956): 26-27.

Heuvelmas, Bernard. *In the Wake of Sea-Serpents.* New York: Hill and Wang, 1968.

Ocko, Stephanie. "The Glouster Sea Serpent." *American History Illustrated* 17 (April 1982): 36-41.

Tatham, David. "Elihu Vedder's 'Lair of the Sea Serpent.'" *The American Art Journal* XVII (Spring 1985): 33-47.

Sex Surrogates

> In view of the statistics there is no question that the decision to provide partner surrogates for sexually incompetent unmarried men has been one of the more effective clinical decisions made during the past eleven years devoted to the development of treatment for sexual inadequacy.

This quotation appeared near the end of Masters and Johnson's book, *Human Sexual Inadequacy* (1970). The text preceding their conclusion provides the first description of the use of surrogates for correcting sexual dysfunction. What William H. Masters and Virginia E. Johnson delineated sounded positively immoral and illegal to the American public. In essence, the renowned sex therapists procured women to have sex with men who paid for the service. The men suffered from any one of five sexual dysfunctions: primary and secondary impotence, premature ejaculation, inhibited sexual desire, or disturbances of ejaculatory function. Via the usual media blitz, news of what many thought was thinly disguised prostitution circulated quickly, so quickly that it appeared the 1970s would out-sex the promiscuous 1960s.

In reality, Masters and Johnson weren't running a brothel or anything like it. Their employment of sex surrogates was all very legitimate. Let them explain:

> Over the last 11 years, 13 women have been accepted from a total of 31 volunteers for assignment as partner surrogates. Their ages ranged from 24 to 43 years when they joined the research program. Although all but two of the women had been previously married, none of the volunteers were married when living their role as a partner surrogate. . . . No attempt was ever made to persuade any woman to serve as a partner surrogate. . . . Of major interest was the fact that 9 of the 13 volunteers were interested in contributing their services on the

basis of personal knowledge of sexual dysfunction or sex-oriented distress within their immediate family. . . . The specific function of the partner surrogate is to approximate insofar as possible the role of a supportive, interested, cooperative wife. . . . [The partner surrogates] are fully sexually responsive as women, and, as is true with most confidently responsive women, understandingly, and compassionately concerned for the frustrations of a sexually inadequate male.

Masters and Johnson did not discuss the details of how treatment progressed. However, after their initial report, other therapists wrote detailed accounts, some of which were intended for the profession and some for public enlightenment. Either way, the accounts of a seasoned woman aggressively tutoring a man about his phallus aroused reader libido and qualified as mild erotica.

Already highly titillated, the public began to hear more about sex surrogates. In a *Time* article for June 17, 1974, a photograph of a shapely brunette named Susan Greene couldn't help but whet the appetite. Her hair flows down over well-toned breasts. Her lips full and inviting, her eyes intelligent and alive, she talks to a patient. In her hand, a pencil dangles above a clipboard. Susan looks very relaxed and self-assured. The article accompanying this vision of an ultra-hip young woman tells the reader that Susan lives near San Francisco, is a graduate of Cornell University, is married and likes to travel, and has "had sexual relations for a fee with two dozen different men during the past year." As noted, Masters and Johnson would not have allowed a married woman to serve as a sex surrogate. In fact, the same year their book came out (1970), Masters and Johnson stopped using surrogates for a variety of reasons— mostly legal ones. Susan is one of three sex surrogates who are part of the Berkeley Sex Therapy Group run by five psychologists. For $2,180, the patient gets ten 2 1/2-hour sessions with the surrogate, followed by an hour's meeting of patient, surrogate, and psychologist. The surrogate receives $110 per session and the psychologist, $90 plus $180 for the initial consultation.

Public reaction to sex surrogates heightened after revelations such as that about Susan and the Berkeley Sex Therapy Group. Plain as the nose on your face, it was open prostitution. Sex therapists who avoided using surrogates worried, not about public reaction, but about the efficacy of the treatment. They suspected that patients helped by surrogates still might not be able to perform sexually outside the clinic. As Masters and Johnson pointed out, the surrogate is a very special woman who can make a man feel like a man. It would be difficult to find another woman like her in everyday life. On the psychoanalytical side, sex experts called surrogates a transitory fix for deep-seated emotional problems. Practically all of the men engaged in sex surrogacy were physically sound, so the cause of their problem was purely emotional. Therefore, having good sex with a surrogate did not necessarily treat the problem, although it might build self-esteem.

An article in *Reader's Digest* for December 1975, entitled "Swindlers in the Sex 'Clinics,'" alerted the public to other suspicious sex therapy practices. Loose in the land were pseudotherapists who used their position of trust for easy profit or sexual adventure. Because sex therapists did not have to be licensed, anyone could open a sex clinic. The article cited several examples of flagrant abuse. A woman therapist in New York made lesbian advances toward a patient who then went into hysterics. Later, the therapist calmly said she was only testing for latent homosexual tendencies. In San Antonio, Texas, a so-called sex therapist frequented singles parties to drum up trade. Later, when new female patients came to him, he had them parade naked in front of other patients. In San Francisco, a sex clinic workshop showed patients as many as six porn films at once on a giant screen, while back in New York at a sex clinic, a dozen naked women reclined on the floor in a circle for simultaneous masturbation. It goes without saying that therapist-patient coupling was a regular outcome of treatment.

In answer, Masters and Johnson, who gave the green light to the pseudotherapists, began conducting ethics conferences; and the Family Service Association of America (FSAA) met with state legislators to pass laws requiring that all sex therapists be licensed. During the 1970s, unrestrained sex clinics attracted considerable public attention. Mostly, the public shook its head at the X-rated fad. But if, at the time, skyrocketing divorce was attributable to the new promiscuity, then sex surrogacy was corruptive.

BIBLIOGRAPHY

Holden, Constance. "Sex Therapy: Making It as a Science and an Industry." *Science* 186 (October 25, 1974): 330-334.

Masters, William E., and Virginia E. Johnson. *Human Sexual Inadequacy*. Boston, MA: Little, Brown and Company, 1970.

Robinson, Donald. "Swindlers in the Sex 'Clinic.'" *Reader's Digest* 107 (December 1975): 82-86.

"Trick or Treatment?" *Time* 103 (June 17, 1974): 90.

Talking to Plants

Almost everyone in the 1970s heard that talking to seedlings produced lofty adult plants in no time at all. A few encouraging words spoken during the day worked wonders. "Grow little plant. Spread your tiny arms and lift your sweet head to meet the sky." Not only words but music accelerated growth. "Had a bad day, little plant? I'll play some Mozart." Water, sun, and soil were not enough if you were to be a good parent.

How did the fad of talking to plants begin? Unbeknownst to the general public, it started with Gustav Theodor Fechner, a German medical doctor and professor of physics. Fechner possessed a roving mind, so it wasn't odd for him to publish *Nanna, or the Soul-Life of Plants* in 1848, a treatise far afield from medicine or physics. His fellow academicians scoffed at him for the nonsense in *Nanna*. Fechner wrote that plants live as human beings do. Plants have nervous systems, so they can feel and experience emotions, and even though the systems do not show up under a microscope, they are there in a spiritual sense. Moreover, Fechner believed plants are superior to humans in some ways. Because plants are happily rooted, with all they need around them, they do not have to toil for sustenance. Flowers communicate with one another by exuding perfume, unlike humans, who greet each other brusquely. A gentle dreamer, Fechner proved to himself — if to no one else — that plants have souls and engage in a life similar to our own. Without saying the words exactly, Fechner advised that we should learn from plants by talking to them at every opportunity. If Fechner was full of moonshine, then what of Charles Darwin? Just before his death in 1882, Darwin published *The Power of Movement in Plants*, which seemed to concur with Fechner's insistence on plants having nervous systems. Darwin described plant movement at certain times of the day that was analogous to animal movement. However, after

575 pages of observation, Darwin left the question of vegetable ganglion unanswered.

The great American horticulturist Luther Burbank (1849-1926) was neither a dreamer nor a speculative scientist. He left his birth-place in the rural Massachusetts village of Lunenburg for Santa Rosa, California, with one thought in mind — to grow plants bigger and better than anyone else. Burbank's success in hybridizing plants made him a legend in his own time, known throughout the world. Virtually unschooled in horticulture, he learned by doing. When interviewers asked him about his methods, this greenest of green thumbs let drop that he talked to plants. Burbank was not sure whether his plants understood him, but he was certain that through some form of telepathy they caught the gist of his conversation. In discussing his development of the spineless cactus, Burbank said, "I often talked to the plants to create a vibration of love. 'You have nothing to fear,' I would tell them. 'You don't need your defensive thorns. I will protect you.'" Interestingly, Burbank applied his vast knowledge of plant development to human development in a book, *Training of the Human Plant*. Believing instinctively that plants have nervous systems without any more proof than Fechner or Darwin, Burbank maintained that children and seedlings were alike. Strict discipline, shutting out love and play, debilitated the nervous systems of both.

Fechner, Darwin, and Burbank — all serious scientists — prepared the ground for the 1970s fad of talking to plants. They were the unperceived progenitors of the fad, while George Milstein and Jerry Baker were the contemporary spokesmen. In 1970, George Mil-stein, a New York dentist, collaborated with Environmental Sound Control, Inc., to cut a record entitled, "Music to Grow Plants By." A reporter for *Newsweek* described the disk as "a mixture of tonal vibrations, camouflaged behind schmaltzy Mantovani-type orches-tration, that induces plants to do deep-breathing exercises that would put seasoned yogis to shame." Milstein said the almost inau-dible vibrations emanating from the recording stimulated plants to grow at several times their normal rate. This was good news be-cause with air pollution worsening, city dwellers needed fast-grow-ing plants to give off fresh oxygen. Milstein's record sold in florist shops and department stores. As silly as it sounds — playing a record for house plants—there was scientific evidence that music affects potted greenery. At the same time that people bought Milstein's record, a Colorado graduate student discovered that plants placed in an environment of soft, semiclassical music remained healthy and grew toward the sound, whereas plants placed in an environment of loud rock music withered and died.

Finally, after a wintry wait of 125 years from Fechner's *Nanna* to 1973, *Talk to Your Plants* appeared. "America's Master Gardener," Jerry Baker, bubbled over in his book:

> I can't believe you will be able to spend many hours in your garden before you will begin to talk to your plants. Believe me, talking to vegetables, shrubs, grass, trees, and flowers is not a kooky or crazy thing to do. Getting to know each plant in your garden, personally through good conversation, will help you become more observant of its general health and wellbeing.

Baker credits his Grandma Putt with teaching him the secrets of nature:

> Grandma said anyone who has been at gardening very long and very successfully, has become a great plant communicator. He is most likely reaping as much news from his garden as there is in the newspaper he uses for mulch.

BIBLIOGRAPHY

Baker, Jerry. *Talk to Your Plants*. Los Angeles, CA: Nash Publishing, 1973.
"Chant of the Plant." *Newsweek* 76 (August 17, 1970): 82.
Tompkins, Peter, and Christopher Bird. *The Secret Life of Plants*. New York: Harper & Row, 1973.
"What Noise Does to Plants." *Science Digest* 68 (December 1970): 60-61.

What makes this tattooed lady particularly interesting is that she wasn't a sideshow attraction—rather, she was a member of the upper class. Note her superior look and exquisite pearl choker. When European monarchs sported epidermal decoration, tattooing became fashionable for the rich on both sides of the Atlantic. (c1900)

Tattoos

The art of pricking the skin with a needle tipped in pigment to incise a design can be traced back to the ancient Egyptians, although tattooing first excited Western man when he ventured onto Polynesian islands and saw the art widely practiced. The Tahitian "tatau," meaning to mark, gives us the word. Since then, sailors the world over have been the best clients of tattoo parlors. Far away from home, salts commemorated their adventures with an exotic memento. In Japan and China, they looked for the best bars, brothels, and tattoo artists, in whatever order. It was almost obligatory for any sailor worth his duffel bag to get his girl's name or an anchor stippled on his forearm. Apart from the steady trade of sailors, tattooing in America has made several faddish appearances.

Around the turn of the century, it was fashionable for socialites to get tattooed. King George V (1865-1936) of Great Britain and Czar Nicholas II (1868-1918) of Russia wore them, thereby making it correct for other members of Vanity Fair to do the same. It must have been quite a surprise for a tattoo artist working the wharf to have a blue blood drop in and look over his designs. In the 1930s, some daring women considered tattooing the answer to their quest for the perfect cosmetic. Instead of fumbling with lipstick and rouge, they had their lips and cheeks tattooed ruby red. And better yet for unsightly eyebrows, they had the hair removed and chic lines etched in.

An article in *Literary Digest* for March 27, 1937, reported the startling statistic that one out of every ten Americans was tattooed. Obviously, the 1930s fad had gone too far. When asked why, psychiatrists labeled the skin-adorned as either exhibitionists or masochists. The clergy repeated Leviticus 19:28, "Ye shall not make cuttings in your flesh for the dead, nor print any marks upon you." But still, people visited the dens of iniquity. In the Bowery section of New York City, a handwritten sign in a tattoo parlor window read: chest pieces $10.00; beauty spots $1.50; nude women $1.00; mermaids $2.00; hula dancers $1.50; and snake women $1.00. Evidently, drawing all the scales in a mermaid's tail cost extra. Not on the sign but often asked for after the Social Security Act (1935) passed into law, some forgetful people had their SS number tattooed on their arm. Loveable cartoon characters were also in vogue; Mickey Mouse, Popeye, and Betty Boop became favorites of the better-heeled clientele. Seeing Mickey tattooed on one shoulder and Betty on the other was truly a beautiful sight. When cubism and surrealism exhilarated the art world, tattoo fanciers asked for similar abstract designs, which the tattoo artist had to copy from Picasso or Dali. Another side of the business was tattoo removal, or rather tattoo disguise. For example a man in love with a girl named Adele had her name tattooed over his heart. But soon thereafter she left him for someone else. Seemingly stuck with the hateful reminder of lost love for the rest of his life, he begged the tattoo artist to help him forget Adele. The artist quickly turned the five script letters into an ornate Napoleonic hat "with the General's countenance below it, moving in a lifelike fashion with the beat of the heart." The 1930s marked the first golden age of American tattooing. The Great Depression forced people to behave in unaccustomed ways, one of which — public acceptance of tattooing — was an odd manifestation.

World War II was the next boon for the tattoo business. Before discussing those years, a couple of basic facts should be mentioned. First, there was no school in which to learn tattooing. The art was passed on from one artist to another, as it still is today. And second, the number of people who get tattooed at any one time is known only to the tattoo artists; the Bureau of Census does not count epidermal hearts and dragons. To hear about tattooing, then, one has to go to the source, such as Charlie Wagner, a busy skin artist during the war years:

> Funny thing about war, fighting men want to be marked in some way or another. High-class fellas, too — men from West Point and Annapolis. . . . And fliers. Had a fine chap from the Air Forces who wanted to be tattooed for good luck before he took off for India, so I put five "Happy Landings" on his

chest. And he got to India and back safely. Better than a rabbit's foot.

Charlie also disclosed that "next to the Crucifixion the Rock of Ages is my most popular design." Often a military man would have a religious motif engraved on one forearm and a patriotic one on the other. "Remember Pearl Harbor, Dec. 7, 1941" was worn with pride.

In the early 1970s in San Francisco, tattoo artist Lyle Tuttle became something of a cult figure. In his clean studio, free from wharf rats and dirty needles, Tuttle incised a small heart on rock singer Janis Joplin's left breast and decorated her wrist with a Florentine bracelet. Not long after, Joplin fans streamed into Tuttle's studio to copy their idol. They were always amazed to see the master greet them in his "body shirt". Tattooed from neck to wrist, front and back, with "Lyle Tuttle" inscribed under his belly button, it was hard not to gawk. Inflation had hit, though, since the 1930s. A simple wristlet, not the Joplin special, cost $20, and a Hindu god or black panther more than $500. Something else had changed in 40 years. Due to the feminist movement, more women got tattooed than men. Usually they asked for dainty designs — flowers, butterflies, or rising suns — discreetly placed. If intimately placed, Tuttle required that a friend accompany the client to avoid any accusations later. Mystical clients asked for occult symbols and astrological signs. Even though flower children constituted a good part of his business, Tuttle still inscribed "Mother" and "Death Before Dishonor" on servicemen. For those who wanted a Tuttle that could be removed easily, a California company came out with SkinSees. After a wild Saturday night at a rock concert, cold cream made the most shocking design disappear without a trace.

Rock musicians have again popularized tattoos. However, gone is Janis Joplin's sweet little heart. In their unceasing effort to look as outrageous as possible, the wild rockers of the late 1980s chose evil monsters and other maniacal motifs to adorn their epidermis. Pale-skinned, shirtless, hair streaming, tight jeans enshrining their gender, the tattooed troubadours strut across the stage. These self-styled denizens of hell greatly affect today's tattoo market. If pop music fans will wear a Michael Jackson silver lamé glove, then a three-color demon is a cinch to be a favorite.

Social scientists have never quite understood the attraction of tattoos. Are they purely sexual in nature due to pricking the skin and implanting the dye? Or are they an outward sign of rebelliousness, telling the world the person wearing them is an outcast? Or are they just ornamental, creating a walking work of art meant to be admired? Whatever the answer, tattooing has embellished fad history with its colorful inscriptions: "The Sweetest Girl I Ever Kissed Was Another Man's Wife My Mother" and the more succinct parcel of wisdom, "Dust Be My Destiny."

BIBLIOGRAPHY

Cumming, Helen. "War Booms the Tattooing Art." *The New York Times Magazine* (September 19, 1943): 38.

Leonard, George. "The Tattoo Taboo." *The Atlantic Monthly* 238 (July 1976): 47-51.

"Needlework: Tattoo Art Traced from Egyptian Tombs to American Social Security." *Literary Digest* 123 (March 27, 1937): 22-24.

"Prosperity Flourishes Unchecked in the Tattoo Industry." *Literary Digest* 114 (October 1, 1932): 32-33.

Talese, Gay. "Twenty Million Tattooed: Why?" *The New York Times Magazine* (November 22, 1959): 42 + .

"Tattoo Renaissance." *Time* 96 (December 21, 1970): 58.

UFOs

People have seen unidentified flying objects in the sky as far back as prehistoric times. Instead of today's sleek spacecraft able to change direction in the wink of an eye, early observers saw colored globes and flying shields. The ancient Sanskrit epics, the *Ramayana* and the *Mahahbarata*, describe aerial chariots called *vimanas* that engaged in laser-like warfare. In Western culture, observers reported seeing a bow-shaped object fly over the Roman Temple of Saturn in 173 B.C., and T. Forcet watched fierce men "striving, struggling and tugging together, one holding a drawn sword" in the air over London on May 20, 1646. The first known reference to the term *saucer* derives from a January 25, 1878, sighting by John Martin, a farmer from Dallas, Texas. While out hunting, Martin saw a rapidly moving orange object in the sky that looked like a large saucer when directly overhead. The extraordinary popularity of dime novels and pulp magazines (1920-1940), following on the heels of classic fiction by Jules Verne, H. G. Wells, and Edgar Rice Burroughs, inspired more sightings.

Perhaps the most influential pulp was *Amazing Stories*, created by Hugo Gernsback in 1929. In the early 1940s, *Amazing Stories* printed a letter written by Richard Shaver, a former mental patient. The author revealed he had personally seen demonic troglodytes called *deros*, who caused countless human misfortunes. Degenerate beings living in the earth's interior caverns constructed the deros. The fanciful letter became known as the Shaver Mystery and boosted the circulation of *Amazing Stories* from 25,000 copies in the late 1930s to 250,000 by 1946. Soon more personal accounts filled its pages, along with drawings of ultramodern spacecraft and bug-like aliens.

With the pulps as appetizer, by 1947 the UFO feast was on the table. A host of sightings occurred, most notably Kenneth Arnold's June 24, 1947 account, which ushered in the modern era of UFO

A U.S. Coast Guard photographer stationed at Salem, Massachusetts took this shot in 1952. While cleaning his camera, he saw flashes of light in the sky and captured them on film. This supposed low-flying squadron of UFOs was but one of many photographed in the 1950s. Later, much of the photographic evidence was shown to be bogus, although true believers maintained that space aliens had visited us.

reports. Arnold described the UFOs he had seen as flying saucers, nine having flashed by in a squadron. According to Arnold, the saucers traversed the 47-mile distance between Mount Rainier and Mount Adams in Washington State in 1 minute and 42 seconds. That worked out to a speed of 1,656.71 miles per hour—nearly three times faster than any known aircraft could fly. Just a few months later, the Technical Intelligence Center of the United States Air Force's Air Material Command began monitoring UFOs. Despite Air Force reassurance that UFOs were explainable, the flying saucer craze burgeoned spectacularly. *Fate* magazine, begun in 1948, capitalized on UFO accounts, while books such as Major Donald Keyhoe's *The Flying Saucers Are Real* (1950), and Kenneth Arnold's *The Coming of the Saucers* (1952) thrilled readers. George Adamski's *Flying Saucers Have Landed* (1953), an international best-seller that ultimately sold more copies than any other UFO title, related the author's meeting with a tanned, long-haired Venusian at Desert Center, California in late 1952.

Hollywood also exploited the UFO craze by producing a galaxy of alien visitation films in the 1950s: *War of the Worlds* (1953), *Invaders from Mars* (1953), *It Came from Outer Space* (1953), *Invasion of the Body Snatchers* (1956), and *I Married a Monster from Outer Space* (1958), to name a few. Despite the prevalence of the monster theme—horrid space aliens bent on enslaving humankind—the most critically successful movie, *The Day the Earth Stood Still* (1951), showed humanoid beings trying to stop earthlings from destroying themselves. The filmmakers had in mind the arms race between the United States and the Soviet Union and its potential for exploding the planet.

In the midst of media sensationalism, a few serious efforts to investigate UFOs got underway. John Spencer and Hilary Evans published a typology of sightings, ranging from those clearly false to ones possessing a minimal chance of being real. The reasons given for the possible existence of UFOs were these:

1. The universe is too vast for highly advanced beings and civilizations not to have evolved somewhere.
2. These advanced beings are as curious about us as we are about them, so they will want to find us.

3. Thousands of people the world over, not just the lunatic fringe, report having seen UFOs.

4. Over 100 people report having been abducted by space aliens for scientific experimentation. All of their reports bear striking similarities.

5. Studies of pulsed microwave radiation might explain some of the unusual phenomenon of UFOs, such as low-pitched humming sounds and high-pitched whistles, which indicate an advanced spacecraft.

6. The U.S. government continues to study UFO sightings in a top-secret effort, not wanting to cause public panic.

7. Civilians have witnessed military clean-up of crashed UFOs after which no reports were released.

8. Certain individuals receive messages from extraterrestrial beings through a trance state called "channelling."

Crash-retrieval evidence offered the best opportunity to render an objective verdict on UFOs. What is now known as the Roswell Incident of 1947 became famous because of an alleged cover-up. This is what happened. A mysterious disc-shaped object slammed into the New Mexico sands. A local ranch manager, W. "Mac" Brazel, discovered the wreckage but did not report his find until several days later when he went into Roswell for supplies. In the meantime, other locals examined the wreckage and described its composition as something like aluminum or lead foil that could not be dented. However, Brazel's son said the thin covering of the object could be wrinkled. Small beams like balsa wood etched with hieroglyphics gave the object structure, and a metallic black box nestled in the debris. When the U.S. Air Force heard about the crash, it confiscated every scrap of the object "not made on this Earth" and flew it to Wright Field Air Base for investigation. Later, a military report declared the object was nothing more than a wrecked weather balloon with a tin foil radar target attachment. Saucer proponents were hardly satisfied with the obvious whitewash of facts. Their strident battle cry became "Remember Roswell."

So much for proof in favor of UFOs, scientists have set forth equally strong reasons why they might not exist:

1. It would require a long trip through space for aliens to visit Earth, whereas a radio message or robot probe would be more economical and less arduous. As yet, we haven't been contacted.
2. Human beings often misperceive natural phenomenon and believe that dreams are reality. Frequent sightings of UFOs confirm this tendency to see things differently from what they are.
3. A number of UFO reports have been proven to be hoaxes. People like to dupe one another.
4. So far, no UFO case merits being called legitimate.
5. UFO investigators are usually untrained and poorly equipped to study a case; therefore, their findings are questionable.
6. UFO investigators are usually true believers and look more to prove the existence of UFOs than to disprove it.
7. Photographs of UFOs are unclear and taken at a distance by only one observer. No close-up photographs have come to light, nor have pictures of UFO occupants.

With no conclusive evidence to go on, the UFO craze subsided to a great extent in the 1960s, although two well-plotted television programs, "The Twilight Zone" and "The Outer Limits," kept the phenomenon somewhat in orbit. To the dismay of social reformers, the fictional aliens drew attention away from real-life concerns like the Civil Rights Movement and LBJ's war on poverty. The 1970s revived interest in UFOs, owing mostly to the huge box office success of the films *Close Encounters of the Third Kind* and *E.T.* Wesley Streiber's best-selling account of an alien visitation, *Communion*, likewise enthralled fans. But these were entertainments divested of the 1950s hysteria. Since then, U.S. and Soviet space exploration has done a lot to calm public nerves. Bogus photographs of UFOs no longer have an air of authenticity, and abduction by space aliens is more a cosmic fantasy as seen at the end of *Close Encounters of the Third Kind.* Moreover, the final report of the Scientific Study of Unidentified Flying Objects (1968), conducted by the University of Colorado under contract with the U.S. Air Force, discredited the majority of documented sightings. Still, ufologists continue to cry out, "Remember Roswell!" They tell doubters that verification of UFOs won't be possible until we reach a level of development comparable to that of our extraterrestrial visitors. Until then, we are pawns of the universe.

BIBLIOGRAPHY

David, Jay. *The Flying Saucer Reader*. New York: New American Library, 1967.

Edwards, Frank. *Flying Saucers — Serious Business*. New York: Lyle Stewart, 1966.

Green, Gabriel. *Let's Face the Facts About Flying Saucers*. New York: Popular Library, 1967.

Randles, Jenny, and Peter Warrington. *Science and the UFOs*. London: Basil Blackwell, 1985.

Spencer, John, and Hilary Evans, eds. *Phenomenon: Forty Years of Flying Saucers*. New York: Avon Books, 1988.

Story, Ronald D. *The Encyclopedia of UFOs*. Garden City, NJ: Doubleday, 1980.

Vallee, Jacques. *Anatomy of a Phenomenon*. Chicago, IL: Henry Regnery, 1965.

Vincent van Gogh

Auction prices paid for four van Gogh paintings in 1987 astonished the world: "Irises" — $53.9 million, "Sunflowers" — $39.9 million, "The Bridge at Trinquetaille" — $20 million, and "Portrait of Adeline Ravoux" — $13.75 million. Without sounding like a philistine, not one of the paintings can be considered great. "Irises" is brightly colored and full of linear energy — both van Gogh trademarks, but many other artists have executed similar studies just as well or better. One of six in a series, the coarse "Sunflowers" is a sentimental favorite because of its evocation of Arles, where Vincent went mad. "The Bridge at Trinquetaille" lacks any sustainable interest; its impasto sky, water, and desultory human figures are truly pedestrian. And the "Portrait of Adeline Ravoux" pictures a plain girl in a stiff pose looking far too melancholy for one of her tender years; she is more a reflection of van Gogh's sullenness at the time. During the same auction year, only Claude Monet's "Dans La Prairie" competed with van Gogh for top price; the Monet sold for $24.8 million. Cézanne's "La Côte Du Galet, à Pontoise" went for $9.24 million, and Picasso's "Souvenir Du Havre" for $8 million. Three years later, in 1990, van Gogh outdistanced the pack once and for all when his "Portrait of Dr. Gachet" exchanged hands for $82.5 million.

At both junctures, the American public asked: Why van Gogh and not Rembrandt, Velasquez, or John Singer Sargent? There are hundreds of other painters more deserving of monetary adulation than the neurotic Dutchman. The art critic for *The Wall Street Journal*, Jack Flam, answered:

The life of Vincent van Gogh represents a kind of apotheosis of the 19th-century image of the artist as scorned outsider, misunderstood by society and answerable only to his own rules of behavior. In fact, his story seems to fill a great mytho-cultural need. Because he is one of the most romanticized artists of all time, his art is often regarded through a cloud of misconceptions centering mostly on his madness and supposed uncouthness.

The latest auction price of $82.5 million makes van Gogh *the* most romanticized artist of all time. The five paintings were completed in the last two years of van Gogh's life when he was overworked and suffering from nervous exhaustion exacerbated by a number of possible causes. His production of these paintings in the face of increasing madness apparently makes them worth a lot more to collectors than his earlier work. Following this kind of acquisitive logic, then, the portrait of Dr. Paul Gachet — who, at his clinic in Auvers-sur-Oise, was Vincent's last caretaker — would be the most valuable. When Sotheby's hammered down the highest bid yet for any painting, the question of actual worth became a moot point. Unwittingly, Vincent aided future sales of his work the day he cut off his ear and gave it to a prostitute, not long before he committed suicide by shooting himself with a pistol. So too did the heartrending letters (650+) Vincent wrote to his brother Theo, the botched friendship with Paul Gauguin, and the poverty Vincent endured for the sake of his art. The world is very familiar with the van Gogh story. Or is it? A good deal of misinformation has accrued over the years.

About the severed ear: van Gogh did not cut off his entire ear as many people believe — only the lobe. He bled profusely because he sliced an artery. The hospital in Arles and Paul Signac, a painter friend who visited Vincent at his bedside, documented this fact. Vincent handed his lobe to a prostitute most likely because she had made fun of his big ears. This conjecture has more basis to it than the assumption that Vincent wanted to impress or distract Gauguin, who was impatient to leave Arles. In a letter dated January 1889 (#569), a little over a week after the ear cutting, Vincent wrote this to Theo:

> I hope I have just had simply an artist's fit, and then a lot of fever after very considerable loss of blood, as an artery was severed; but my appetite came back at once, my digestion is all right and my blood recovers from day to day, and in the same way serenity returns to my brain day by day.

In Vincent's mind, the act was not catastrophic. But the world thinks otherwise and conjures up the image of Oedipus. A year and some months later (1890), Vincent shot himself in the stomach, not gruesomely in the head or heart. It took him two days to die in bed. The romanticized version has him drenching a field with blood while crows circle overhead, because the year of his suicide he painted the portentous "Wheat Field with Crows." Furthermore, to dispel legend, he did not kill himself because he was unrecognized as an artist or a burden to Theo or the loneliest of men. Vincent ended his life because he had mistreated his body too long and couldn't go on working.

The fad of buying van Gogh paintings for outrageous sums and the interest it generates worldwide has a rider—the fad of wanting to know what caused the painter to pull the trigger. Two recent articles in the *Journal of the American Medical Association* suggest different answers. The first, a 1988 article, posits what it calls the thujone connection. Thujone is a compound found in absinthe, a green liqueur made from wormwood. Drinking absinthe was a popular pastime in France among artists and hard-core alcoholics. Vincent's liking of absinthe deteriorated into an addiction for thujone, which was also present in turpentine and paints. Rumor had it that Vincent, to satisfy his craving for thujone, drank turpentine and ate paint, thus driving himself mad. The second article (1990) asserts that Vincent had Ménière's disease, an inner ear disorder that causes dizziness and vertigo. A loud ringing deep in the ear is also a symptom which, in the opinion of the medical investigators, drove him to cut off part of his ear for relief. In his letters, Vincent did complain about suffering from an ear problem, among many other maladies.

A personal doctor of the van Goghs diagnosed both brothers as having hereditary epilepsy and neurasthenia. Theo van Gogh survived his younger brother by only half a year. One month after Vincent's death, Theo already showed signs of nervous debilitation; thereafter, his health declined rapidly. Theo had lived a moderate life, Vincent, an immoderate one; both died prematurely because their genes were against them. But naturally, it's more exciting for the public to visualize Vincent gnawing on a tube of cadmium yellow, a razor in one hand, while holding a can of turpentine to his trembling lips with the other. The truth is, anyone who lived and worked as hard as Vincent did probably would have succumbed to mental illness even with good genes. Improper nutrition, long hours at the easel under hot sun or in winter's chill, his obsession with finishing a body of work before "his time was up" — these things aggravated his fragile genetic condition. Mad at times he may have been, but the three volumes of letters Vincent left behind reveal a sane man who wanted to get on with the business of being an artist.

Faddish interest in the death-cause debate will continue as long as van Gogh paintings sell for the cost of a Hollywood movie. Art lovers like to remind the awed public that a van Gogh represents the height of artistic permanence, whereas a film like *Batman* is ephemeral. So the $82.5 million paid for the "Portrait of Dr. Gachet" wasn't that ridiculous. What was absurd was the merchandising of van Gogh in 1990 for the centenary of his death. No one knows how many Americans made the pilgrimage to Amsterdam to participate in the celebration. But those who did could buy a Gentleman Vincent van Gogh Pen Set by Waterman, a "Vincent" bust (with both ears) by Theo Melchiors for $530, Van Gogh Perfume (an article alien to Vincent) from International Flavors and Fragrances Ltd., a 1990 Vincent Extra Brut Cava (what about Extra Brut Turpentine?), and the usual assortment of T-shirts, watches, shawls, and ties. Visitors ate potato meals at rough-wood tables to commemorate van Gogh's quaint scene of "The Potato Eaters." They dined more sumptuously at restaurants in the van Gogh village, where planter boxes burst with "le Midi" sunflowers. Posters of van Gogh as jack-in-the-box proclaimed "Amsterdam keeps you surprised." The 236-mile Van Gogh Homage Bicycle Journey wound its way from Vincent's birthplace, Zundert, to Auvers-sur-Oise, Vincent's and Theo's gravesite. For the centenary there was so much to see and do in Amsterdam that waiting in long lines to view van Gogh paintings was a matter of choice.

BIBLIOGRAPHY

Arenberg, I. Kaufman, et al. "Van Gogh Had Méniere's Disease and Not Epilepsy." *Journal of the American Medical Association* 264 (July 25, 1990): 491-493.

Arnold, Wilfred N. "Vincent van Gogh and the Thujone Connection." *Journal of the American Medical Association* 260 (November 25, 1988): 3042-3044.

Flam, Jack. ". . . I Apply Myself to My Canvases with All My Mind." *ARTnews* 89 (March 1990): 153.

Turner, Jonathan. "The Merchants of Vincent." *ARTnews* 89 (March 1990): 155.

Zemel, Carol. "What Becomes a Legend Most." *Art in America* 76 (July 1988): 88+.

Veterans of Future Wars

Early in 1936, few people doubted that a second world war was inevitable. Historical events pointed dramatically to a renewal of hostilities. World War I had not settled a thing and in fact, had only served to stir up a greater hornet's nest. This time global war would be more cataclysmic and painfully obvious, there seemed no way to avoid it. A Princeton student, Lewis J. Gorin, Jr., while sitting around with fellow classmates debating the Harrison Bonus Act, tossed out a novel idea. The purpose of the Harrison Bonus Act was to demonstrate America's appreciation for those who fought in WW I by paying money to all veterans and to the families of dead combatants. Since Princetonians and other young American males were to fight in the next war — unannounced as yet, though incubating in Nazi Germany, Fascist Italy, and Imperial Japan — they also should get a war bonus while still alive and able to enjoy it. With this in mind, Gorin and his classmates penned a manifesto:

We [Veterans of Future Wars], therefore, demand that the Government make known its intention to pay an adjusted service compensation, sometimes called a bonus, of $1000 to every male citizen between the ages of 18 and 36. Furthermore, we believe a study of history demonstrates that it is customary to pay all bonuses before they are due. Therefore we demand immediate cash payment, plus three percent interest compounded annually and retroactively from the first of June 1965, to the first of June 1935. It is but common right that this bonus be paid now, for many will be killed or wounded in the next war, and hence they, the most deserving, will not get the full benefit of their country's gratitude.

Later additions to the manifesto asked for:

1. Future Veterans' preference . . . in competitive examinations and in all forms of promotion and retention in the public service.
2. Loan of equipment for annual convention . . . from the War Department to the Veterans of Future Wars.
3. A Bill to incorporate the Veterans of Future Wars of the United States . . . to grant a Federal charter.
4. A Bill to exempt all real and personal property of Veterans of Future Wars, Inc., and of any and all members of Veterans of Future Wars, Inc., from any Federal, state, or local taxation.
5. A Bill to provide for the immediate refund of all interest paid in the future by Veterans of Future wars on loans secured by service compensation certificates.

This mordant humor was nothing more than an intellectual exercise played out for amusement until Robert G. Barnes, Princeton correspondent for the *Philadelphia Inquirer* and secretary of the University Press Club, sent the manifesto to several national newspapers. Immediately it struck a sensitive nerve, and as a result, new chapters of the Veterans of Future Wars appeared on campuses across the country. Then the fad got even more sardonic. One of the Princetonians, Thomas Riggs, Jr., went to Washington, D.C., to register as a lobbyist. He began and ended every appeal for consideration by reciting the VFW national slogan, "Equal Justice for All—Especially the Future Veterans." A Home Fire Division of the VFW claimed to have enrolled 100,000 college girls who were to visit their future husbands' and sons' gravesites at the earliest opportunity. At Cornell, the Future Munitions Workers organized. At Rensselaer Polytechnic, the Future Profiteers called for advances on contracts-yet-to-be-let. At Sweetbriar, the Future Gold Diggers unhesitatingly agreed "to sit on the laps of the profiteers while they drink champagne during the next war." Just over the Canadian border, University of Toronto Vets implored their Alumni Association to erect cenotaphs on campus "in memory of our coming sacrifice in giving our lives to our country."

But not everyone laughed. The national commander of the other

VFW, the Veterans of Foreign Wars, James E. Van Zandt, dismissed the instigators of the fad as "a bunch of yellow monkeys." Not to be outdone, Arkansas Congressman Claude Fuller blasted the Princetonians and their followers by saying, "This movement is saturated with communism, foreign influence, and a total disregard of true American patriotism." On the other hand, abetting the rich satire of the Princetonians, the *New York Herald-Tribune* suggested that all young women should "insist upon pensions in anticipation of widowhood and allowances for unborn orphans." And Democratic Representative Maury Maverick of Texas swore on his Stetson to sponsor a House bill to pay the Veterans their advance bonus. The Veterans of Future Wars did not break under censure, nor did they get cocky when applauded. Theirs was the good fight, and they sang their official song proudly, set to the tune of "Over There":

> Fall in line — fall in line,
> Now's the time — now's the time,
> To collect our bonus
> That Franklin D. will loan us
> So we won't fight him over here.
>
> So raise your beers and give three cheers
> For the war that's comin' to keep us hummin',
> And we won't be there till its over
> Over here.

BIBLIOGRAPHY

"Bonus: 'Equal Justice for All — Especially the Future Veterans'." *News-Week* 7 (April 11, 1936): 10-11.

"Bonus: 1965's 'Veterans' Want It Now — With Interest from 1965." *News-Week* 7 (March 28, 1936): 32.

Riggs, Thomas, Jr. "We Call Upon America." *North American Review* 241 (June 1936): 264-273.

Walden Two

The famous behavioral psychologist B. F. Skinner wrote *Walden Two*, a utopian novel, in 1945. Three years later when the book was finally published, a few critics took notice, but the reading public, as Skinner said, "left it alone for a dozen years." Then, on the threshold of the tempestuous 1960s, America awoke to the importance of Skinner's themes: small is beautiful; the simple life is the best; unwanted human behavior can be changed; and the less people consume, the less they have to work. These themes and others glowed like neon for young readers caught up in a decade of dissatisfaction with their inherited society.

The title alluded to Henry David Thoreau's *Walden* (1854), which outlines utopian living for one. *Walden Two* visualizes communal living for 1,000 with the inference that many such settlements could usher in a golden age of peace and harmony for all humankind. The plot of the novel is simple. T. E. Frazier, the founder of Walden Two, tries to convince a skeptical visitor, Professor Burris, that his settlement answers every human need while eliminating every human ill. Unlike other communes, Walden Two has a master plan which Frazier, through long hours of discussion, reveals to Dr. Burris. Persuaded at last, Dr. Burris quits university teaching and joins Walden Two. Frazier's master plan is what sets this utopian novel apart from others in the genre. Skinner explains, "I suppose the main theme of the novel is this: that with available behavioral technology it should be possible for any group of men of goodwill to construct a good life."

It is somewhat unusual for a scientist who deals with the concrete to write imaginative fiction. But in Skinner's case, it was the best way to breathe life into behavioral engineering and at the same time project an image of an ideal society. Born in 1904, Skinner had already achieved considerable success in his chosen field of psychology. His name was synonymous with the behaviorist school of which he was the leader. Since he could not run an experiment using human subjects on a large scale to prove that behavior modification worked, he chose to write *Walden Two*. Skinner, following in the footsteps of the Russian physiologist Ivan Pavlov, had shown the world that rats and pigeons could be trained to complete simple, repetitive tasks. He conditioned them with food to do his bidding by rewarding good while ignoring bad behavior. With humans, the reinforcement would be encouragement for doing the right thing, not a handful of grain. A mother would not spank her child when it did something wrong, instead she would ignore bad behavior. When her child acted according to her wishes, she would lavish affection. Soon the child would stop all wrong behavior to get attention for correct actions. Substitute a scientist or some other authority figure for the mother and this—in a nutshell—is the basic premise of behavioral engineering and *Walden Two*.

Although reinforcing good while ignoring bad behavior sounds simplistic and nothing more than common sense, alert readers feared Skinner. Some of their arguments were: Who determines what good behavior is? If it's so easy to manipulate human behavior, then what if an evil genius gets hold of the power? Hasn't Hitler already shown the dark side of behavioral engineering? If everyone acts in response to conditioned reflexes, won't we have a world full of robots? Skinner foresaw these criticisms and thought he had covered them in his novel. His intention was to correct the behavior of criminals, warmongering politicians, polluters, and other obvious malefactors. Yet many readers thought Skinner a Big Brother from George Orwell's antiutopian novel, *1984*. Any loss of freedom was abhorrent to them—even the freedom to engage in wrongful actions. Given the power, a Skinnerian society could say "no" to premarital sex, drinking wine, socks on the floor—anything, no matter how pleasurable or insignificant.

Some 20 years after Skinner published *Walden Two*, a group of young people attempted to follow his precepts. Not 1,000 but 35 adventurers founded Twin Oaks, located in the foothills of the Piedmont region of Virginia. This commune was much different from others currently in progress. Twin Oaks was not a haven for pot smokers, free love, and grumbling about society. A reporter for *Time* magazine filed this eyewitness account:

> Work is allocated by an intricate system of labor credits so that none of the 35 members have unequal burdens. . . . No one is allowed to boast of individual accomplishments, to gossip (negative speech), or to be intolerant of another's beliefs. Behavioral engineering goes on every minute of the day. A member who gets angry, who makes demands or who gives ultimatums is simply not "reinforced," to use the behavioral term. He is ignored. What is considered appropriate behavior — cooperating, showing affection, turning the other cheek and working diligently — is, on the other hand, applauded, or "reinforced" by the group.

In 1970, turnover at Twin Oaks was close to 70%. Those who left did so because they could not be that self-effacing. Some members saw themselves as natural leaders and issued ultimatums anyway — the most egregious crime — and not being able to say anything negative created immense pressure among the rest. Throughout *Walden Two*, Skinnerian social thought played out beautifully, but in real life it produced irritation and disharmony. Often asked the central question, Skinner replied:

> Why don't I start such a community myself? I could do it, with a little money. I'd have hundreds of people ready to join, and I could probably raise the money from a foundation. But I'm too old . . . And now I've gone way beyond Walden Two, in a sense. One has to design one's own life, after all.

Skinner said those words in 1970 at age 66. By 1976, when he wrote a new introduction for a reissued *Walden Two*, he basked in the glory of his novel having sold over a million copies. His panacea for the ills of the world had repaid him handsomely. Misunderstood by his detractors and with Twin Oaks as a sorry reminder, Skinner still firmly believed in behavioral engineering.

BIBLIOGRAPHY

Skinner, B. F. *Walden Two*. New York: Macmillan, 1976.

"Skinner's Utopia: Panacea, or Path to Hell?" *Time* 98 (September 20, 1971): 47-53.

Todd, Richard. "'Walden Two': Three? Many More?" *The New York Times Magazine* (March 15, 1970): 24 + .

Index

DATE DUE

DEC 4			

Demco, Inc. 38-293